RECKONING
AT
EAGLE CREEK

RECKONING AT EAGLE CREEK

◊ ◊ ◊

The Secret Legacy of
Coal in the Heartland

JEFF BIGGERS

NATION
BOOKS

New York

Published by Nation Books, A Member of the Perseus Books Group
116 East 16th Street, 8th Floor
New York, NY 10003

Nation Books is a co-publishing venture of the Nation Institute and the Perseus Books Group.

The names of some individuals in the book have been changed to protect their privacy.

All maps courtesy of the author. Lyrics on page 183: "Black Waters" ©1967, 1971. Reprinted with permission from Jean Ritchie Geordie Music Publishing Co. ASCAP.

Books published by Nation Books are available at special discounts for bulk purchases in the United States by corporations, institutions, and other organizations. For more information, please contact the Special Markets Department at the Perseus Books Group, 2300 Chestnut Street, Suite 200, Philadelphia, PA 19103, or call (800) 810-4145, ext. 5000, or e-mail special.markets@perseusbooks.com.

DESIGNED BY JEFF WILLIAMS

Library of Congress Cataloging-in-Publication Data
    Biggers, Jeff, 1963-
    Reckoning at Eagle Creek : the secret legacy of coal in the heartland / Jeff Biggers.
        p. cm.
    Includes bibliographical references and index.
    ISBN 978-1-56858-421-8 (alk. paper)
    1. Coal mines and mining—Illinois—Eagle Creek Region—History. 2. Coal mines and mining—Social aspects—Illinois Eagle Creek Region—History. 3. Shawnee National Forest Region (Ill.)—History. 4. Mountain life—Illinois—Eagle Creek Region—History. I. Title.

TN799.6.I3B54 2010

                                                                    2009032686

10 9 8 7 6 5 4 3 2 1

To
Cora Bell and Bob Followell, Frankie and Henry Stilley,
and all those who lived on Eagle Creek;

Richard and Jerretta Followell,
keepers of our family trees;

Gary DeNeal,
poet errant of the Shawnee Hills; and

in memory of Shera Biggers Thompson,
who reminded me of the importance of family heritage.

◊　◊　◊

CONTENTS

CHAPTER SIX

The Short Swift Time of Clean Coal on Earth:

They who are strong have claimed an earthly peace
Gathering their strength in this treasured hour
When the winds hush, the muted waters cease
And fog with misty wings has raised a tower
Of silence as a harbor for the stars;
When hills have cleft the sky with brooding peaks
Thrust in the purple bowl, raised solemn bars
Against all utterance, he who then speaks
Shall in this mighty breathlessness be heard.
They shall be heard, the weary and the spent
The broken at the wheel, the fledgling bird
Each grievous thought, each yearning here unspent
Shall have its reckoning when the hills confide.
They shall find strength where peace and time abide.

—JAMES STILL, *"Reckoning"*

Strip mining Eagle Creek. *(Photos by Jerretta Followell.)*

◊

Prologue

IN COAL BLOOD

> Something like a shadow has fallen between the present and
> past, an abyss as wide as war that cannot be bridged by any tan-
> gible connection, so that memory is undermined and the image
> of our beginnings betrayed, dissolved, rendered not mythical but
> illusory. We have connived in the murder of our own origins.
>
> —EDWARD ABBEY, *Shadows from the Big Woods*

I stood with my mother and Uncle Richard at the rim of a lunar
expanse of ruts and rocks and broken earth. We had to protect
our eyes. A dark wind swept along the ridge. Howling little eddies
of fury. Huge trucks stormed in all directions. Blocks of sandstone
abounded like nameless tombstones on a battleground of slate and
clay. Colorless somehow. It looked like an earthquake had devastated the area.

How green was our valley of Eagle Creek, when my mom and
I last walked these hills together. Corn and sorghum tassels had jutted out from the slopes like ancient signposts next to the barn that
slumped with stories of accidental and nearly fatal hangings. Our
porch was weighed down with tables of chicken legs and gizzards,
catfish, okra, garden vegetables, beans, corn bread, and heapings of
rhubarb pie.

The rolling forests seemed eternal in those days, protected by sentries of hickory, oak, maple, gum, beech, dogwood, and wild grapevines that thickened up the ramparts of Eagle Creek with the intrigue of danger. Pine was a latecomer, an entry of reforestation. I was told yellow pine was a sign of death. The pioneers who had first entered these Illinois hills would plant two pines in front of their houses, which eventually served as the wood for their coffins. Coffin pines, we called them.

Our family homestead, known since 1849 as the Oval Hill Farm, sat on a knoll in the eastern shadows of the Eagle Mountains, which withdrew to the upheavals of 400-million-year-old faulted ridges that were older than many American ranges. To the northeast, across the nearby Wildcat Hills that infested my grandmother's stories of panthers and wolves, hid the ruins of the Great Salt Spring that fed the largest prehistoric civilization north of Mexico City and drove legal slavery into the land of Lincoln and Obama. On the southeastern horizon, the promontory outlook of the Garden of the Gods Wilderness area, one of a handful of such protected areas in the American heartland, retreated into the traces of the Shawnee National Forest boundaries that looped around the panhandle of our hollow with the intransigence of a national border.

On a clear day, as a child, I once pretended to be an eagle and took flight down the hill, rose above the forests, and soared beyond the Ohio River and Kentucky, which lay only twenty miles away.

"I can't believe this," my mom whispered.

"Beyond description now," Uncle Richard said. "Just wasted."

Richard was a tall, peaceful man in his seventies, still all legs, blind in one eye, whose soft Kentucky accent spun words with an ancient borderland dialect that my first ancestor had planted in these hills in 1805 and distinguished family from outsiders. My mom may have been his older sister, but she moved faster, had sat confidently in the passenger's seat at the age of sixteen, while her father drove across two county lines and left her at the redbrick wonder of Southern Illinois University with just enough time to get back to his place at the coal mines. She measured her soft-spoken words in an accent that left no traces of her past.

We could see the route of destruction. The first explosions had taken place in the summer of 1998. The coal company had set off the ammonium nitrate–fuel oil blasts in the surrounding Eagle Creek Valley, gnawing away at the edges of our family hill. One thousand six hundred pounds of explosives sat in each hole like a land mine, set to ripple across the valley with enough thunder to bring down the walls of Jericho.

In this last phase, Loeva's place along the lower creek went first. She was still a teenager the first year she taught my mom and Uncle Richard at Central, a one-room schoolhouse on the muddy trail between the hills. From the porch of the Oval Hill Farm, where cousin Juanita would rest and put on her boots and lipstick before cutting through the forest, you could have seen the valley crumple into ashes, as if the New Madrid earthquake that had laid waste to the region in 1811 was returning for a second reckoning.

For years, our family's homestead leaned down the crest like an overburdened hickory. Not anymore. My mom's cousin Leon, the last occupant of the old homeplace, had told and retold the story until he could tell it no more, no longer cared to talk about it, no longer wanted to have the memory conjured up by outsiders like a living nightmare. He didn't even want us around, poking into his despair, his affairs, a muck of betrayal that only he could fathom. He had just remodeled the log cabin for the eighth generation of our extended family set to reside there—had even put on a new porch.

And it shook with every blast. Permits were renewed and modified to move the explosives closer, until harassment became a legally authorized tactic. Dishes shot off the cupboards. Frames unhinged. Every three days the machines moved in closer, carving a rusty horseshoe two hundred feet deep.

We were on the wrong side of the official Shawnee National Forest and first designated Illinois wilderness area border for one reason; our land possessed "resource attributes." Our family hollow and hillsides were endowed with five rich seams of coal. Dekoven, Davis, Springfield, Herrin, Survant—quaint names that meant nothing to me, but that could change the register of any coal baron's voice with glee.

Family names and so-called clans—our Colberts, Stilleys—had defined Eagle Creek since their arrivals as the first pioneers from various southern states in 1805. But in modern times, kinship had been replaced by seams of coal.

Both sides of the border, though, stretched in stands of temperate deciduous hardwoods: white oak, black oak, some beech, gum, ash, elm, hickory, and tulip poplar. In his letters from 1818, English settler Morris Birkbeck had described these same forests on his passage from the Ohio River to eastern Illinois: "To travel day after day, among trees of a hundred feet high, without a glimpse of the surrounding country, is oppressive to a degree which those cannot conceive who have not experienced it. Upwards he sees the sun and sky and stars, but around him an eternal forest, from which he can never hope to emerge."

Birkbeck and his English followers, coming from the coal-fired industrial Old World, hated the woodlands. They had little love for our backwoodsmen. The collision over the coal and the forest, and the dwellers in between, had rattled the bones of the region for two centuries.

Now we had reached the final battle.

The Wisconsin glaciers that had encamped on the Midwest never reached our boot-heel range of southeastern Illinois. The dense forests crowning our hillsides and hollow, like most of the Shawnee hill region from the Mississippi to the Wabash River, once rivaled Appalachia or the Ozarks for plant diversity. Some even called it the Illinois Ozarks. It was that rare main chain of mountains and hills to stretch east to west. Over 1,100 plant species, 270 birds, twoscore of mammals and reptiles. A sea of serpents; you could have snake-fenced the entire region.

The back slope of our hollow butted against Colbert Hill on one side, with outcroppings of rock formations and sandstone caves, and then dropped into the Eagle Creek basin, dotted by a handful of slumping farmhouses and cleared fields.

I can hear my mother's voice. *That would have been Dallas's house right here. He'd put on his peg leg every time he went looking for work; stood behind the others so as not to be seen. We've made ice cream in that yard so many times. There's a creek we'd jump and fall into and get wet. Alfred built the next house, and Addie and I would stay out in his car and listen to the stories on the radio until the battery died. Get so mad. Once he couldn't get the car started in the middle of winter, so he crawled down and made a fire under the oil pan. 'Bout burned up the car. Our homeplace was up here on the hill. Dad rose before dawn, milked the cows, did the chores around the farm, before he'd head off to the mines.*

The rumble of coal trucks cut off her voice.

Before the blossoms on the four wild plum trees turned and fell, the explosions from the next valley had managed to crack the well between the barn and the old homestead in the summer of 1998. Debris clipped the walls, thin loess soil, and bricks colored the water like blue john days, when the rope broke on gallon jugs of stored milk in the well.

Then came the reckoning on our hillside along Eagle Creek.

After harassing and intimidating our last remaining cousin on Oval Hill, a coal mining company had bought most of the hollow where my extended family had lived for two centuries and blasted away the old homeplace.

The throttle of machinery, an industrial cocktail of explosives, and a handful of large equipment drivers removed our Oval Hill farm and leveled the ridge by the end of the fall. Flattened the knoll to its knees, and then to ashes. The old pond, the four plum trees, the sorghum and cornfields, the garden, the barn, and the one-hundred-fifty-year-old log cabin were buried in a crater formed before the Paleozoic era. The forests had been torn asunder, in King James's terms. It looked like a black amphitheater fit for an epic tragedy with no characters but receding trucks, bulldozers, and front loaders.

My granddaddy was a coal miner; he bent his towering frame into the narrow underground shafts under the hills in this region. Now this work had become the dominion of anonymous heavy-equipment operators, nonunion transients, who plowed the wound of stripped pits into scabs and then disappeared.

It was all gone.

We weren't supposed to be standing on this mining site. It was someone else's land now. Danger signs warned of explosives. The coal trucks left behind the tracks of tanks.

A representative from another company that had leased the land from the first coal company eventually arrived in his truck. He mistook us for a family on the other side of Eagle Creek and assumed we wanted to discuss making a lake as part of the mine's reclamation process. He was halfway through his sentence before he reached us.

"I've been doing this for twenty-nine years, and every time we do this someone wants a lake after they've seen their neighbors with a lake." His nasal midwestern accent blended the folksy with the devious; it seemed so at odds with our southern Illinois ways. He spoke fast, as if he had gone over this script many times. "Like I make these lakes with goose-nesting areas out in the middle of the island so the coyotes can't get to them. And we'll make nice peninsulas that come out. We make really nice lakes."

"What happened to the log cabin?" my uncle interrupted.

The company representative had the answer.

"Well, they numbered the logs, disassembled it, and reconstructed it." The more he talked, the more he became convinced of his false story. He didn't know that we knew the answer—the truth. All he lacked was a straw hat and he could have been a dead ringer for Zephaniah Scadder, the unscrupulous agent of the Eden Land Corporation who sells swampland in southern Illinois in Charles Dickens's biting novel, *Martin Chuzzlewit*. "Ah, no, you can't see it from the road. They put it up by a pond. But, I've heard good things about it."

He turned his back on us and swept his arm across the ruins.

"We'll slope all of that down and flatten it out. And we'll put a minimum of the topsoil back. And eight foot of clay. It'll be better now than it was then. Of course, the difference is how long it takes the trees to get back to maturity, but, you know . . . you have to get rid of the overburden to get to the coal." He laughed.

Mining jargon referred to the forests, hills and hollows, all flora and fauna—anything on top of the coal—as the "overburden."

Our two-hundred-year-old family history was nothing more than overburden to this company hack.

But it wasn't just our family history. It also included a thousand years of bones of the first natives in the region, the modern Shawnee encampments and farms, the pioneering squatters and homesteaders in our family, and the slaves and coal miners in one of the first settlements in the nation's heartland—all of which had been churned into dust in the race to strip-mine the area. Like the gaping black ruins of Pompeii, I knew this forsaken land now hid the dark legacies of our past in ashes.

There were a lot of secrets in those ashes—secrets that implicated the legacies of our American heroes Thomas Jefferson and Andrew Jackson, Abraham Lincoln and Tecumseh, and labor leaders like Mother Jones and John L. Lewis.

As the wind whipped up the blasted dust, which howled in the destruction, I had this strange feeling that I was not only witnessing the stripping of a hill and its ancient flora and inhabitants, but also the shredding of a great library of stories that had shaped this region, and our nation's history.

Zephaniah Scadder nasaled on with his monologue. I noticed my mom and uncle had lost interest; they had shifted their gaze at a massive pile of rocks and mud to the side of one slope, not far from where my grandmother and great-grandmothers had tended their gardens and canned enough food to last the wintry months of hunger. A patch of corn remained, growing out of the rubble in defiance of the strip mine. There was a mixture of awe and family pride. My mom gripped my uncle's arm. He wiped at his eyes.

I realized I needed to make this journey to witness that powerful sight.

"Damn their souls," I heard someone say.

"No," another voice replied. "You need to raise the dead and tell the stories of those they have just destroyed."

RECKONING
AT
EAGLE CREEK

State militia posted at a Peabody mine near Kincaid, IL, 1932. *(Photo by Greg Boozell.)*

◊

Introduction

MR. PRESIDENT, WELCOME TO THE SAUDI ARABIA OF COAL

I come from a coal state and so I am a big proponent of clean-coal technology and I want us to move rapidly in developing those sequestration technologies that's required. We're not going to immediately move off coal. A huge percentage of our electricity is generated by coal. What we need to do though is to put clean-coal technology on the fast track and that means money. It means investment in research. That's something that we should have already been doing. We had a project called FutureGen, a billion-dollar project that was slated to go up, and the Bush administration canceled it after the siting decision was made and it wasn't in Texas. I think that's a mistake. We're the Saudi Arabia of coal.

—**SENATOR BARACK OBAMA,**
campaigning in the Montana presidential primary, May 29, 2008

The United States is the Saudi Arabia of coal, but we have our own homegrown problems in terms of dealing with a cheap energy source that creates a big carbon footprint.

—**PRESIDENT BARACK OBAMA,**
Ottawa, Canada, February 18, 2009

As the *Washington Post* reported during the 2008 presidential campaign, President Barack Obama first visited the southern Illinois coalfields in 1997 on a golf outing with a fellow state legislator. On those tree-lined fairways near the town of Benton, he most probably heard stories of the coalfield heydays in the area, when 1,110 miners crouched into the cages and sank two football-field-lengths below the putting green into the largest coal-mine shaft in the world at the nearby New Orient No. 2.

Not that the young legislator from Chicago didn't already know about coal. As a community organizer in Chicago's South Side, President Obama must have wondered about the origins of the coal that fired up the Fisk Generating Station in his neighborhood. Despite a rack of violations, the coal-fired stack and its nearby counterparts billowed out thousands of tons of sulfur dioxide, nitrogen oxide, and carbon dioxide emissions, as well as 117 tons of particulate matter that led to an estimated 300 heart attacks and 14,000 asthma attacks every year.

President Obama's hosts at the Benton driving range, though, had a different view. Burning coal was Chicago's problem; extraction was theirs. They wouldn't have wanted to dwell on the details of the dirty old town—that was Chicago's burden. Here in southern Illinois, they wanted the young legislator to know that he was standing on the biblical stones of fire, the largest bituminous coal reserves in the nation.

Over 38 billion tons of coal, "a vast natural resource that could produce more energy than the oil reserves of Saudi Arabia," as the Illinois Office of Coal Development liked to boast, lingered like black gold for the taking in the state of Illinois.

The hosts were no fools. They were pounding nails into the green to keep the eternal springtime of coal alive. They dragged out the sepia images of their granddaddies, coal miners and operators all, and played the nostalgia trump card in those moments when the romantic past belied the wasteland realities of the present. They conjured images of great lines of coal trains and tipples, and huge ranks of coal miners emerging out of the depths of the earth in an endless parade of employment opportunities.

The young legislator must have listened politely. How could he not have been touched by the gravity of the situation? In the late 1990s, eight counties in southern Illinois hemorrhaged on the edge of economic despair, dealing with some of the worst poverty rates in the Midwest. He knew that the coal industry—the single engine in the region's economy—had collapsed, the state's high-sulfur reserves betrayed by the new restrictions in the Clean Air Act of 1990. Opting to buy low-sulfur coal from western states, the Illinois and other midwestern state utilities managed to sidestep the investment in plant scrubbers required to reduce sulfur dioxide emissions—the cause of acid rain.

The Clean Air Act, passed precisely to protect the senator's ailing constituents in the shadows of the Fisk Generating Station and the acid rain–draped forests in the north, had transformed a level of resentment into sheer denial in southern Illinois. And this denial invoked the two great death-defying myths that had ensured the constancy of the stars in the coal basin: that coal is cheap and coal is clean.

Acid rain, in the minds of nostalgic coal enthusiasts, was a hoax, just like the concerns of climate-change activists today who ranted that 40 percent of all carbon dioxide emissions came from coal-fired plants like the Fisk Generation Station in Chicago.

But denial, like nostalgia, suffers from amnesia.

The golf pros in Benton most likely didn't tell the young state senator that their fathers and grandfathers and great-grandfathers had carried on this same conversation with politicians from Chicago for the past century. That by 1905, virtually all southern Illinois mineral rights had been bought up by a torrent of Chicago and absentee speculators and coal operators. And that the region had been relegated to the vassal status of a supply-and-demand extraction colony subject to the whims of the senator's own constituents.

No one probably confessed to the fact that the region's coal industry had peaked in 1918, and while little spurts of demand had taken place during the Second World War, the mines had been on a slope of decline for decades. Over 100,000 miners produced more than 100 million tons in the early 1920s; a little more than 3,000 miners churned out 30 million tons today.

By the 1930s, according to the government report "Seven Stranded Coal Towns," those same Chicago coal companies had abandoned the region and left a picture of "almost unrelieved, utter economic devastation." As one of the most depressed and vulnerable places in the country, the southern Illinois coalfields had been given over to "hopeless poverty."

While some communities made small attempts at developing a diversified economy, the region simply waited out the lull in the coal market for the next boom—or war. Those 38 billion tons of coal burned under their feet. They burned under the chambers of commerce. The communities wondered aloud: Why would any town ever consider any other industry? All they had to do was find a way to bring back the Chicago investors to the coal mines, at whatever cost.

In the meantime, abandonment had also taken a toll on the land. Out of the 1,300 mines that had been opened in the state, less than 25 remained by the end of the twentieth century, leaving the federal and state governments with a bill for billions of dollars to clean up the dangerous sites and toxic waste seeping into the region's watersheds. Thousands of fertile farmland acres and lush

Shawnee forests had been strip-mined and left to the unmanaged spoils of weeds, foreign grasses, and sterile creeks. Cancer and health problems soared.

The coal miners, too, had been abandoned: Their town squares and schools had been boarded up; their hard-earned property values were wiped out. No one would have told the young senator that 10,000 coal miners still died each decade from black lung disease, according to a recent study by the National Institute for Occupational Safety and Health study. The bill for this cleanup program, too, had cost the taxpayers billions of dollars.

No one on that golf course would have paused for a moment, pointed to a landmark a few miles away to the south, and recalled an explosion on the last working day before Christmas in 1951, when mining safety violations were ignored and a buildup of methane gas ripped through the nearby New Orient No. 2 mine and took the lives of 119 miners.

Here in the heartland of the nation's first labor battleground that created the earliest mining unions, every mining safety law had been assembled from the fractured bones and lost lives of the coal miners and their families. In the Saudi Arabia of coal, miners had been as expendable as the tree lines that stood in the way of the bulldozer. In their haste to extract the coal at the cheapest price, coal companies had resisted every piece of legislation for operating safety in a state of permanent violation.

The shattered lives of those coal miners near Benton prompted the Federal Coal Mine Safety Act of 1952, which called for annual inspections in underground coal mines, and charged the Bureau of Mines to issue citations and imminent-danger withdrawal orders.

But even those laws had now been denied. The largest mine in southern Illinois was owned by the same operators fined by the Mine Safety and Health Administration for "violations that directly contributed to the deaths of six miners" in the Crandall Canyon disaster in Utah in 2007. Blatantly in defiance of over 2,000 annual violations, the company's headlong operations awaited the next disaster.

In a largely mechanized and computerized industry, less than 3,000, mostly nonunion, miners now sank into the shafts for $18–$25 an hour.

This was the real Saudi Arabia of coal, where coal remained the merciless king, and the land and its residents defended themselves against the daily onslaught of the monarch's extraction for more wealth.

In 1997, Obama would have also heard the parable of "clean coal," a marketing phrase that had been first used by the golfers' great-granddaddies in selling the hot-burning Btu's of "smoke-free clean coal" in the 1890s in Chicago. Every couple of decades or so since, the "clean coal" slogan had been trotted out as the standard response to any questionable element in the industry, whether it was in the mining, processing, burning, or storage of coal-fired ash and coal-fired emissions. It had been drafted in the 1970s to sell the illusory "clean coal" cars and their coal-to-liquid gas plants; it had been adapted to the Clean Air Act scrubbers to winnow out the sulfur emissions in the 1990s.

Today, they simply dusted off and refashioned the "clean coal" slogan to address the increasingly urgent findings of climate destabilization and the illusory possibility of capturing and storing carbon dioxide emissions from coal-fired plants.

Was this not the state where the French first discovered coal in the Americas in the 1600s?

Was this not the state that gave birth to the commercial strip-mining industry in the 1860s with its horses and scraping plows?

And why shouldn't this state be the first to launch FutureGen, the chimera of all denials in the age of climate destabilization, the experimental venture to capture and store carbon emissions from coal-fired plants in the twenty-first century?

Dating back to 1981, the state had bankrolled the largest coal research and development program in the country. By 2002, the state of Illinois had launched the unabashed Coal Revival Program, invoking the outdated images of coal-inspired boomtowns that had not existed for over a half century. Caving in to the demands of the still-powerful coal lobby, millions of dollars in taxpayer subsidies would be handed over to Peabody Energy, the nation's largest coal company, and ExxonMobil, one of the largest corporations in the world, at the expense of other sustainable economic development schemes for the impoverished region. Two other smaller coal operators, both of which had featured prominently in the news, also received significant subsidies: International Coal Group, which owned the Sago, West Virginia, coal mine that lost twelve lives in a mine accident in 2006, and Murray Energy, the company denounced for the Crandall Canyon coal disaster in 2007.

In 2008, ranking fifth in the nation in coal power generation, Illinois was considering the construction of sixteen new coal-fired plants to add to the emissions-belching ranks of its twenty-three graying old plants, the most proposed in any state in the country.

Coal-fired plants, whether they were clean, green, or downright dirty, meant one thing to the golfers in Benton: More coal would be mined, money made, and the illusion of the halcyon days of last century's coal industry could finally return to modern times.

On that golf course in southern Illinois in 1997, the young legislator from Chicago not only kept company with coal enthusiasts, but also the apparitions from two hundred years of a nightmare struggle to extract coal from the land and its people at any cost.

In truth, the coal boosters in the Saudi Arabia of coal were not only denying the dirty realities of coal. They were hiding the two-hundred-year-old secret legacy of coal in the heartland.

A legacy that started with Eagle Creek.

◊ ◊ ◊

HOW COULD I MAKE this dark and beautiful secret down in these Eagle Creek hills real for our president?

How could I reveal the human and social costs of two centuries of coal mining that had quietly disappeared from our history books and, worse yet, seemed to have lost any connection to our contemporary times?

Unlike an underground mine that had been forever sealed after a disaster, the strip mines at Eagle Creek stood in the wake of the explosives and draglines and bulldozers like a historic battleground that had been transformed into an unholy war cemetery, bereft of gravestones and faded flags.

I wanted our president to know what had died on that battleground.

I wanted our president to know that the strip mines did not only obliterate our family homeplace and farm: they ripped out the roots of invaluable historic sites and stories, such as a secret black slave cemetery that had helped to give birth to the coal industry, and churned them into unrecognizable bits of dust. History did not only vanish—it was covered up—the same way a native and lush Shawnee forest was wiped out and replaced, through a faux coal mining reclamation program, with foreign grasslands, and the aquatic life of Eagle Creek itself disappeared with the toxic runoff from the slurry pond.

But dead fish don't tell lies. Nor did our ruins. As Mexican writer Octavio Paz wrote in his Nobel laureate address, the ancient past in his country never truly disappeared; it remained a presence; it breathed its spirits into our contemporary decisions. It churned out bits of cautionary tales that reflected our choices and ways of living today.

In many respects, the judgments that allowed the strip-mining of Eagle Creek—that commerce trumped community and economic profit ruled over human rights and environmental protection—had been made two hundred years ago.

The more I stood at the abyss of the mines and watched the frenetic pace of the bulldozers and coal trucks to cover up what had been lost in Eagle Creek, the more I became convinced that I had stumbled onto the scene of a crime. Not only a crime against nature and our communities. As a society, we had willfully forgotten our tragic history.

Or rather, we had silently committed a crime against our history—literally stripping away the most troubling issues of the coal industry from our historical memory. Here, in the Saudi Arabia of coal, we never discussed the fact that Native people, such as the Shawnee, Kaskaskia, and Kickapoo, had been removed as part of a national policy by Thomas Jefferson to extract our minerals; that the first coal industry, even in the supposedly slave-free territories under the Northwest Ordinance and in the land of Lincoln and Obama, had been launched and sustained with black slaves; that the first union movement for coal miners in the nation emerged and battled a policy of negligent homicide by wealthy coal operators and governmental partners for generations; that the environmental havoc unleashed by strip mining had not only poisoned some of the most diverse forests and vibrant waterways in the heartland, but also systematically wiped out our contemporary woodland cultures and families.

Here in the American heartland, Eagle Creek, like most coal-field areas, had been the staging ground of a collective act of historicide: the murder of our history.

This act of historicide not only served as an indictment on our selective viewing of history, but also unveiled an important cautionary tale of how we were repeating the same injustices and errors of the past, precisely because we had erased our memory of this history.

Coal had created a stunning anatomy of denial in every generation, including today.

There was a haunting irony about invoking the image of crime in southern Illinois: No region, outside of Appalachia, seemed to have been so maligned and unfairly saddled with a reputation for violence by outside writers. Since the 1790s, traveling chroniclers, journalists, and novelists had been obsessed with painting the region with an unending chain of colorful and often gut-wrenching crimes: family feuds, river bandits, counterfeiting gangs, slave traders, bootleggers, Klansmen, and "bloody" coal miners.

The most important scholarly book written about the region for a popular readership, *Bloody Williamson: A Chapter in American Lawlessness* by historian Paul Angle, came to the conclusion that after a century of bloodletting, the inhabitants "almost without exception" were "hot-blooded, proud, obstinate, jealous of family honor, and quick to resent an insult. Given what they considered sufficient provocation, they could kill with little compunction." In 1988, a *New York Times* bestselling true crime book, *Murder in Little Egypt* by Darcy O'Brien, hailed our county as the "murder capital of rural America," second only to the bloody coalfields of Harlan County, Kentucky.

At the crossroads of the great American experience, I wanted to shatter these demoralizing half-truths that had plagued my beloved southern Illinois homeland by chronicling its extraordinary history of resilience and resistance to the machinations of King Coal.

And yet, in the Saudi Arabia of coal, the true crime in southern Illinois had never been reported.

Robert and Cora Bell Followell family. *(Courtesy of the author.)*

◊

Chapter One

4.5 HOURS

The Choices We Made

Let my heart rest this purple hour
With slow wandering in dull passages of breath.
In unwoven air, in sleep withdrawn from death,
And voiceless spans the mountain's crumbling tower.
Let me lie here unstirred, unwaked and still.
Let my heart lean against this fallow hill.

—JAMES STILL, *"Let This Hill Rest"*

To understand Eagle Creek and its legacy, I knew I had to meet Gary DeNeal, the poet errant of southern Illinois hills.

I don't recall when I first met Gary, but I do know that he was on the pudgy side, slightly disheveled in appearance, and that he wasn't wearing shoes but sandals with socks. That was how he always dressed, whether it was a sweltering day in the cypress swamps, a step ahead of the chiggers and ticks let loose like hounds, or a bone-chilling cold on Stoneface bluff in January, when the retrenched spirit of the wintry forest granted us that brief period to gaze across the Eagle Mountains for miles. His wavy hair and oversized glasses hadn't changed much since the oil crisis in the mid-1970s. He never made eye contact, but he talked, talked a lot, asked questions like a revenue agent more envious than suspicious of moonshine activity in our backwoods of southern Illinois.

Not that Gary didn't already know all of the answers. He was officially the publisher and a founder of *Springhouse Magazine*, a stapled country journal he launched with two other self-proclaimed "hillbillies" in the Illinois Ozarks in the fall of 1983. Hillbilly in that self-deprecating manner of literary wags who listened to Mozart, idolized Emily Dickinson, and were born and raised and chose to live in this "kingdom of hollows" and didn't need to act contrite about it. Gary and his mates appreciated the aroma of burnt walnut, tarried in the chat of barnyard conventions, and relished the ever-changing details about a panther's cry in someone's new version of an old tale.

Springhouse wasn't all tall tales, though. The lead story in the debut issue featured "alternative energy pioneers," about a couple that lived off-the-grid with solar panels and wind turbines in the woods near Womble Mountain.

The other two founders, a former mercenary who lived on Possum Ridge and a local business contractor, eventually lost the thrill of publication drudgery and let Gary and his wife, Judy, take over in 1984. Gary placed an image of Don Quixote on the cover. They churned it out from their A-frame home off a dirt road in the woods, a couple of miles from a shoulder-in-the-road-sized postal community called Herod.

For the next twenty-five years, the couple lovingly laid out each page, collected and wrote stories and historical tidbits and recipes, and eventually took to reprinting forgotten chronicles from the nineteenth century. At some stage in its evolution, *Springhouse*'s chaotic layout reflected more of its publisher's wanton disregard for convention than any amateurishness.

I bring all of this up to introduce Gary, as I first met Gary, because this is how I had viewed him then: as a middle-aged publisher of a country relic, an author of a well-received biography on Charlie Birger—the infamous Jewish gangster and bootlegger in our beleaguered coalfields—a poet of some regional acclaim, and a talented artist.

It wasn't until after I spent years trudging behind him in the hollows, or climbing up death-defying rock faces, or lingering in the silence of abandoned cemeteries and watching hawks light atop bluffs, or sitting against a shag-bark hickory as he read his poetry in the forest, that I realized Gary's waggishness—this backwoods élan—had more to do with a deep cracker-barrel desire to reconcile his lifelong struggle for a sense of place in one of the most enigmatic but scorned places in our country—the coalfields of southern Illinois. That was his story.

And why is it, Gary would ask me repeatedly, that *you* keep coming down here?

"Eagle Creek is gone," he told me, just about every time we met. "You're too late."

Much to my irritation, Gary often reminded me of John Prine's classic tune about coal mining, "Paradise," in these moments.

> When I was a child, my family would travel
> back down to western Kentucky, where my parents were born.
> There's a backwards old town, that's often remembered,
> So many times that my memories are worn.
> Daddy, won't you take me back to Muhlenberg County,
> Down by the Green River, where Paradise lay.
> Well, I'm sorry my son, you're too late in asking,
> Mr. Peabody's coal train has hauled it away.

In one of the oldest settlements in the heartland of the American Midwest, tucked away in the back hollows of the Shawnee forest in southern Illinois, Eagle Creek's two-hundred-year-old farms and homesteads had been hauled away by Mr. Peabody and a handful of other coal companies.

As my Virgil, Gary always arrived at our meetings in midsentence, a tiny dog-eared notebook opened to questions and poems that he had scribbled at night when the whippoorwill sounded. *When the old women knew it was time to cut stove wood.* He answered my questions with vague self-deprecating riddles of his own, as if he needed a nip of our family gossip to keep the gristmill in his mind churning out ideas for poems and stories. He mocked my presumptions, often feigned indifference, and then an email would arrive a couple of days later with a cryptic reply:

> Ever notice
> >how men
> >love to talk
> >about the size of things?
> >Drag lines, bulldozers
> >you know what I mean.
> >It's a man thing
> >Best I can figure.
> coal bleeds
> >Your grandfather
> >wore a coal tattoo
> >on his cheek,
> >mine lost three fingers
> >at Wasson.

At times, I found Gary's intensity and tricksterlike quips unnerving. He asserted he had no politics at all; that he, like everyone else in the region, had no truck with the coal industry any more than they would question the sun rising or the barking roadside dogs.

"Coal has always been a matter-of-fact part of life here. How dare you question it."

His wife, an Audubon member, also had a subscription to the United Mine Workers newsletter—don't you? Besides, Gary's brother worked in one of the largest coal mines in the region as a reclamation expert. One of Gary's close friends, another writer of historical crime sagas, served as a public relations spokesman for the Illinois Coal Association. And furthermore, Gary had never taken a stand on any hot-button political issue.

"Except one time," he said to me a couple of days later, returning to his broken-down truck with a handful of corn kennels he had scavenged from a plowed field. He tossed the corn into the truck bed with a clatter—Gary liked to subversively treat the deer to corn in his patch of protected woods. He also smeared peanut butter on his trees for the titmice and nuthatches and raccoons.

"I spoke up at a Harrisburg city council meeting to keep Charlie Birger's tommy gun on display at City Hall." A wide grin swept across his face. "Now there was a cause worth a bloody nose."

But soon I realized that he was turning the table on my own inquiries, as if the secrets I was searching for in these woods had to first be discovered in my own family history.

Not long after that meeting in the cornfields, I thumbed through a *Springhouse* magazine Gary had handed me. Next to a column by the "Rebel Without Applause," which declared he had "sold turnips, sweet potatoes, sweet corn and ginseng, but I have never sold out," Gary had hand-sketched a quotation from Henry David Thoreau:

"If a man walks in the woods for love of them half of each day, he is in danger of being regarded as a loafer; but if he spends his whole life as a speculator shearing off those woods and making earth bald before her time, he is esteemed as an industrious and enterprising citizen, as if a town had no interest in its forests but to cut them down."

In the spring of 2004, Gary quietly let me know that a hammer had come down on his fate. He sent the address of a type of hospice in St. Louis, where he was recovering from a major throat cancer surgery. There was very little hope of survival. He had been faced with two options—a tracheotomy and subsequent surgery to remove the cancer that would have allowed him to eat, but speak through a vocal box; or another form of surgery that would inhibit his ability to swallow and force him to eat and drink via a feeding tube in his stomach, but allow him to speak.

Gary was the first person in his doctor's career to choose the speaking option.

Once he returned to the woods, Gary picked up his morning role on a no-holds-barred talk radio show out of nearby McLeansboro. He traded banter with "Cuzin' Eddie." They once took turns reading James Joyce's *Ulysses* in its entirety across the airwaves of southeastern Illinois.

We were trundling down the back slope of a canyon in a wilderness section of the Shawnee National Forest. Three years later Gary had defied the odds. He was not only alive but more vibrant. His weight had plunged. He was still disheveled, his glasses seemed even more oversized, and he was sandal-clad; this was his silent rebuke to the northern stiffs who had mocked the region's shoeless poverty. But there was a light in his eyes that I had never seen before. There was a country boy defiance that knew no consolation now.

Perched on a bluff one day, we sat for a spell, watching a couple of turkey vultures stitch a pattern in the cloudless sky. It was a beautiful fall day. I don't know what we chatted about—perhaps the name of a rare plant or tree, the direction of an Indian trace, the poetry of Robinson Jeffers, the antics of our brothers or kids—but there was always the faint echo of a coal truck in the hollows.

"You're not going to make anyone happy with this book, you know," Gary said, standing up. He withdrew a discolored plastic feeding bag and a long tube, then strung it to the limb of a yellow pine tree, emptied a can of a liquid nutrient into the bag, uncoiled the tube for several feet, and then sat down and attached the tube to his stomach. "But sometimes you've got to make choices."

I didn't know what to say, so I pulled my sandwich out of my bag and pretended to eat. And then we just sat in silence and watched the Eagle Creek valley unfold in front of us with a sense of wonder.

◊ ◊ ◊

WHEN I LOOKED into that staircased pit of destruction of the strip mine, I felt a profound sense of severance, as if my disconnection from Eagle Creek, and my family, had been finalized in an irreversible manner. As if some creature of fate wanted to cruelly remind me: You have no family history now.

But it didn't happen that way.

The strange irony of the situation was that instead of closure, the strip mine opened up a wound that I couldn't heal. I wanted to know: What was the real cost of strip-mining that hill and our homeplace?

In truth, my disconnection to my family, and our ancestral homeplace, mirrored my disconnection to my use of coal. I had no idea where my electricity came from, or the journey coal took from extraction to cleaning to transporting to its burning and storage of ash at a coal-fired plant.

Coal furnishes roughly 42 to 45 percent of our electrical needs in the United States: the lights in our homes, schools, hospitals, airports, offices, religious centers, our air conditioners and electrical heaters, refrigerators and freezers, appliances, computers, phones, iPods, TVs and entertainment systems, medical care units, security systems.

Whether I wanted to admit it or not, I was connected to coal, like every other American. As Jeff Goodell wrote in his classic, *Big Coal: The Dirty Secret Behind America's Energy Future*, I consumed about twenty pounds of coal a year.

I was part of the problem.

The incident at Eagle Creek forced me to confront this connection head-on. The invisible bedrock of coal that had fueled my world suddenly turned into a crucible I couldn't overlook. It stood before me in a gaping hole of oblivion.

When I stood for the first time in years at our Colbert family cemetery in Eagle Creek, a section of land draped by dogwoods and oaks and flanked by slabs of granite and limestone that dated back nearly two centuries to the first families, I wondered what it meant to lose Eagle Creek to the coal company—for my grandfather to lose his breath to black lung. Coal haulers from the strip mine roared by as we rustled our shoes in silence, as if to remind us of the biblical vision that we should let the dead bury the dead.

"You're kin to everyone in this place," my uncle Richard had reminded me.

As a peripatetic writer who left home in my teens, I had spent virtually all of my adult life far away from any family and now I was surrounded by seven generations of them. It was a powerful feeling. Why, I wondered, after living in many of the great cities and regions of the world—New York City, Washington, DC, the Bay Area, the American Southwest, the Sierra Madre of Mexico, Kerala, India, Berlin, Madrid, and Bologna, Italy—did this forsaken backwoods cemetery in the southern Illinois coalfields feel like home?

It made me ask myself: How could I have ignored the dirty reality of coal these years when it had been all around me?

◊ ◊ ◊

IN THE FALL OF 1989, as a freelance journalist, I sat on a hill over-looking Wenceslas Square in Prague, awaiting the fall of the Iron Curtain. The stark image of the Soviets' industrial mayhem hovered in the form of a dark cloud of smoldering lignite, as a haze of sulfuric acid, mercury, lead, and fly ash from the massive coal-fired factories cloaked the beautiful city in sheer darkness.

Even after his death, Kafka would have never returned to this coal-smothered city of his past. In my mind, coal had strangled Prague to death.

I washed off the muck and the black air and left. For years, I thought I had rid myself of its anachronistic clamor, that coal had gone the route of steam engines and piped itself out of existence.

In the late 1990s, living in a remote indigenous community in the Sierra Madre canyons of Mexico for a year, I began to read closely for the first time about the growing effects of global warming and climate destabilization. I saw it firsthand. During my tenure in a canyon village whose sparse cornfields had been wracked by deforestation and erosion, Mexico went through the most prolonged drought in its modern history. Living among an indigenous people that largely subsisted on corn, I experienced the despair and famine of farmers who saw their fields dissolved into the gray shards of a wasteland. The drought in the Sierra Madre had effectively endured over a decade.

According to many reports, deforestation of the world's woodlands not only eliminated valuable carbon sinks, but also contributed heavily to global warming with the release of carbon dioxide emissions; in 2006, a United Nations Food and Agriculture Organization study concluded that the felling and burning of the world's forests accounted for 1.6 billion tons of the greenhouse gases released into the atmosphere.

In the process, to my astonishment, I also learned that more than 40 percent of CO_2 emissions came from coal-fired plants.

Coal? We're still burning that much coal in the twenty-first century? As I delved further into the debate over climate change, coal suddenly emerged as the prime contributor to our emissions crisis.

I made a note in Mexico: We all live in the coalfields now.

And then, weeks later there in Mexico, strangely enough, my mother forwarded a letter from my uncle Richard about the strip-mining of Eagle Creek.

When he got word that our last cousin had succumbed to the intolerable blasting, a broken well, and unlivable conditions wrought by the coal company, and the strip-mining of our family homestead had begun, he had written an urgent letter to my mother to come back to Eagle Creek.

"A part of our lives now exists only in our mind," Uncle Richard wrote, "and will completely be erased when we die; as if it never existed."

He had actually written "when I die," and then crossed it out and added "we die," as if reminding my mother of some kind of burden.

After returning to the States from Mexico, I felt I needed to face this dilemma: I could either walk away and forget about Eagle Creek for the rest of my life, or attempt to reclaim its history as a writer, and as one of its offspring.

My uncle Richard just watched me one evening at his home in Kentucky, as I recounted some of my experiences abroad. I told him stories about Prague, about the Sierra Madre, about Appalachia. He nodded his head politely. My aunt Jerretta, who had dedicated her retirement years to her passion for genealogy, disappeared one evening as I spoke and then returned with an armload of three-ring binders. She disappeared again and then emerged with another armload. Soon the coffee table was stacked like a communion table.

"What are you waiting for?" Uncle Richard asked. "That's your family. That's your history."

The struggle of man against power is the struggle of memory against forgetting, author Milan Kundera wrote about his native Prague. "Thus what terrifies us about death is not the loss of the past. Forgetting is a form of death ever present within life."

◊ ◊ ◊

SOON AFTER MY VISIT to Eagle Creek with my mom and uncle, I returned to Appalachia to work on a new book. I felt I had another debt to repay. It dated back to the summer of 1983. I had been a dropout from the University of California. I had gone through a wild nine-month tour of duty in Berkeley's corridors, spending more time in jail and at political meetings than in classrooms. I failed to finish my last quarter that spring. Returning from a stint in jail for a demonstration in central California, I was involved in a tragic car accident, which resulted in the death of a young woman. I had been at the wheel.

Still in a daze, I eventually took a Greyhound bus across the country and then started hitching and hiking through the Appalachian Mountains. I was angry, resentful, and adrift. I worked on farms across the Blue Ridge—haying, mainly, tossing fifty-pound bales onto tractors and into the barns—and slept in the forests, barns, under bridges, and at lean-tos along the Appalachian Trail.

With less than ten bucks in my pocket, I accepted the ride and an offer to visit a folk school in West Virginia, after I had inadvertently insulted the driver. I had made a bad joke about hillbillies. He stopped the car; told me to get out. When I had responded that *I was a hillbilly*, that my family came from the southern Illinois hills, also known as the Illinois Ozarks, as if that somehow justified the comment, he gave me the option of getting out at the next exit or going with him across the state line into West Virginia. He took me to the Appalachian South Folklife Center in Pipestem, West Virginia.

At dawn, I was milking cows and soon listening to the history lectures and poetry readings of the folk school's founder, Don West, a ramrod-tall educator, poet, preacher, and radical labor organizer, who reminded me of my grandfather. There was one difference: As a young man I considered my John Henry–like grandfather, who had been a coal miner in southern Illinois, as a casualty of commerce, part of the beaten-up hill folk whose one attribute that drew respect from the industrial bosses—his brawn—had been abused and struck down by black lung, among other ailments.

There was an impervious working-class conceit about West that demanded respect. He could bring an elitist to his knees with his textbook memory of Shakespeare or Tom Paine. He had dedicated his life to reclaiming Appalachia's progressive heritage and traditions, which he felt had been strip-mined by a century of concerted misinformation.

I often tagged along on West's trips in his pickup to some of the most remote hollows and settlements. He toted crates of food and books, and often hiked them into the backwoods. One day we visited a family that lived in an old cabin on the edge of a ridge. Their roots went back to the Revolutionary period; the hollow and mountain carried their name. But due to some gerrymandered tax law, their family managed to keep the homestead but had lost the land several decades ago, unable to pay the back taxes in a period of extreme poverty. Standing to the side like a wolf in waiting, a coal company had paid the taxes, purchased the land, clear-cut the forest, and stripped the side of the mountain with such a devastating sheath that it appeared as if the old cabin had been displaced by an earthquake and now rested on the opposite side of a chasm of ash.

I'd never forget lugging a heavy pail of water from a nearby well. I followed a black trail of coal dust back to the house, as drops fell onto the dark earth like spots of blood. I sat on the porch and listened to an older woman tell her family stories. Three generations of this family had been underground coal miners; some had even worked on the crew that had stripped their ancestral land.

"Wasn't no other work around," she said.

"The abuse of the land has always gone hand in hand with the abuse of the miner or woodsman," West lectured me. "It's easy to take and strip-mine someone's land if we have convinced the world that its inhabitants are disposable, poor white trash. Bunch of hillbillies."

In those volatile days of political conflict, when environmentalists were pitted against miners in the coal companies' classic strategy of divide and conquer, West's folklife center was one of the few places that brought both sides together. He celebrated the land, and he celebrated the progress of unions in defending the rights of miners.

"You can't talk about mountains without mountaineers," West insisted. "You can't talk about mountaineers without mountains."

In the evenings that summer, I often loitered near West's front porch, where I would join him for long walks along the back roads. He answered my youthful questions; he recounted various episodes of his often harrowing life as a labor organizer and civil rights advocate in the South in the 1930s. He trotted out his beatings, imprisonments, and blacklistings like red badges of courage.

One evening, he turned the tables and questioned me about my understanding of southern Illinois history. I failed the test. I realized that I knew nothing about my grandfather or my family's history, nothing about the region—other than its own well-endowed slight as the crime-ridden, impoverished, and racist embarrassment of Illinois, a hilly range of boarded-up coal-mining and river towns that had been left behind.

Southern Illinois had always shared a similar history with Appalachia; it had always dealt with the same stereotypes of poverty, pity, and the picturesque, framed in the backdrop of the violent coalfields. Historically, in fact, the first wave of immigrants in the Shawnee forest came from the Appalachian highlands. In 1873, an article in the popular *Lippincott's Monthly Magazine* even associated the backwoods inhabitants of southern Illinois with Appalachia, as "A Strange Land and Peculiar People."

"Do you know that Mother Jones is buried in southern Illinois?" West suddenly asked me.

I didn't, of course. I assumed the legendary "Miner's Angel" and labor organizer had been buried in West Virginia.

"If you don't know your history," West admonished, "someone else will write it for you, and it will most likely be wrong."

West told me to leave West Virginia and go back to southern Illinois. I shook him off.

Why couldn't I go back to southern Illinois? In my mind, as a young man, it represented all that I wanted to forget: a family past of the farm, of the hollows and forested hills, of the coal mines, of the failure of the American pastoral.

West dug out a tape recorder from a trunk the next day, and soon I found myself accompanying him into the back hollows, where he delivered food and recruited students for his various camps and courses. I began to interview coal miners and their wives and widows, farmers, musicians, and families that had been displaced by strip mining and the collapsed coal towns. Burl Collins was one of the liveliest, even if he was the one closest to death.

Burl was an irascible old coal miner in West Virginia. After thirty-five years underground, he struggled to conjure his breath to match his storyteller verve, as if the iron hoops of a whiskey barrel had been strapped around his lungs.

While Burl spit every few minutes, I held up the small tape recorder, edging closer to his faint words. At one point, he rolled up his pant leg and showed me where he had been crushed in a mining accident. The scars snaked down to his ankles.

"My grandpa was a coal miner," I said, without thinking.

Burl wheezed. "Where does he live?"

"He's dead," I said.

Burl labored to catch his breath. He stared at me with a confounded look.

"Ever interview your granddaddy?"

I shook my head. Burl read my mind; I wouldn't have found any value in interviewing my grandfather in those days.

"The hell you interviewing me for?" he spit.

I nodded, picked up my tape recorder, and walked away; walked back through the forest and valleys and lonely country roads to West's farm. For the first time in my life, I felt like I had betrayed my grandparents. I had never made any effort to understand their lives, when they were living.

◊ ◊ ◊

"THE RAPE OF APPALACHIA," Harry Caudill declared in his classic portrait of Appalachia, *Night Comes to the Cumberlands*, "got its practice" in Illinois. He was referring to the fact that the nation's first commercial strip mines took place in eastern and southern Illinois in the 1860s.

There was one other strange connection between Appalachia and my southern Illinois coalfields: Like the unintended consequences of outsourced war from a peace treaty, the Clean Air Act not only dismantled the high-sulfur coal industry in Illinois in 1990, but also shifted our nation's demand to Appalachia, wildly escalating the process of mountaintop removal—the process of literally blowing up mountains and dumping the waste and overburden into the valleys and waterways.

When I returned to Appalachia in 2001, I couldn't believe the level of devastation that had taken place since my first visit in 1983. I finally understood what Caudill and Don West had forewarned:

The abuse of the land was always connected to the abuse of the people.

One story in particular grabbed my attention. After witnessing five hundred mountains in central Appalachia get blown to bits by strip mining, a community of coalfield activists at Coal River Mountain in West Virginia was drawing a line in the sand. The verdict was in on mountaintop removal, which had been launched in 1970 as a quick and dirty option to cheaply procure coal. Thirty-odd years and a million and a half acres of destroyed hardwood forests later, mountaintop removal had run its course in the region with appalling effects. It had not only destroyed the natural heritage, it had also ripped out the roots of the Appalachian culture and depopulated the historic mountain communities in the process.

Over 1,200 miles of waterways had been sullied and jammed with mining fill. Blasting and coal dust had made life unbearable for anyone in the strip-mined areas. Wells had been busted and polluted with toxic waste. Given the mechanization of aboveground mountaintop removal, and its shakedown of a diversified economy, coal-mining jobs had plummeted as poverty rates rose in strip-mining areas.

The history was clear: Coal was not cheap, and coal was not clean.

Facing an impending 6,600-acre mountaintop removal strip mine that would destroy their historic communities and the last mountain in the Coal River Mountain range, the residents on Coal River Mountain had come up with their own plan for an industrial wind farm, which would have provided more energy, more tax revenues, and more sustainable jobs than the proposed mountaintop removal operations. They presented their community of coal miners with a simple message: We have a choice.

The Coal River Wind Project—and the protection of the last mountain on the Coal River Mountain range—was ultimately rejected by the county and statewide officials, who allowed the mountaintop removal operation to proceed. The stranglehold of the Big Coal lobby on local and national politicians, and our history, had never been so obvious.

I realized it was time to go back to Eagle Creek.

◊   ◊   ◊

I WAS RAISED, like most children at the tail end of the baby boomers, on the concept of coal-fired industrial progress. Our parents weathered the hardscrabble days of the Great Depression and never let us forget it. They took part in the great fracture of rural America, that postwar exodus that released the hand from the plow or pick, became the first generation in the front row of state universities, and then returned to their coal-mining hometown to scratch out their own generational niche above the dirty collars of their past.

My mother would be the first person to remind me that she attended Southern Illinois University, thanks to the heydays of the coal mines. Her father's low but livable union wages in the underground mines allowed her to study for four years, paid the rent at a boardinghouse. He'd put on his church suit jacket, on top of his overalls, and shuttle her back and forth between Harrisburg and Carbondale every Sunday afternoon with the same dedication and pride that made him rise before dawn, huddle into the cage, sink hundreds of feet below the ground, and detonate explosives.

That kind of steady job meant something to those who lived in a boom-bust-boom-bust region that had witnessed unemployment rates near 70 percent during the lean years. It meant even more after the mines shut down in the early 1950s, and my grandfather rambled from one labor crew to the next, unable to maintain the stable paycheck of those coal mine years for the rest of his life.

He was a proud coal miner in southern Illinois—that's the image I wanted to preserve. I was proud of coal miners, because I was proud of my grandfather. My grandfather had dug the coal that powered the nation's progress, not the coal barons; and my grandfather, like other coal miners, had paid the ultimate price with his health and life.

The coal mines remained a memory of stability for my mother. Still, the sound of that haunting whistle of an accident at the mines remained an echo of fear in her mind for years.

Coal had always been part of our family's and our region's life. My mother's grandfather, Charles Stilley, had been a backwoods blacksmith in Eagle Creek, who pounded those red-ribbon irons over the hot coals. In the deforested era of the 1930s and 1940s, the fireplace in their hillside farm at Eagle Creek burned coal, not wood. There were no Yule logs; my grandfather placed slabs of Yule coal in the fireplace. Chunks as big as an oak stump.

Coal was so prevalent that my uncle recalled feeding slack coal to the pigs, who gobbled it up like a furnace. One of my mother's uncles even had his own dog-hole coal mine at the basin of his hillside property at Eagle Creek, where a little dynamite in the evening brought a morning's wagon of coal.

My grandfather Bob Followell was a specimen of a man, folks liked to say. Tall, broad shouldered like an ox, a hammer's strength in his hands at hog-killing time. "You have his build," my mom once told me, "except he actually had muscles." But he was a gentle man, said he had always wanted to be a preacher. Instead, he had left the back hills as a young man, worked in the Harrisburg brickyards, as a migrant worker in the West, and in the canning factories in Terre Haute, Indiana. When the Second World War broke out and gas was rationed, Bob packed up his family, traded for enough gas coupons to cannonball the Wabash, and returned to the old homeplace in the Eagle Creek hills of southern Illinois.

The Oval Hill homestead had been part of his wife's inheritance. My grandmother Cora Bell Stilley had begrudgingly left behind the Eagle Creek hills as a teenager to marry Bob on July 4, at the first courthouse in the next county over. He was ten years older; he was already white haired. Packing up her belongings in a cardboard suitcase, they left immediately for Terre Haute in 1930.

Nonetheless, for the next thirteen years, raising three kids, Cora insisted on returning to the hills every two weeks. Eagle Creek was home. When her father fell ill in 1943, she didn't want to be cut off from the family during the war. Kinship mattered more than money. Cora Bell decided it was time to go back to Eagle Creek, even if it meant giving up her husband's steady factory job, her children's good schools, and the conveniences of electricity and indoor plumbing.

Eagle Creek had none of that. They were moving back to the woods.

When they returned, the area ranked as one of the most impoverished regions in the entire country. "Less than two decades ago," the government report "Seven Stranded Coal Towns" chronicled, "the southern Illinois coal field was riding the crest of a prolonged and spectacular boom." Three out of four coal miners now looked for work; the rest of the region hoed at their dirt farms and cursed their region's doomed fate.

My mom and her family arrived in their overloaded truck that night to an ominous sight. As they bumped down the rutted dirt road along Eagle Creek, Bob and Cora Bell swore they saw a ring of strange mineral lights hovering around the old homestead on the hill. Perhaps the stones of fire from the book of Ezekiel, the tail of Lucifer. The mineral lights disappeared as they approached the cabin. The curse of death remained.

The homestead on the knoll provided the basic foods—pigs, chicken, corn, sorghum, a large garden—but it wasn't enough to

make a living. Nor was Bob a young man. In his forties now, he re-
luctantly turned to coal mining as a last resort. He considered himself lucky to get a job; his brother-in-law had a union connection.

Born in 1901, coming of age in a generation when every father
in the county had escorted his teenage son to the booming mines,
Bob had somehow eluded the fate of coal. Perhaps his own father,
a rough-edged farmer, bootlegger, and shopkeeper who had also fled
to Indiana with an Eagle Creek wife in the 1890s, only to return
because of her homesickness for the hills, cared more for his son
than he had ever managed to show. In fact, he had quietly taken his
teenage boys to Colorado during the draft for World War I.

Even in an era of unthinkable sacrifices and bootstrap-molasses
poverty during the Depression, as long as the tipple purred with
coal, my grandfather never had to deny my mother those little details in life that remained in her memory like balms of Gilead. On
the way home from the mines, he would stop at the general store at
Herod, tie a block of ice on the back of the bumper, and then thrash
down the dirt road through the Gap, across mud-sucked ravines and
up the hills until he arrived in a cloud of dust at the farm at Eagle
Creek. About half the ice block would be left. But Norma Jean liked
ice in her homemade sweet tea.

And that was why he got up every morning before dawn,
slopped the hogs, worked on his hardscrabble hillside farm, and
eventually moved into the coal-mining town of Harrisburg, despite
his love for the country life at Eagle Creek. He had to be closer to
his work in the coal mines; only a dozen miles away, the winding trip
out of the hollows of Eagle Creek to Harrisburg and the mines became too long; took too many expensive tires to repair. The mud
ravines that served as roads turned to quicksand after the rains. Bob
loved his family, so he moved from his beloved Eagle Creek hills, because coal mining was the only way to make a living.

My father's parents weren't coal-mining people, though. They had only shoveled coal into their basement furnace like the rest of the town of Harrisburg. It was part of their daily chores, not their daily bread. They didn't think much of those strange winters, when their white Christmas snow was covered in black soot before they went to church in the morning. Every spring, they bought a pack of putty, scrubbed the blackened walls of their rooms until the patterns of the floral wallpaper came back into bloom, and then aired out the sour smell of ash from their house.

My father studied journalism at the University of Illinois, in central Illinois, where he had to ward off mockery of his southern region's reputation as a coven of violent, backward people. My father was intent on a newspaper career, but his older brother, a war hero and chemist, talked him into derailing that dream for a more bona fide position in the accepted confines of Our Town.

So, he ended up at law school, hitchhiked home on the weekends, and then returned to Harrisburg as an ambitious young assistant state's attorney, whose first case was to prosecute backwoods stalwarts for their coon-on-a-log fights. It was a strange case. Moonshiners, for the most part, chained a raccoon on a log, cast it from the edge of a lake, and then released two hounds to see who could knock off the raccoon first. There was plenty of bloody action in the process.

In his early days, my father had eavesdropped on enough of his father's tales from the bank to despise the miners' union. My grandfather never forgave the gall of the John L. Lewis union stiffs who walked the picket line in the middle of the Second World War.

And then my father married a fierce union member and coal miner's daughter.

My father straddled the line between working-class angst and middle-class ambition, the son of a low-level bank clerk who had

put on a tie and cowered in the presence of the coal company executives and bank officers all of his life. They ruled the town; he
pushed the pencil and kept their books. But my grandfather considered himself one of them and memorized the rituals to earn his
Masonic ring, even if he was only a shadow in the back rooms of the
power brokers who bankrolled the coal mines. These were the men
who ensured the bricks and mortar for the mainstream churches
and Masonic lodges and main-square storefronts. The message was
clear: The bankers and coal company executives built Harrisburg,
raised southern Illinois out of the pits of agricultural failure, lived
in their mansions on Main Street, and nobody was to forget that.
And they paid my grandfather's rent.

After my father lost an election for state's attorney in Harrisburg in the mid-1950s, my folks packed up their suitcases and
moved to St. Louis, Missouri.

They followed the well-worn hillbilly highway that had carried
the unemployed miners, bootleggers, and dirt farmers for several
generations out of southern Illinois. But, my parents were not unemployed miners—they were the first children of mining communities that had left on their own terms, not in desperation. They
arrived as a successful lawyer and a dynamic schoolteacher, anxious
to be part of the middle-class American dream that rested on the
rise and fall of the urban smoke stacks from the coal-fired factories
and mills and industries.

This great city on the Mississippi River had been built with the
sweat of their fathers. Coal, indeed, was not a dirty word; coal was
the key to our nation's industrial future.

Within a few years, my parent's exile was over, so they moved
back to Illinois and began to raise their three children in the modern suburbs. Life had moved on; gas-generated furnaces had replaced the coal burners. Coal and its enduring legacy in their lives
had not lost its temper; it had merely retreated like bark on the

trunk of an oak tree that had grown limbs and blossomed in a new era. By the time I was born in 1963, coal mining had been put away in my parent's personal closet like a relic from a different life. My grandfather's coal-mining helmet sat on the mantle of our fireplace with the nostalgic air of his .22 single-shot long rifle—two characters in search of a play.

In 1970, my folks packed up our family and dog and piled us into a 1960 Chevy, and we followed the stream of sunbelt migrants to the New West suburbs outside of Tucson, Arizona.

They made the choice to move on. Illinois made the choice to hang on to coal. It went through another Tin Pan Alley coal boom in the 1960s and mid-1970s, before it came to a screeching halt in the late 1980s with the Clean Air Act. Illinois' mostly dirty sulfur-ridden coal couldn't compete with the cheaper Wyoming and Appalachian coal basins.

On our vacation trips back to Harrisburg and Eagle Creek over the years, my parents never really discussed the past or the present reality of the strip mines that had engulfed the area like a battlefield and eventually turned the depleted coal mining towns and surrounding areas into empty apparitions of their former lives. We remained aloof, as if we had been spared the lingering sadness of the busted coal economy and its boarded-up future.

A few years later, when the market decided that coal was "cheap" and "clean" again in Eagle Creek, a different fate awaited our family homestead in the Shawnee Hills.

We returned to Eagle Creek, as if we were returning to a funeral.

◊ ◊ ◊

THE IMPACT OF A MURDER on a family, Thornton Wilder wrote, is ultimately what shatters history and time and our sense of place. In his novel *The Eighth Day*, a coal miner in southern Illinois is accused of killing the boastful Breckenridge Lansing, the mine operative. A mysterious group, though, springs the miner from prison before his execution; he sets off for South America, while his children attempt to make sense of a family unraveled and forced to reinvent itself at the mercy of industrial machinations.

The Eighth Day, which won the National Book Award in 1967, is an American parable of good versus evil, though who is good and who is evil is limited to the witness's narrow view of history: "No eye can venture to compass more than a hand's breath." History, even for the moralizing Wilder, unfolded like an illusive tapestry with multiple interpretations. He wrote: "There is much talk of a design in the arras. Some are certain they see it. Some see what they have been told to see. Some remember that they saw it once but have lost it. Some are strengthened by seeing a pattern wherein the oppressed and exploited of the earth are gradually emerging from their bondage. Some find strength in the conviction that there is nothing to see."

The day after the murder, Wilder conjured, another history began: "Man is not an end but a beginning. We are at the beginning of the second week. We are children of the eighth day."

My eighth day began on July 18, 1998, when the daily newspaper in the nearby coal-mining town of Harrisburg, Illinois, recorded a sale in ten lines under its Land Transaction section. Technical phrasings buried in the back pages opposite the cartoons: Warranty Deed (WD) or Quit Claim Deed (QCD), Grantors and Grantees. The Downen mining company. Land purchase on Eagle Creek Road. No obituary or note about the death of the old homeplace. It was a business deal.

"Hell, son, don't know what happened to those logs," an older representative with the local coal company told me on the phone one day. He projected a very matter-of-fact, blunt, but likeable rural air of chitchat, as if he were another wizened uncle playing with all of his cards on the table, even when he was bluffing. "You know how those country people want to get out of the hills and into town. So we helped your cousin out."

This small coal company would never admit in a thousand golden summers that it had rattled the bones of our last cousin at the Oval Hill Farm to the point of despair. That it had carved a black sea of ruin around our Eagle Creek knoll, their massive machines clawing at the foothills; that its explosions took the peace and property titles out of the trembling hands of the children of the first pioneers who had cleared a path in the virgin forests and established Illinois. This company wasn't the only coal operator in Eagle Creek, of course. Large-scale mining outfits from Chicago had been razing the hollow since the 1930s. With a massive strip mine on the east end of Eagle Creek in the 1960s and 1970s, Peabody Coal had wiped out the first historic mining town, Bowlesville, which had supplied Union army ships with coal during a critical moment in the Civil War.

With his retirement only a year away, our cousin had recently remodeled the old homestead. He was preparing for the eight generation in our family to reside at the Oval Hill Farm. His daughter, who had lost her own husband in an underground coal mining accident, understood its family legacy.

Like the mine operatives in Wilder's novel, the small coal company in Eagle Creek didn't share this family story. With unusually low sulfur content for Illinois, the coal in the Eagle Creek, according to the company report, was one of the best strikes in their history. They stripped 12,000 tons of coal an acre out of our original homestead (of 160 acres). That was the first seam; they were just getting started.

"We're stewards of the land," the aging representative of the company told me with an air of nostalgia. Once they harvested crops, like tobacco; now they harvested the coal.

By 2001, the small outfit leased several of their Eagle Creek operations to Illinois Fuel, whose parent company, Appalachian Fuels
in Ashland, Kentucky, operated some of the most aggressive and
ruthless mountaintop removal operations in Appalachia.

The rape of Appalachia may have got its practice in our Illinois
hills, but now it was our turn again in Eagle Creek.

◊   ◊   ◊

THE ILLINOIS DEPARTMENT of Commerce and Economic Opportunity never tired of reminding the country that Illinois was the
"Saudi Arabia of coal." Every state report began with this mantra:
"Illinois is sitting on a vast natural resource, with coal reserves that
can produce more energy than the oil reserves of Saudi Arabia."
More so, Illinois liked to claim that it possessed the largest bituminous (soft) coal reserves in the nation; or at least, the largest strip-
pable bituminous reserves, notwithstanding its costly high-sulfur
content. And Saline County, home of Eagle Creek and some of the
heartland's most diverse wilderness areas, produced more coal than
any other county in Illinois.

This was only the outlandish marketing buzz, of course. Out of
the 1.1 billion tons of coal produced in 2007, nearly half of it came
from the Powder River Basin of Wyoming. The next five states—
West Virginia's coalfield juggernaut included—barely matched
Wyoming's output. And then came Illinois in a distant ninth, at 32
million tons, not even within reach of honorable mention, limping
along as the costly high-sulfur stepchild that resented being left out
of coal's great inheritance.

Not that it stopped anyone from strip-mining Eagle Creek for its
last seams.

Nearly a hundred and fifty years after the hearthstone had been
placed on the foundations of our old homeplace at the Oval Hill
Farm, an estimated 960,000 tons of coal were stripped from our an-

cestor's original farm and adjoining areas. Shipped to a medium-size coal-fired power plant, it would have generated roughly 2.06 MWe of electricity, based on typical estimates of burning coal.

That would have been enough electricity to supply American demands for approximately four and half hours. That was the choice we made.

Now it was my turn to discover the real price we had truly paid for those four and half hours.

It was time for a reckoning at Eagle Creek.

Barney Bush. *(Photo by Charles F. Hammond.)*

◊

Chapter Two

IN THE NAME OF
THE SHAWNEE

Removing the Earth's Liver

In them he had seen his face a
thousand times over seen
headless bones of ancestors
scattered over hillsides over
stripmine dumps left by
looters who sell even the
fleshless skulls

—**BARNEY BUSH**,
"A Single Proselyte"

Barney Bush had these enormous feet, and the first time I visited him at the double-wide mobile home headquarters of the Vinyard Indian Settlement, he was nursing a toe infection at a springhouse on the property. A narrow cowboy boot rested to the side like a spent shotgun shell. Barney limped with the disposition of a harried middle-aged community organizer (with cropped hair and a short ponytail) who wouldn't hesitate to take to the barricades again, even if he had to crawl.

This time, though, the jutting canopy of dogwoods and hickories dwarfed his grounded figure. He peered from the spring with a look of pain in these two searingly blue eyes that reflected his turquoise earrings; his big toe was crimson-tinged. The hounding of coal trucks on the nearby state road, heading to Herod and the turnoff to the Gap and Eagle Creek, sounded for a moment before we exchanged greetings.

Barney had summoned my visit. Over the past year or so, we had swapped the kind of exploratory emails and phone calls that eventually filtered out the familial courtesies and initial suspicion of unsolicited contact. After dealing with a lifetime of indifference and ridicule in his homeland, Barney's voice always sounded with a war veteran's edge of zero tolerance for bullshitting chitchat.

What is it that you want? Barney would ask me.

Gary DeNeal had first told me about Barney and his efforts to resurrect a Shawnee Indian settlement in our hills with his usual droll nonchalance. He had mentioned Barney's noted career as an award-winning published poet, translated in nearly a dozen languages, anthologized in scores of collections. Not that anybody in the area ever considered this side of Barney's otherworldly life; not that anyone had a copy of Barney's French-produced CDs of his *Left for Dead* poetry performances accompanied by acclaimed British musician Tony Hymas. Barney's Shawnee presence was like goldenseal, that rare medicinal plant in the hills that everyone considered eradicated, and yet it cropped up in the most unusual places for a handful of backwoods roamers.

And while their fathers had played baseball against each other on the rural grounds over three-quarters of a century ago, they had never really connected as friends until Gary published his first book of poetry with a press out of Philadelphia. *Butterfly, Flutter By*. Barney had already packed his suitcase to hitchhike and escape town. He wrote Gary a note of profound appreciation; poetry had also been Barney's refuge in an otherwise joyless education. Their friendship began, thus not as country boys but as writers, or as Gary had written as an eighteen-year-old poet, lonely walkers who "talk to trees."

But Barney didn't want to talk only to trees. He grew up listening to the stories of a pair of aunts and uncles who had worked in the Indian service, including stints at Native American schools in Montana, South Dakota, and the infamous Carlyle Indian School in Pennsylvania—whose founder sought to "kill the Indian and save the man." Still in his teens, he journeyed off to initiate himself into a life and fatherhood on Indian reservations in Oklahoma and the northern plains, and in the academic corridors in Colorado, New Mexico, Idaho, North Carolina, and Wisconsin.

Despite the geographical divide, Barney always alerted Gary to his occasional returns to the Shawnee forests or visits to his mother in Harrisburg. He had even stayed at an old cabin in the woods on Gary's parents' property for a period in the late 1980s, early 1990s. In fact, Gary mused, Barney had never failed to keep in touch with Gary's octogenarian mother, a childhood friend of his own mother.

In one book of poetry, *Petroglyphs*, Barney had written, "Sometimes I think of all the recent lives I've been a part of and find it hard to believe that my childhood is a part of my present lifetime."

In the late 1990s, Barney returned one day with the idea of reestablishing a more formal Shawnee Indian settlement in the area. For the first time in anyone's memory, Barney unveiled the saga of a nearly two-hundred-year history of his Shawnee family's elusive presence in a nearby range called Karbers Ridge, just over the valley from Eagle Creek. Prior to the arrival of the namesake Karber, the story went, a large German-Irish family by the name of Vinyard had provided refuge for a band of Shawnee Indians around 1810 or so in a hollow north of High Knob around Karbers Ridge. The Shawnee band had fled Ohio and, prevented from joining the

Tecumseh-led resistance at Prophetstown in nearby western Indiana, had attempted to ditch the pursuing militia in the southern
Illinois hills. They camped, hunted, traded, eventually assimilated
into the Vinyard, Eagle Creek, and Hardin County families, inter-
marrying and assuming more of a backwoods than Native appearance. Those in the know referred to them as the Vinyard Indian
Settlement. After the death of Barney's grandfather in the 1950s,
any semblance of Shawnee culture had vanished into the mountain
fog—or so people thought.

The problem was that no one in the contemporary Vinyard fam-
ily knew or even accepted this history; some genealogists among the
Vinyards, in fact, had openly objected to any connection with the
Shawnee.

After years of planning and cultivating the territory for a sym-
pathetic hearing, Barney answered one of my emails with a cryptic
reply: "We need to talk," he told me on the phone one day. "There's
a story down here you need to hear, and your family's part of it."

I assumed my "family's part" had to do with Vinyard inter-
marriage with our Colbert clan in Eagle Creek, or even a lingering
Chickasaw connection that had fascinated my aunt Jerretta for years.

We straggled to the front porch of the trailer, which Barney had
purchased a few years ago. Tucked into the densely forested valley,
the moss-covered trailer was located right off the main road to
Herod, which eventually led to Karbers Ridge and Eagle Creek. The
trailer sat at the base of a hill; the property climbed the ridge for
twenty acres in a thick stand of oak, hickory, dogwoods, and pine,
among other trees. When a wildcat logging company dropped by
one day, offering Barney a considerable amount of money to clear-
cut the property, he told them to get lost.

"We'll stay here for now," he told me, resting his foot on the
steps of his porch. "But once the settlement grows and we can raise
enough money, we plan to eventually move back into our homeland
on Karbers Ridge."

Barney had estimated three hundred people in the area with Vinyard Indian connections. Still, there was a solitary air about the trailer that didn't suggest a burgeoning movement of Native revival. Nonetheless, he had formally incorporated the settlement as a nonprofit agency, replete with an official council and governing body. Several people had committed themselves to DNA testing, as required for federal recognition.

Barney's gruffness disappeared quickly. Still, he kept his shoe off. Like every soul I would visit in the area for years, he put on a spread of southern hospitality: coffee and stew had been prepared. You never left a home without eating or drinking in abundance, often before you engaged in any real discussion.

Blue eyes notwithstanding, Barney was no Indian wanna-be that churned out academic polemics or haunted the edges of pow-wows and genealogy forums with romantic notions. In fact, much of his writing mocked "whites" searching for some tribal identity, "stripping and tearing at / the earth devastating native / lives in whose eyes yet lurk / the seven cities of Cibola." Unlike others in his family, he had embodied and hog-wrestled and defended a Native identity with bare-knuckled fortitude, whether assumed or adopted, and it had transfigured his life completely.

In his early sixties, Barney eased into a tenor-pitched drawl that sounded like my uncle. He could mimic various accents with ease, including that distinctive staccato voice of non-Native English speakers. Barney referred to Natives with the colloquial "In'din."

"I know why you're here," Barney began. "I took my mother over to Eagle Creek the other day. She's almost ninety." He paused for a moment, looked away. "We couldn't even figure out where we were, considering how much it's been changed by the strip mines. And we just stopped the car and looked in amazement. And then we just sat there and wept."

Barney's parents did not raise him at his grandparent's home-place on Karbers Ridge, but at another forest settlement a few miles to the west, just south of Harrisburg. It was called Battle Ford; some local historians even suggested the name was acquired from conflict with the Shawnee. In his memoir of the 1840s, W. S. Blackman didn't recall problems with the Natives, but the terror of wolves in the Battle Ford woods that obliged farmers "to pen all small animals each night or run great danger of losing them." Fish stocked the streams in abundance in those days; trappers had their pick of plentiful wild game.

In the post–World War II years, Barney and his brother roamed the edges of their valley, where a branch of the creek provided fresh water and a wonderful swimming hole in the summers. The boys disappeared into the forests for days. They fished and hunted. They made bows and arrows; they conjured the spirits of their Indian past.

Although Barney's childhood had been a joyous romp through the woods, his primary years at a one-room schoolhouse had been painful. The teacher had been a disgruntled soul whose singular act of goodness, in Barney's mind, was to gift him a stone ax found in the area. Barney likened his treatment to that of Indians at the mission schools in the West. When the teacher announced that Barney's family were savages because Native Americans had never possessed the wheel, the young student turned to the encyclopedia and discovered drawings of wheeled instruments in prehistoric Mesoamerica. He excitedly showed his finding to the teacher, who turned and brutally beat the fifth-grade student with a leather belt for his insolence.

Those beatings remained a bad memory, but the "massive scars" in his life arrived when he turned thirteen. "Near the end of the eighth year came the strip miners," he wrote in an essay, "another of that world's great war machines against nature and humanity."

Barney rubbed his toe, as he recalled the evening the lawyers for a coal company arrived on his family's front porch, towing their wives along, as if to give their deal a domestic touch. The adults went inside. Barney and his brother listened from the front porch, where they slept each night. The lawyers offered a fairly small sum of money for his parent's land in the forest, along the creek of Battle Ford.

Barney's parents resisted, as they had done on earlier attempts. Despite the reasoning for money, or the guilt-ridden harangue of jobs and local commerce connected to the strip mines, they had no intention of selling their ten acres. So, the lawyers changed tactics, threatening to employ an act of eminent domain to take the land—without payment. Barney's naive parents didn't entirely understand the legal dynamics; that the lawyers, in fact, had bent the intent of the laws into an unrecognizable mockery of truth.

"Either take the price we offer," the lawyers said, "or lose the land completely."

They signed the contract at the kitchen table, under the faint light of a coal oil Aladdin lamp. As they left the house, the lawyers crossed through the porch, reached into their pockets, and handed each boy a dollar bill. Barney took it, walked over to the corner, and dropped it into his chamber pot.

"I detest strip mining with every fiber of my being," Barney told me. "When they strip-mined our forests and valley, they strip-mined me. I could literally feel it. Like they had removed part of my body."

He held a hand to his side, as if in pain.

◊ ◊ ◊

EMINENT DOMAIN, of course, had been used to remove citizens from their private property for centuries, dating back to common law practices in England. When the concept was incorporated into the Fifth Amendment of our Constitution in 1791, the American Congress strictly relegated its application to public use—such as railroads or utilities, like the largely forgotten removal of untold numbers of families in rural Appalachia for the Tennessee Valley Authority dams and coal-fired plants in the 1930s and later; or state or national parks, such as the Land Between the Lakes recreation site in western Kentucky. *With proper compensation,* as the bureaucrats who served the eviction notices to seventh-generation elderly homesteaders, liked to say.

Not that this had anything to do with Barney's family or the Shawnee, or my family for that matter. His folks, intimidated by the legalese of the coal company attorneys, were probably bilked out of their property by fraudulent means for the most part, under the guise of *proper compensation.* Either way, there was an element of colonialism in the exchange, back in the late 1950s, that still reared its head today like a diamondback rattler when it came to coal claims.

This was Barney's lesson: The roots of the colonialism of coal preceded both of our families. They branched off with their arrivals into legislative acts that shaped our pioneering economy. And they still blossomed in the twenty-first century with their disingenuous skewing of our modern terms of mining and population removals.

My Colbert family, the first of our extended clans to enter the Eagle Creek area in 1805, knew that their name preceded them with an element of intrigue. For years, family tradition had it that our ancestors descended from James Logan Colbert, a legendary Scottish American trader—pronounced "Kalh'bert"—who married three Native women over the course of his life, spawned several generations of Chickasaw leaders, and made the last raid on the western front in the American Revolution, attacking Fort Carlos on the Arkansas River.

Alas, there was no Elisha Colbert, our enigmatic first ancestor in the region, on the well-combed Chickasaw Colbert lists, or any credible link, outside an unidentified third Chickasaw wife. Another elusive Colbert connection resonated in southern Illinois. Since René-Robert Cavalier de La Salle had claimed the Mississippi River Valley on behalf of the French king Louis XIV in 1682, the first colonists had always referred to the Mississippi as the River Colbert, in homage to their foreign minister Jean-Baptiste Colbert.

La Salle, an adventurous merchant who had given up the priesthood, became the first European to navigate the mysteries of this great Colbert River that connected France's northern colonies in Canada with its future Louisiana colonies on the mouth of the lower Mississippi. He also took something else back to France with him: a pair of Shawnee Indians and a handful of coal from Illinois.

One of those Shawnee visitors to Paris never returned. But he would have choked on the smell and fumes of the "stone coal" spewing from the furnaces along the River Seine. The faculty from the School of Medicine in Paris had debated the health hazards of burning fossil fuels a century before; while the first recorded imports from Newcastle, England, took place in 1325, France used only a fraction of the coal in comparison to England, which by 1700 consumed more than ten times the amount used by the rest of the world. By the time a delegation of Cherokee visited a coal ash–ridden London in the 1730s, the first basic steam engine had already been converting coal into power for two decades. Recognizing England's industrial prowess, France began to levy more taxes on coal imports as a way of boosting its own domestic production.

Their eyes remained on the treasure of coal in the Mississippi Valley.

The "discovery" of coal in the United States, as much as that phrase denotes such an anachronistic European viewpoint, actually took place in Illinois a few years before La Salle's arrival, when French explorer Louis Jolliet and his Jesuit companion, Jacques Marquette, stopped at an Indian encampment on the Illinois River in 1673 and sketched the black banks of *charbon de terre* on their maps. (Some historians also question whether French Jesuits recorded the use of coal by "Poulak Tribes of the Assiniboine" in Minnesota in 1659.)

La Salle's discovery, though, was not as an ethnographer or cartographer; he was an entrepreneur and he recognized the potential wealth of trade and mineral resources along the vast Mississippi River Valley. As historian Eric Hinderaker noted in his survey of the elusive empires on the western frontier, "The Illinois country, in short, was the linchpin of French territorial expansion in North America." The minerals, as part of its imperial wealth, underscored the élan for that expansion.

La Salle never enjoyed the benefits of those mines and minerals. Equipped by the king to return to the Mississippi Valley to launch his own private feudal state and serve notice on Spain's legendary mines in northern Mexico, La Salle's ship went off course and landed in Texas. A bereaved mutineer eventually killed the French entrepreneur and his longtime Shawnee slave in a gruesome fashion on their search for the River Colbert.

By then, however, the incursion of French Canadian *coureurs de bois,* or forest runners—fur trappers and traders who generally operated outside the bounds of treaties, and often cohabited within the mores of Native wives and settlements—had already begun to reshape the order of business in the Illinois country. Few of the forest runners would ever get their names in the history books, but their presence forever changed a continent. European contact did not simply open a new frontier inhabited by Native people; it redefined the frontier as an international theater of war and diplomacy, and a staging ground for the some of the most important exchanges of commerce in the New World.

In essence, it turned the American heartland into a catalogue for wealth and wealth-seekers in Europe and along the East Coast, long before the region was downsized into a place for pioneer settlement.

In the process, it triggered an upheaval of Native American social
and economic ways of life, village structure, and tribal identity and
loyalty in a very short period of time.

When La Salle first stumbled onto the coal banks on the Illinois
River in 1682, he also met with an estimated one thousand Shawnee
in the area, who had splintered from other Shawnee in the Wabash
and Ohio river valleys. While the anthropologist Charles Callender
referred to the Shawnee as a "singularly restless people," they had
often found themselves in conflict or faltering treaty with other nations, on the run from the Iroquois, or making alliances with fellow
Algonquin-language tribes, only to migrate again within a generation. The Shawnee ranged from the Mississippi River to the Great
Lakes to the Appalachians and as far south as the low country of
Georgia.

The advent of British and French colonization of North America forced the Shawnee farther into the gray zones of tribal alliances.
In truth, those tribal alliances were trading alliances. By the late
1690s, the well-known hunting grounds in the Ohio River Valley
resembled a busy corridor of commerce, far more than the idyllic
scenes of untamed wilderness painted by untrained eyes a couple of
centuries later. Southern Illinois, especially, was becoming a crucial
burning ground of competing entrepreneurial interests.

Beyond the facades of the palisades, front porches, and gabled
windows of the first French towns in southern Illinois, such as Cahokia and Kaskaskia on the eastern side of the Mississippi River in
the early 1700s, the emergence of an interethnic society centered
mainly around the businesses of the day: furs, hides, skins, bear oil,
some corn and grain, salt, and other minerals, such as coal.

This is how my Colbert family of Eagle Creek, and Barney's
Shawnee, most likely came together for the first time, albeit a century later. A Revolutionary soldier who had roamed from Georgia
to Alabama, Elisha Colbert first appeared on the rolls in 1805 as a

squatter living and working at the Great Salt Spring operations around Eagle Creek.

The story of coal in Eagle Creek, in fact, begins with salt. The two treasures were inexorably encased in the region's destiny, and both foretold the depths of brutality our nation would accept to withdraw their wealth.

Salt was the first precious mineral in the area to be mined, culled, and shipped away. It had generated a prehistoric industry for centuries—long before the Shawnee. All trails and trading networks in the vicinity, dating back to the stomped earth of ancient mastodons, led to the area known as the Great Salt Spring near Eagle Creek. They were part of a larger trade network that stretched from the Great Lakes to the lower Mississippi River, once referred to by an early Illinois governor as the "Appian Way" of the heartland.

The prehistoric salt trails that laced the great regional mound cities—from southern Indiana and Ohio, across the Ohio River in Kentucky, and throughout southern Illinois to the Mississippi River capital of Cahokia—evolved into Shawnee traces, including the contemporary Shawnee Hollow Trail still found on today's maps.

These trails did not elude the French. In 1702, French Canadian Charles Juchereau de St. Denis, who had received a royal patent from King Louis XIV to set up a tannery for buffalo (among other animals) at the southern tip of Illinois, reportedly slaughtered thousands—some estimated 13,000 buffalo for hides and tongues—and packed them in salt and shipped them down the Ohio and Mississippi rivers to the new Louisiana colonies.

According to some historians, however, the nature of these trading centers did not suit the imperial aims of France. In effect, the traders-of-fortune and their Native allies pledged allegiance to their goods, not so much to the Crown, and this concerned the royal courts. Missionaries, despite their presence in founding Cahokia, seemed to have had little influence. So, when France reorganized its fledgling Illinois settlements into Louisiana jurisdiction, one of the first acts of the king was to send a mining engineer by the name of Phillipe Renault to Fort Chartres near the Kaskaskia settlement, under the auspices of the Company of the Indies in 1722.

Renault founded a village in his own name, and then employed nearly five hundred African slaves from San Domingo in his search for coal and other minerals. A French military officer, Jean Paul Le Gardeur de l'Isle, wrote a cheerless letter about his experience of searching for coal in 1722 with Renault and his cadre of slaves. Renault failed to mine any coal of note, but he did succeed in finding lead; for the next twenty years, his mines in Illinois and Missouri produced enough lead to load untold boats on the Mississippi River, much of which was shipped back to France. When Renault abandoned the mines in 1742, he vanished from American history; his black slaves became a part of the southern Illinois and Missouri settlements.

Slavery, of course, was not limited to Africans, as the death of La Salle's own Shawnee slave indicated. In the 1752 census of the six French settlements in southwestern Illinois, 134 male heads of the household listed 445 black slaves and 147 Indian slaves. Even the Jesuit missionaries in Cahokia and Kaskaskia owned African and Indian slaves.

The slavery of Natives continued well into the American takeover of the Illinois country. On Christmas Eve in 1778, the heroic American commander George Rogers Clark, who would wrestle Illinois away from British control, issued a proclamation to prevent "too great liberty enjoyed by the red and black slaves, a liberty that prevents them from accomplishing the different pieces of work in which their masters employ them." Other edicts about the proper treatment of Indian slaves in southern Illinois appeared as late as 1791—the same year the rest of the country adopted the Bill of Rights.

The context of the Shawnee experience, therefore, was tenuous, despite their longtime presence in southern Illinois's revolving doors of conquest. But viewed with some historical irony, the peripatetic Shawnee might have been the most stable and grounded of any tribe or European settlement, if there were any constant in the inhabitation of the region. The Great Salt Spring near Eagle Creek underscored their centuries-old occupancy.

According to most historians, the French and Shawnee came to a trade agreement in the late 1730s, which allowed the Shawnee and various Wabash-area tribes to settle near and operate the salt wells. This served the French as a buffer zone of sorts, positioning their allies on the trace of a major thoroughfare of potential conflict. French traders also worked the wells or contracted with the Shawnee for the lucrative fur trade. In the process, the Shawnee founded a small community above the Saline River, as well as others in the Eagle Creek Valley and near the confluence of the Wabash and Ohio rivers. One settlement would eventually become one of the first American townships in Illinois: Shawneetown.

For Ernest Gates, a high school teacher in the Harrisburg area during the early twentieth century, who spent decades wading through the archaeological sites and studying Native ways, the lack of written documentation allowed revisionist historians to diminish the role of contemporary Indians like the Shawnee. In his chapter on Natives for a centennial history of Saline County in 1947, Gates noted that most explorers—French, British, American—stayed along the water routes, therefore missing any chance to truly observe the settlements of the woodland Indians.

Out of sight, out of the historical record. Gates wrote: "Prior to the time of the conquest of Colonel Clark, there were practically no written reports about the Indians in Southern Illinois except the reports of the French about the Indians living in or known to the American Bottom."

One of the few exceptions was the celebrated ornithologist John James Audubon, who spent Christmas Day in 1810 in a Shawnee village at the mouth of the Cache River. He marveled at the hundreds of trumpeter swans, whose feathers the Shawnee used to trade.

The deep woodland ways of the Shawnee fascinated Gates, who responsibly amassed a collection of artifacts from prehistoric and Shawnee settlements, farms, burial sites, and the salt wells during a time when no laws prevented weekend honeycombers from sacking archaeological sites. He concluded that the Shawnee were not only hunters and salt gatherers and traders, but also the oldest contemporary farmers in the region. He noted that the Shawnee made their own pottery and fashioned nets for fishing.

Gates's remarkable collection of flint and stone implements would rival many national museum collections. They now sat in the dark attic of his son's home near Harrisburg, but in their neglect they gave evidence of the Shawnee's and prehistoric cultures' longtime agricultural prowess. Gates wrote: "The Shawnee were the first tobacco raisers in Saline County, and many pipes fashioned out of sandstone or clay have been found in and about their graves."

◊   ◊   ◊

FOR ALL OF THE DIPLOMATIC memorials and poetic memoirs on the sweeping "uninhabited wilderness" that awaited French or British or American pioneers, the truth is that all eyes were focused on the prize of the valuable "resource attributes" in this paradise along the Ohio River Valley.

George Croghan, a wily Irish American trader and British Indian agent, understood this reality better than anyone in North America in 1765. In the annals of great American trailblazers, the legendary Daniel Boone and Christopher Gist might be Croghan's only peers. He served with George Washington in the French and

Indian War; he participated in many of the key battles, Indian treaties, and land surveys along the Ohio River Valley frontier during the mid-eighteenth century.

Two years after the French relinquished their control of the Illinois country to the British, Croghan survived a tomahawk wedged into his skull at an encampment only a few miles away from Eagle Creek, in pursuit of his greatest scheme: the creation of a colony in Illinois that could corner the market on the fur and mineral trades.

That tomahawk came courtesy of a rival Kickapoo band that attacked Croghan and his Ohio Shawnee escorts in the summer of 1765. Despite a British Crown proclamation in 1763 that prohibited land acquisition from Natives west of the Appalachian Mountains, and despite a law that prevented British Indian agents from investing in any trade agreements, Croghan's illicit mission sought to lay the groundwork for the control of commerce in the Illinois country.

Croghan's injury, strangely enough, served his purpose. The guilty Indians escorted him to the old French fort community of Vincennes along the Wabash River, north of the Great Salt Spring. In his later journals about the painful trip, Croghan not only spied the outcroppings of the valuable salt basin, but also noted the presence of "several very fine coal mines."

After arranging his own freedom, the veteran trader went on to single-handedly negotiate a peace agreement among various Wabash and Illinois tribes, as well as with the Native resistance leader Pontiac, allowing for an English takeover of the former French areas. Croghan's success, without firing a weapon, ranked as one of the great achievements in British-era diplomacy.

Not that it helped his Illinois trading schemes. Croghan's hopes were grand: "Let all mines and minerals belong to the owners of the land in which they may be found, except those denominated Royal Mines." Despite the fact that he had returned a hero and soon garnered the participation of Benjamin Franklin, among other colonial and British leaders, in his Illinois colony idea, Croghan's plan was turned down by the Crown in 1767. Franklin wrote the dismayed trader: "I hope you may in time obtain suitable rewards." While Croghan went on to other real estate adventures in New York and Pennsylvania, Franklin and another cunning group of merchants-of-fortune made another business attempt on Illinois that would have permanent bearing on the Shawnee, Eagle Creek, and the future coal industry.

◊ ◊ ◊

WHAT A STRANGE CUSTOM to name our modern places of living in the memory of the very Native people we have defeated, destroyed, and removed. *The Shawnee Hills. The Shawnee National Forest. Shawneetown.* The second newspaper in Illinois—the first in Shawneetown—was briefly called the *Shawnee Chief* in 1819, only six years after the same community had waged a bitter war and participated in the battle that killed Tecumseh, the last great Shawnee military leader.

When the famous mining surveyor and ethnographer Henry Rowe Schoolcraft made a study of southern Illinois in 1821, he naturally sketched in the hilly range as the "Shaunee" or "Oshawano" mountains, as if the Natives still determined the landscape. The first two government land districts in 1814, in fact, had been divided in the name of the vanquished tribes, Kaskaskia and Shawnee.

Thomas Jefferson, forever with his head in the classics, proposed dividing Illinois into three states and referred to southern Illinois as Polypotamia.

Does naming matter? Of course. The naming of Saline County, one of the few counties in the heartland to be identified with a mineral, not a tribe or pioneer or American political leader, only passed after a fierce debate in the 1840s. Many favored the name of Moredock County, in honor of John Moredock, a member of the territorial legislature. Moredock's infamy as an "Indian killer," however, "who never in his life failed to embrace the opportunity to kill a savage," and as an often debt-ridden gambling drunk who had reportedly sold a free black woman into slavery, was immortalized as "the Indian Hater" in James Hall's bestselling accounts of frontier life in the 1830s. He also became a dubious character in Herman Melville's novel *The Confidence Man* in 1857. His name was thankfully refused.

The power to determine the naming or fate of a place, and its people, might be the greatest power in the spoils of war and conquest. What is named, therefore, remains. What is not named is removed from our memories. In the process, people are also removed from our memories and erased from our histories. In *Translations*, Brian Fiel's modern Irish theater classic, the translation of placenames in Ireland by the British literally transformed the landscape.

For some academic observers, this eradication of people from history, or historicide, is tantamount to killing a people, or at least killing their presence in history. As Southern Illinois University anthropologist Jonathan Hill wrote: "Historicide, the removal of people from their histories, is radically disempowering because it obscures the historical processes that have produced the racial hierarchies that prevail in the Americas today."

The counter to historicide, perhaps for Hill, as he analyzed the revival of Native and immigrant African ethnic identity movements in the Americas, was the process of "ethnogenesis" or rebirth of an ethnic community. This called for a deliberate and deep endeavor of historical consciousness—a total recall, so to speak, of one's history. More so, it also recognized a people's effort to simply exist.

I first thought about this concept of historicide, or removing people from our historical memories, when I revisited my family's brief residence in the eastern Illinois town of Danville. My folks used to take us to swim and play in the nearby Kickapoo State Recreation Area, an area today of wooded hills and riparian bottomlands off the Middle Fork of the Vermillion River. There was never any discussion about what happened to the "Kickapoo" part of the Kickapoo recreation area, or more important, the historic role of Kennekuk, the Kickapoo diplomat who lived in the area. Nor did we know or discuss the fact that any remains or memory of the Kickapoo had been physically removed in the 1850s, in this historic place of the birth of commercial strip-mining of coal in the United States. The Kickapoo villages presumably turned into ashes and spoil piles, stagnant mine ponds and pits; the first mechanized strip-mining machines rattled their blades across the land cleared of virgin forests, creeks, and thousand-year-old Native settlements until 1939.

Strip mining more than stripped the land; it stripped the traces of any human contact. It resulted in a form of historical ethnic cleansing. Although the recreation site would now be lauded for its reforestation (albeit slight in diversity compared to the virgin forests) and fun recreational sites as the first state park developed from denuded strip-mined pits, it seemed like a cruel joke to rename the land for the removed Kickapoo and their obliterated settlements. They existed in name only: not with a history or within a historical context. Unlike the dogwoods and the duck ponds, the Kickapoo would never return. Even worse, their history had been relegated to the scrap pile of a vanished past.

◊ ◊ ◊

NORTH OF EAGLE CREEK at the basin of the Eagle Mountains, Gary took me to a bronze statue of the Shawnee leader Tecumseh. This was reportedly the only statue dedicated to Tecumseh in the country, and certainly the only official monument to Shawnee Indian habitation in the region. Not that Tecumseh ever lived in the area, or southern Illinois; this hadn't prevented a half dozen other towns across the country to be founded in his name.

Gary read a plaque at the statue that recalled a brief history of the Shawnee, their resistance to white encroachment in a "holy war," and declared: "Before the past is forgotten, we honor this great people and remember their presence with us in this beautiful place." In a dramatic radio voice, Gary concluded reading the plaque with a statement attributed to Tecumseh:

"Where today are the Pequot? Where are the Narrangansett, the Mohegan, the Pokanoket, and many other once powerful tribes of our People? They have vanished before the avarice and the oppression of the White Man, as snow before a summer sun.

"Will we let ourselves be destroyed in our turn without a struggle, give up our homes, our country bequeathed to us by the Great Spirit, the graves of our dead and everything that is dear and sacred to us? I know you will cry with me, 'Never! Never!'"

Tecumseh stood in bronze, clutching a bundle of twigs, a reference to his famous charge for Native unity: You can break one stick, went the saying, but you cannot break a bundle.

Gary informed me that the brainchild behind the statue project was John O'Dell, who headed up the Saline County Department of Tourism. Gary said John had done more than anyone over the past decade to generate local and national interest in the Shawnee Hills.

On first glance, I assumed John would be a likely advocate for Barney's Shawnee revitalization crusade. He was wearing a beaded outfit made of buckskins, carried a long knife on his belt in an impressive sheath, and was en route to watch the firing of an old musket when our paths first crossed at a Saline County festival in Harrisburg. John didn't just dress the part of a pioneer. He looked like a pioneer. In his sixties, he carried himself with the muscular gait of a ruddy woodsman who knew how to use an ax, spent most of his time outdoors, and spoke with a thick barked voice that had little patience for the formalities of bureaucrats.

On the other hand, he was the director of the county tourism office located in a renovated log cabin. Although he took his job seriously, you could immediately sense that heritage and eco-tourism for John were not an occupation but a lifelong commitment to the region.

His list of projects was impressive. Festivals, films, statues, and recreation and outdoor events. In the mid-1990s, John shepherded the longtime dreams of many hikers into the official development of the River to River Trail. The historic path stretched across the Shawnee National Forest for 160 miles, from Battery Rock on the Ohio River to the Devil's Backbone on the Mississippi River.

A kind of pioneer religiosity appeared often in John's writing and speech, especially when discussing nature. John was not only an avid hiker and birder. He was also a preacher in a local Primitive Baptist church, a tiny but vibrant sect in southern Illinois and the Appalachian south that still held to the ways of foot-washing river-dunking a-cappella-singing predestination.

Spreading out a collection of French maps of the Shawnee settlements in Illinois on a table one day, John recalled his first introduction to the Native presence in the land. He grew up in the town of Cahokia, the first French settlement in Illinois in the 1690s. The revered Ottawa military leader Pontiac, who took refuge in Illinois after the failure of his rebellion in Detroit, was murdered in Cahokia in 1769. His body was transported across the Mississippi River and buried in St. Louis, where historian Francis Parkman wrote: "The race whom he hated with such burning rancor trample with unceasing footsteps over his forgotten grave."

As a child, John roamed the ruins of the nearby Cahokia landscape, the stretch of six miles that served as the heartland of the prehistoric Mississippian culture. According to some archaeologists,

Cahokia had been the crossroads of America; it had been continually inhabited for 10,000 years. At one point in our contemporary Dark Ages, roughly at the time William the Conqueror invaded England, Cahokia's population and over one hundred mounds would have rivaled London. Some argued that its ceremonial Monks Mound, a massive four-floor earthen pyramid, stood as the highest building in the United States until 1867.

After John retired from his post as superintendent of a school district in southern Illinois, he set aside his PhD in education, strapped on some hiking boots, and tended to a forested plot outside his wife's native Harrisburg. Within days, he felt a call to revive the region's interest in its heritage and hills, especially if it could help the local economy.

For John, ecotourism went hand in hand with heritage tourism, which meant the Shawnee National Forest also needed to celebrate the Shawnee Indians. Tecumseh, as one of the most celebrated Native American leaders in the country, emerged as an obvious icon. John said he genuinely admired Tecumseh for his spiritual quality and respect for the views of others. Hadn't everyone? William Henry Harrison, the Indiana governor that led the attack on Tecumseh's brother and forces at Tippecanoe, had raved in a letter in 1811: "If it were not for the vicinity of the United States, he would, perhaps, be the founder of an empire that would rival in glory that of Mexico or Peru. No difficulties deter him. His activity and industry supply the want of letters."

On a quiet fall day in 2002, John sponsored the dedication ceremonies for the Tecumseh statue. He invited representatives from the Loyal Band of Shawnee in Oklahoma. The local media showed. Pictures were taken. And whether John was unaware of Barney and his Vinyard Indian Settlement band or not, no local Natives took part in the event.

Barney was incensed. He and other Native families in the area eventually denounced the statue in less than diplomatic terms as a tourist stunt at the expense of the Shawnee. John took offense. Both considered each other fraudulent. John, like many genealogists in the extended Vinyard families, even raised doubt of Barney's Native ancestry.

In effect, they asked: Did anyone have the right to claim Shawnee blood or recognize Shawnee heritage in the area today?

As part of the fallout, the Vinyard Indian Settlement went into high gear. Reaching out to various cousins, cousins of cousins, and other people who claimed Native ancestry in the area, Barney purchased the double-wide trailer near Herod, organized an elected council, formally incorporated the Vinyard Indian Settlement as a nonprofit organization, received unofficial state recognition as a tribal affiliate (a symbolic gesture, since only the federal government can actually determine tribal status), and began a slow public relations campaign to reintroduce the history of the Vinyard Indian Settlement.

In the end, you might say, at least for Barney and his Shawnee band, it came down to a question of ethnogenesis versus historicide.

Barney not only had to struggle to prove his Shawnee existence. He had the burden of reminding the region of his ancestors'—and his own family's—calamitous removal from the land because of its mineral resources.

◊ ◊ ◊

ON A CLOSER LOOK, Barney's stories of the Vinyard Indian Settlement did not seem so remote from the truth about the changing fate of the Shawnee in the area. Nor would his family have been spared from the machinations taking place in diplomatic and business circles around the control of the Great Salt Spring and coal mines.

In fact, genealogy entries for his Tyer family, including an anti-slavery advocate from Arkansas named John Tyer who married into the Vinyard family, noted that Karbers Ridge was originally called Vinyard Settlement.

Writing in the *Journal of the Illinois State Historical Society* in 1931, William Nelson Moyers referred to such settlements as the "Isolated Indians," Natives who quietly blended in to the hunting trade areas. "What became of them?" Moyers asked his readers. "It is the opinion of one writer that they were absorbed by amalgamation, and that their descendants are still here—some of the descendants being proud of their ancestry, others very sensitive about it, and a majority, indifferent."

Closer to Eagle Creek and Karbers Ridge, local author Elihu Hall directly referred to Shawnee hiding out in the nearby hollows as "stowaways." In a history of Hardin County, he added: "A few scattering families hiding in the Ozarks here and there remained here many years. . . . They had dodged officers in their work of moving Indians to western reservation, but they gave settlers no more trouble in the way of warfare."

A century before, the German duke of Württemberg wrote of his astonishment at the "frequent intermixture of white blood" with the Shawnee and European and American settlers in the Eagle Creek and Shawneetown area. The mixed-blood Natives quietly lived and hunted in the forests and along the rivers. As many historians noted, the concentration in southern Illinois of Shawnee from Ohio had greatly increased after the loss of the salt wells and trade grounds enacted in the Greenville Treaty in 1795.

So why would Barney's family story of the Vinyards providing refuge to Ohio Shawnee in 1810 or so even be questioned? Shawnee families abounded in these forests; I stumbled on more stories of Shawnee-related families in self-published memoirs and county narratives than I could keep up with.

These stories reminded me that revisionist historians in the last century had essentially allowed infrequent violent conflicts with Natives to overshadow the greater intrigues taking place in the corridors of government and the largest trade companies in the country.

In truth, during the first decade of my pioneering ancestors in the Eagle Creek area, there were more government-addressed petitions by salt well operators to stop the encroachment of squatters and wildcat loggers than concerns with Native attacks. A government official even considered setting fire to the cabins of squatters. In the winter of 1814, responding to repeated complaints from the salt well operators, the U.S. commissioner of the General Land Office in Washington, DC, even authorized the use of the militia on squatters and wood poachers.

Moyers, as a voice in the wilderness of southern Illinois history, wrote:

> Historians have magnified wars, sieges, battles, and the heroes of blood and thunder, and our newspapers thrive on the recital of vice and crime; while little attention is given to the ninety-and-nine that go not astray. In just such a manner has the Indian been given a black record. Writers have portrayed the worst examples; artists have painted the most fiendish looking. The Indian's vices have been magnified and the virtues forgotten. The man who said the only good Indian was a dead Indian, might just as well have said that the only good Negroes were slaves; or that the only good poor men were bound to a master, or to a hoe handle.
>
> During the territorial period, 1809–1818, there were several war scares, apparently started by jingoes who hoped to get into the army in order to get "free land" which was offered for such service. But there is no record of any battle with the Indians in the old Reservation; the few Indians remaining here were much more afraid of the whites than the whites were of the Indians. It is related that Stacey McDonald carried the mail along the old "Goshen" road from Shawneetown to Kaskaskia for two

years around 1812, without missing a trip, and that he did not
see a single Indian in all that time.

James Hall, the editor of a Shawneetown newspaper in the early
pioneer period, recognized the undue hatred for the Indian as early
as the 1820s. He concluded: "Is it to be wondered at, that a man
should fear and detest an Indian, who has always been accustomed
to hear him described as a midnight prowler, watching to murder
the mother as she bends over her helpless children, and tearing,
with hellish malignity, the babe from her maternal breast?" The
children of the pioneers, he surmised, "have only heard one side,
and that with all the exaggerations of fear, sorrow, indignation and
resentment."

As Moyers pointed out, Native Americans had hardly cornered
the market on violent lawlessness. The bloody episodes of outlaw
gangs along the Ohio River Valley had become legend as early as the
late 1790s.

The exception to this took place in 1813, on the tip of southern
Illinois near present-day Mound City. A band of roaming Red Stick
Creek, reportedly inspired by Tecumseh's war calls, slaughtered two
American families in cold blood. Within a year of other attacks and
retaliations, Andrew Jackson would rise to fame with his defeat of
the Red Stick Creek in Alabama.

Facts notwithstanding, the fallout over Tecumseh's revolutionary upheaval and the collapse of any unified Native resistance into
violent bands after his death, led lawmakers in Illinois to pass a dra-
conian, if not lucrative, act on Christmas Eve, in 1814, "to promote
retaliation upon hostile Indians." It granted $50–$100 for "incur-
sions into the country of hostile Indians" and "each Indian killed,
or squaw taken prisoner."

My pioneering Colbert family, paradoxically, stood to gain from
more Indian warfare, not less, especially when it came to land grants.

One of our oldest family documents dated back to 1855, when a ninety-six-year-old woman climbed out of her wagon, stepped across the mud, pressed down her long skirt, and walked into the office of the justice of the peace in Tuscaloosa County, Alabama. To the ear, of course, Illinois seems far from Alabama; on the map, however, the Shawnee range along the southern tip of the state was only a short boat ride up or down the river; Chicago was over three hundred miles and another generation away from settlement. The clerk notified the judge that the woman was sound of mind. Accompanied by her attorney, my ancestor Mariann Colbert declared that she had come to make a sworn statement to request the bounty land due to her, on behalf of her husband's service in the Illinois militia in 1811 at the salt wells and around Eagle Creek during the War of 1812.

Nonagenarian Mariann Colbert's story was remarkable. She had married her husband on February 9, 1791, in Elbert County in eastern Georgia. Those were good times. Her husband, Elisha Colbert, had served in the Georgia militia in the American Revolution and received a land bounty for that war, as well. Instead of homesteading, they had followed the excitement with the opening of the Alabama territories and then followed the lead of Andrew Jackson and headed to the Great Salt Spring in the Shawnee Hills of Illinois.

Like most salt workers, Elisha Colbert had been enticed by the credit system to buy public land in Eagle Creek, but he could not afford the minimum required amount of acreage. Benefiting wealthy absentee land speculators more than pioneers, investors had to purchase 160 acres, at $2 an acre, and provide a down payment of 15 percent. Elisha and Mariann, with four children at this point, settled as squatters in a craggy area called Hog Thief Creek.

Colbert had served in the mounted Illinois militia from 1811 until 1815, in case of Shawnee attacks. Although Congress authorized the enlistment of ten companies of mounted rangers with four companies to be placed in Illinois and Indiana, British policy ended up preventing a bloody frontier war from enveloping southern Illinois by shifting the action to the Detroit and Indiana area.

Nonetheless, in the minds of the pioneers, peace did not arrive in southern Illinois until Harrison routed Tenskwatawa, the Shawnee prophet, at the much ballyhooed Battle of Tippecanoe along the Wabash River in 1811, and Tecumseh, the celebrated Shawnee leader, fell at the hands of southern Illinois and Indiana troops in 1813.

This had been promised to the pioneers: With the passing of the Indian Relocation Act of 1830, no Shawnee should have been left standing east of the Mississippi River.

Mariann's first son, James Colbert, had even succumbed in 1834 to cholera, while serving in the Illinois state militia in the Black Hawk War, the last battle against Native Americans east of the Mississippi.

Hadn't President Andrew Jackson defined our nation's view of the Shawnee, and our natural resources at play in this region, in his extraordinary presidential address in 1830? Jackson had proclaimed:

> What good man would prefer a country covered with forests and ranged by a few thousand savages to our extensive Republic, studded with cities, towns, and prosperous farms, embellished with all the improvements which art can devise or industry execute, occupied by more than 12,000,000 happy people, and filled with all the blessings of liberty, civilization, and religion
>
> The present policy of the Government is but a continuation of the same progressive change by a milder process. The tribes which occupied the countries now constituting the Eastern States were annihilated or have melted away to make room for the whites. The waves of population and civilization are rolling to the westward, and we now propose to acquire the countries occupied by the red men of the South and West by a fair exchange, and, at the expense of the United States, to send them

to a land where their existence may be prolonged and perhaps made perpetual. Doubtless it will be painful to leave the graves of their fathers; but what do they more than our ancestors did or than our children are now doing?

And is it supposed that the wandering savage has a stronger attachment to his home than the settled, civilized Christian? Is it more afflicting to him to leave the graves of his fathers than it is to our brothers and children?

Jackson had not only issued a stunning rejection of the Native's right to existence. He had effectively launched the first proclamation of the industrial revolution.

In 1855, Mariann Colbert could have never realized that her own family's fate would be eventually caught up in the machinery of this same policy of removal. Nor did she know that the entangled schemes over the mines and minerals in the greater Eagle Creek and the Great Salt Spring had included none other than Andrew Jackson himself.

◊ ◊ ◊

IN 1778, during the Revolutionary War in the Illinois country, the American commander and hero George Rogers Clark once sat spellbound and listened as the Kaskaskia elders recited their history through storytelling. In a letter to a museum in Philadelphia in 1789, he wrote, "I see no reason why [their traditions] should not be received as good history, at least as good," as Clark considered our own written American history.

But oral stories, inasmuch as we appreciate storytellers and oral historians, have rarely been accepted as good history. Especially from Native American perspectives.

For Barney, his literary endeavors were a "last resort" to "make known to those people in places of social power our spiritual sense of balance with all life—known and unknown—hoping that this might make a difference to indifferent lawmakers."

Nonetheless, he struggled to translate what had been an oral tradition in his life, relating to his Shawnee family, into a written form.

"There are mysteries about being who we are that have no definition, at least to me."

As a teenager, Barney recalled going through a period of not being able to explain his own questions about his identity. The Eagle Mountains on the horizon, in his childhood, had always hovered as a place of intrigue, and refuge, for him. In his late teens, he set out one summer to live on the western slope of the Eagle Mountains, finding an overhang in a forested part of Stillhouse Hollow—a once famous moonshine area. Barney packed in his mother's 10-gallon Crock-Pot and made his own home brew. He built a *wikiwa* out of canvas. He attempted to follow a ritual of fasting, roaming the hills, talking to no one but the trees and animals. Sleeping on the ground or under bluffs, he considered this his reintroduction to his ancestors.

At this point, numerous strip mines had begun to devour the Eagle Creek basin to the east and northeast, and the Big Ridge area to the northwest. Strip mines had also turned once densely forested sections across the Battle Ford and Mitchellsville area of Barney's childhood into scarred pits and black slurry ponds.

Barney went on. "I wondered, if they can remove relatives by force . . . what could you do about these people strip-mining your homeland? That bothered me."

In his late teens, Barney wrote a letter against strip mining and then showed it to a Forest Service employee and friend of Gary's father. The older man shook his and handed back the letter. "Sorry," he said, "but there's nothing we can do about this."

There were two options in Barney's mind: surrender to a sense of powerlessness or commit to a sense of resistance.

In 1982, Barney's beloved grandfather from Karbers Ridge died. Barney returned to the Shawnee Hills for the funeral. In a poem, "Last Song for Granddad Clyde," he wrote:

> He   the last that grandchildren
> know as ancients is looking for
> our grandmothers trail   I am
> the clinger   the beggar   the singer

His mother gave him a box that had belonged to a great-grandfather. It contained kernels of green corn used in ceremonies, as well as some cherry pits. Barney planted eleven kernels of corn in 1988; seven stalks rose. From there, he and his mother cultivated their own fields.

Historian Carla Freccero explored the role of the dead in our lives, the "non-living present in the living present." She referred to it as "hauntology": "We inherit not 'what really happened' to the dead but what lives on from that happening, what is conjured from it, how past generations and events occupy the force fields of the present, how they claim us, and how they haunt, plague, and in-spirit our imaginations and visions for the future."

A few years before the deaths of his grandparents, struggling with his life, a story that haunted Barney merged into a short novella, "Abbey of the Bear," which would eventually be published in his book, *Inherit the Blood.* He based it loosely on the image of his great-grandmother, Hannah Foster Tyer.

In the story, Omar Little Light, a veteran of the urban streets and reservation struggles, returns home to White Bird Creek. Annie, his *nohkohmis*, or grandmother, is a midwife and healer. One day, representatives of the Ozark Mining Company confront her to test her land for coal and sell out "the final removal area, the last land that the Greedy Ones didn't want."

Annie asks her grandson Omar: "Do you know why you have come home?" He doesn't.

The story unfolds like a homecoming for Omar, and a look back at his derailed life of drinking, wandering, getting lost. He listens as his grandmother recounts visits by the coal company and her continual resistance.

"The revenue from the coal will provide a lot of jobs for your people. Industry needs this coal. Take a little more time to think this over. We don't think you realize the magnitude of this situation. Other tribes have gladly sold leases to mine coal. They want to help out their country. They want businesses moving in on their reservations," said the one attorney whose fingers and neck were laden with turquoise jewelry.

"Yes," Annie had said. "Greed has affected lives among all the tribes. We heard Crow, Cheyenne, and Navajo tell us stories about the coal mines. They say the big machines came and devoured the earth like any monsters, spit out the remains and left orange water in their holes. . . . When our people make deals with you, there is only death. Your own history says it is so, yet you continue without regard for the balance of life. . . . Our home is alive now, and we will not see our mother."

Omar remembers his grandfather's last speech at a green corn celebration. "He senses that there is something in tradition, in human memory that cannot be passed on without ceremony, cannot be recorded for history, but passes into the winds, into the soil and rivers until that time that someone must pick it up again, must use it to dignify survival, to give life to beauty."

Annie is eventually harassed and physically attacked by thugs sent by the coal company, and a battle ensues. Amid the confusion, Annie and Omar are killed along the creek by the corrupt relative and coal company thug, who declares: "You can buy a lot of booze and good times from money from the strip mines."

Nature, though, refuses to relent. P'quay the bear comes and devours the coal company thug in the mud of White Bird Creek.

◊   ◊   ◊

THE FAILURE OF George Croghan and Ben Franklin to establish their Illinois Colony and "all mines and minerals" in the late 1760s only served to inspire another round of mercenary land-schemers based in Philadelphia. Not that Franklin actually gave up the ghost on this project; as late as 1770, he had continued to provide updates on the Great Salt Spring to the British secretary of state of the American colonies.

This time, though, the newly formed Illinois Land Company sought to manipulate the brewing American revolutionary confusion in 1773 as a way to circumvent the British authorities altogether. These land speculators understood the natural laws of the western territorial land market; the greatest gains would come directly from Native losses.

Following Croghan's example, Pennsylvanian merchant-of-fortune William Murray traveled to Kaskaskia on July 5, 1773, as the trade representative for the company, and hammered out a deal for 23,000 square miles with a very select group of ten Native representatives—the Shawnee and other salt tribes excluded. At the same time, the Great Salt Spring area, encompassing Eagle Creek and the vicinities, was a key factor in demarcating the boundaries.

In exchange for the massive land grab, Murray's offer was noteworthy in its parsimony: He gave the Indians a total of 250 blankets and a wagonload of shirts, stockings, some gunpowder and lead, brass kettles, three dozen gilt-looking glasses, among other items, and five shillings in money.

The handful of Native representatives accepted, especially since they had little control over the designated areas, such as the salt wells. The British commander in charge of the territory, when

presented with the deed, was more bewildered by Murray's legal-
istic shenanigans. Fully aware that the British proclamations
forbade land purchases from Indians, Murray offered the Camden-
Yorke opinion as evidence of his land rights. The Camden-Yorke
document actually granted individuals the right to buy land from
Indians *in India*. Unsure how to proceed, the British commander
allowed Murray to conclude his land deal, though he was not permitted to found any settlements.

This land scheme became the most important landmark
Supreme Court case on Native American land rights. But it didn't
happen overnight. In fact, it took fifty years of litigation before the
Illinois Land Company—and an additional Wabash Land Company
partnership—lost their challenge to British precedence.

But one merchant's failure, once again, proved to be another
merchant's boon. By declaring that "discovery gave title to the government by whose subjects, or whose authority, it was made," the
1823 Supreme Court case, *Johnson v. McIntosh*, effectively established the legal grounds for subsequent removal of Indians east of
the Mississippi. The Supreme Court ruling concluded that though
the Indians were "the rightful occupants of the soil," the principle
of "discovery" by the Europeans, gave the exclusive title to the
discoverer.

Indians, therefore, were only tenants, never landlords.

As legal historian Lindsay G. Robertson showed in his riveting
examination of the case, the Supreme Court ruling would be cited in
virtually every case in the Jackson era of removals. In effect, the successful removal of the eastern tribes, including the Cherokee, Creeks,
Chickasaws, Choctaws, and Seminole, and salt well tribes like the
Shawnee and Piankashaws, could be traced back to the "unintended
consequences" of this fateful land scheme in southern Illinois.

When the Cherokee camped in the snow-covered forests of
southern Illinois in the winter of 1838, an attending Rev. Butrick al-

lowed himself to finally divulge his true feelings in a diary he had kept during their now infamous Trail of Tears. On New Year's Eve, he wrote:

"For what crime then was this whole nation doomed to this perpetual death? This almost unheard of suffering? Simply because they would not agree to a principle which would be at once death to their national existence, viz. that a few unauthorized individuals might, at any time, set aside the authority of the national council and principal chief, and in opposition to the declared will of the nation, dispose of the whole public domain, as well as the private property of individuals, and render the whole nation houseless and homeless at pleasure, such a treaty the President of the United States sanctioned, the senate ratified, and the military force was found ready to execute. And now we see some of the effects. The year past has also been a year of spiritual darkness."

Between the Illinois Land Company's illegal forays into southern Illinois in 1773 and the Supreme Court ruling in 1823, the region witnessed a level of brinkmanship over the mineral rights that went beyond spiritual darkness.

◊ ◊ ◊

IN THE SAME YEAR Croghan filed his reports on the wealth of the Illinois country and the several fine coal mines he stumbled across on the Wabash River, Thomas Jefferson recorded the presence of coal mines along the James River in his *Notes on the State of Virginia*. Near his estate of Monticello, the area was "replete with mineral coal of a very excellent quality" and had been worked "to an extent equal to the demand." Although Jefferson's vision of the yeoman farmer citizen is well known, we tend to overlook his foresight in anticipating the industrial revolution.

That revolution, of course, required a lot of coal and mineral-rich land. And it took its marching orders from the hounds of

industry in the very country we had decisively rebelled against—
Britain and its vanguard iron and coal producers.

In 1786, while visiting England, Jefferson was astonished by the
technological prowess of England's coal industry. He had oftentimes
witnessed England's great coal-fired navy that controlled the waterways. Author Daniel Defoe, a half century before Jefferson's first
arrival in London, had written about the "wonder" of the "prodi-
gious fleets of ships which come constantly in with coal."

But on this particular trip, Jefferson was the first American to
make note of what historian James Parton hailed in his *Life of
Thomas Jefferson* as the "most important piece of mechanical in-
telligence that pen ever recorded—the success of the Watt steam
engine, by means of which 'a peck and a half of coal performs as
much works as a horse in a day.' He [Jefferson] conversed at Paris
with English industrialist Matthew Boulton, who was Watt's partner in the manufacture of the engines, and learned from his lips
this astounding fact."

Coal not only could provide fire; it accelerated an energy-
efficient power. It would fuel the industrial revolution and a nation.

Back in the States, Jefferson was soon investigating the dynamics of coal importation versus the quality of American coal. Although the steam engine and other technological advances were
another generation away from taking hold in the United States, Jefferson forever shaped his frontier American policies with an eye
perennially cast back across the water.

Dating back to Jolliet's discovery of coal in Illinois in the 1660s,
surveyors continued to note the prevalence of coal in the Ohio River
Valley throughout the mid-to-late eighteenth century. In 1780, the
French inhabitants of Vincennes, up the Wabash River from the
Great Salt Spring and Eagle Creek, appealed to their French ministers to not forget the "coal, and different metals" superior to those
in Virginia. In 1796, former French governor Victor Collot raved
about the coal and salt reserves in the Great Salt Spring area.

Not that Jefferson needed any prompting. He had reported on the Great Salt Spring in his overview of the Northwest Territories in the late eighteenth century; he championed their procurement in his presidential State of the Union address in 1802. It was not merely salt, though, that intrigued him. With an eye on Europe's progress, he also admonished every surveyor, such as the legendary Meriwether Lewis and William Clark, readying to depart in 1803 from southern Illinois on their epic journey across the West, to note every deposit of coal, which enviously advanced England's industrial revolution.

In his journal of 1803, Captain Meriwether Lewis found "fine mines of *pitt* Coal," in the southern Illinois country, including one on a riverside bank "whence boats ascend in common and high tide" to fuel the works of "blacksmiths and other artisans."

One thing stood in the way of Jefferson's view of progress: Indians. And the Shawnee, and other tribes in the Great Salt Spring area, blocked the passage to the mineral deposits unrivaled anywhere in the Ohio River Valley and Illinois country.

The complexities of Jefferson's views didn't exclude contradictions. He had once exclaimed to his friend in disgust: "Money and not morality is the principle of commerce and commercial nations." And Jefferson had also lectured a French politician in 1786: "It may be regarded as certain that not a foot of land will ever be taken from the Indians without their own consent. The sacredness of their rights is felt by all thinking persons in America, as much as in Europe."

Yet, in the spring of 1801, when Jefferson learned of Napoleon's intent to establish a new French empire in Latin and North America, he dramatically shifted his view of transforming the Illinois country as the western boundaries along the Mississippi River and Ohio River Valley. The threat heightened in 1802, when Spain closed the commercial traffic on the Mississippi River to Americans, as the French landed an army in Haiti to put down the extraordinary slave revolt that would eventually lead to Haitian independence.

Meanwhile, the line of land speculators and merchants-of-fortune grew at the Great Salt Spring. The letters to Jefferson piled up with increasing pressure to remove from the region the various Natives who still controlled the salt wells in the area. A young entrepreneur and military leader from Tennessee, Andrew Jackson, stood at the front of the line.

In an 1802 speech honoring the role of the Pilgrims, future president John Quincy Adams presented the viewpoint behind much of Jackson's eventual reasoning for the Indian Removal Act of 1830. In essence, Indians were only hunters, not industrialists. Adams declared:

"The Indian right of possession itself stands, with regard to the greatest part of the country, upon a questionable foundation. Their cultivated fields, their constructed habitats, a space of ample sufficiency for their sustenance, and whatever they have annexed to themselves by personal labor, was undoubtedly *by the laws of nature* theirs. But what is the right of the huntsman? . . . Shall the lordly savage not only disdain the virtues and enjoyments of civilization himself, but shall he control the civilization of a world? Shall he forbid the wilderness to blossom like the rose? Shall he forbid the oaks of the forest to fall before the ax of industry and rise again transformed into the habitations of ease and elegance?"

The venerable historian Frederick Jackson Turner once noted that salt determined the opening of the West. The profit from its extraction, like coal, also determined the removal of the Indians.

Jackson and his business partner, John Coffey, had made initial inquiries into the status of the Great Salt Spring area as early as 1800. In 1802, Jackson wrote directly to Jefferson in Washington, DC, explaining that he represented a company to "benefit our country and not self aggrandizement," intent on breaking up the unfair monopoly of the salt trade in the western states of Kentucky, Tennessee, and the Ohio River Valley. The Great Salt Spring area, according to Jackson, would supply "all the western world." There was just one problem: It was in the hands of the Indians. To be fair, Jackson asked Jefferson to arrange a lease with the Indians, as opposed to outright removal. Either way, the Indians were squandering an opportunity for profit.

According to historian John Jakle, the American government quickly understood that "depriving the various tribes of their Ohio Valley salt springs" would shatter their trade-dependent economy and adopted way of life.

Despite the Native demands to lease the salt wells, not sell the land, territorial governor Harrison took a hard-line position in negotiations, departing from previous policy or even Jackson's recommendations. For Harrison it came down to an issue of commerce. In the spring of 1802, he explained his views to Albert Gallatin, the secretary of the Treasury:

"While the chiefs who were at the seat of government lately expressed a desire to lease, my opinion is, that it would be altogether improper to comply with their request considering both the present advantage of the Indians and the interest of white settlers, now and in time to come. The spring alluded to is perhaps the very best in the whole extent of the country from the Allegheny Mountains to the Mississippi."

Despite Napoleon's retreat from any imperial designs on the Mississippi River Valley and North America in the early spring of 1803, the increasingly ruthless Jeffersonian Indian policies had been set in motion by Harrison. Not that Jefferson had any misgivings about Harrison's uncompromising approach to land cessions. In a letter to Harrison in February 1803, Jefferson openly favored a deplorable scheme of encouraging debt to bring the tribes to their knees:

"When they withdraw themselves to the culture of a small piece of land, they will perceive how useless to them are their extensive forests, and will be willing to pare them off from time to time in exchange for necessaries for their farms and families. To promote this disposition to exchange lands, which they have to spare and we want, we shall push our trading uses, and be glad to see them run in debt, because we observe that when these debts get beyond what the individuals can pay, they become willing to lop them off by a cession of lands. . . . "

By that summer in 1803, Harrison convened a reluctant gathering of representatives from nine tribes, including three members of the Shawnee, at Fort Wayne, Indiana. Harrison had threatened to withhold annuities if representatives failed to attend. No one appeared happy with the proposed arrangements. Disagreements over land claims ensued. According to historian Robert Owens, the Shawnee representatives walked out of the meeting at one point and proposed to go directly to Washington to meet with Jefferson. The relentless Harrison would not be derailed in his mission. Whether the whiskey flowed, as some Shawnee contended years later, lamenting the diminished role of "whiskey chiefs," or whether Harrison browbeat and cajoled his way to victory, the Indians relented to an agreement on June 7 that ceded most of southern and central Illinois.

As the son of a signer of the Declaration of Independence, Harrison pulled off a remarkable denouement to a yearlong effort to wrangle over 1,800 square miles from the Natives. And the price? As Owens noted: "Because the tract was now considered part of the original Greenville Treaty [in 1795] the national government paid no additional annuities for the land, other than 'a quantity of salt not exceeding one hundred and fifty bushels' to be divided yearly among the tribes."

Andrew Jackson was denied a lease on those salt wells near Eagle Creek. He applied again in 1806. By that time, as the surrounding forests were quickly destroyed to fuel the boiling pans of industrial salt production, as we will see in the next chapter, coal began to emerge as a key factor in determining the region's extraordinary trade.

Salt may have opened the door to the frontier of the heartland, but coal would fuel its plunder.

In the end, Jefferson's removal of the Shawnee would have more bearing on his prophetic vision of a coal-fired industrial revolution than his commitment to defending a frontier boundary.

Harrison's and Jefferson's conquest of the coal-rich Illinois reserves from the Natives was not lost on the French, though. In 1912, *La Chronique Industrielle*, an economic journal in Paris, lamented France's discovery and ceding control of coal reserves throughout the Louisiana Territory. The headline declared: we have had great coal wealth.

"We have spoken of the possibility of discovering in America coal supplies in which we are so deficient. We had them, alas; for the gifts by Napoleon to America deprive us of inexhaustible coal deposits discovered by the French. . . . In conclusion, is it not curious to think that we have possessed all these great deposits of coal in the Upper Mississippi?"

◊   ◊   ◊

I ATTENDED A Vinyard Indian Settlement council meeting one evening. Barney was visiting from New Mexico, where he had been teaching at a Navajo high school. As the secretary read the notes of the prior meeting, and a council member seconded them, the council followed an agenda with a strict adherence to rules. Items were discussed, suggestions were solicited, all in favor said "aye." Motion overruled. The secretary counted the hands—a half dozen of them, but a fervent half dozen that recognized the fledgling organization had a long way to go, and they were in it for the long haul. For all of the apparent officialdom, I felt a real sense of excitement in the room. Of something grand in the making, or remaking.

They had also just released the first official printed history of the Vinyard Indian Settlement.

"I'm not into this 'let's all hold hands and dance around a circle,'" Barney told me the next day over a cup of coffee and a bowl of stew. "I am definitely opposed to having someone tell me which aspect of God's people I am. We want our resurrection here. Our action to resurrect our homeland is more important than discussing family trees. We've got things to do. The Ohio River has to be cleaned up. I want to know there are places here in this world where we can go and be at peace, and understand why we were placed in this world."

That vision was not confined to the Shawnee Hills of southern Illinois. Like Tecumseh, Barney took part in a transnational Native American movement still trying, in his words, "to find something to break through the colonial mentality, the steel door of ignorance."

In dealing with his students of the Dine, or Navajo, Nation, that meant Barney felt obliged to discuss the strip mines of his childhood and in their own Navajo lives. Our meeting, strangely enough, coincided with the startling eleventh-hour announcement in the winter of 2008 that the disastrous George W. Bush administration planned to give a green light to reopening the scandalous Black Mesa strip mine on the ancestral lands of the Dine and Hopi.

Within a few days of our meeting, the U.S. Office of Surface Mining (OSM) released a "Record of Decision" on the "Black Mesa Project" Final Environmental Impact Statement, granting Peabody Energy, the world's largest coal company, which got its start in southern Illinois and had strip-mined much of Eagle Creek, a "life-of-mine" permit to reopen and expand one of the nation's largest coal strip mines.

Like a voice in the wilderness, Arizona congressman Raul Gri-jalva had recently written to Bush's secretary of the Interior, Dirk Kempthorne, to request that the OSM suspend "hurriedly conduct-ing a deeply flawed environmental review."

Like mountaintop removal in Appalachia, and strip mining in southern Illinois, the decades-long battle over Black Mesa and the ensuing Hopi-Navajo Land Settlement Act have been symbols of the shameless disregard of human rights and environmental pro-tection for the sake of extraction-industry profits.

It was an old story, of course, dating back to the discovery of one of the largest coal deposits in the country on Black Mesa last century.

Over a decade ago, documents emerged that proved that the main lawyer hired to represent the divided Hopi was secretly on the payroll of the Peabody coal company, and helped to gerrymander the massive land deal and subsequent settlement acts. This not only resulted in unfair royalty payments and virtually no environmental safeguards, but also managed to bitterly divide tribal interests and relations.

In the process, an estimated 12,000 Natives were forced to relo-cate, while one of the largest strip mines in the nation swept across the northern Arizona desert.

As investigative reporter Judith Nies wrote:

"In Los Angeles, air conditioners hummed. Las Vegas embarked on an enormous building spree to make gambling a family vacation. Phoenix and Tucson metastasized out into the desert—building golf courses and vast retirement developments with swimming pools and fountains. Few realize that much of the energy that makes the desert 'bloom' comes from the Black Mesa strip mines on an Indian reser-vation. Even fewer know the true costs of such development.

"And water, in this upland desert, was pumped away. As part of a 273-mile slurry line, billions of gallons of water were siphoned from the Navajo aquifer for decades. Not only the main water source for the native farmers and ranchers in the area, this caused wells and springs to dry up, groundwater levels to plummet and native vegetation to vanish.

"I try to get those kids to understand what is happening to their land," Barney went on. Holding his side as if in pain, he explained to the kids that the traditional Navajo and Hopi referred to coal as the liver of the earth. Remove it, goes their traditional saying, and the earth will die.

"Those draglines tearing up Black Mesa. I make them write poems and papers, do research. And I sit up there and cry like a bitch every time."

◊   ◊   ◊

ONE HOT AND SWEATY AFTERNOON, Gary and I parked my car at the ruins of the Sulphur Springs Church and headed up to Cave Hill, on the northwestern side of the Eagle Mountains. I looked back at the dilapidated church—the abandonment of religious landmarks had always unnerved me with its symbolism. Carrying a book of poetry, and no water, Gary walked in an almost reckless fashion, refusing to stay on any trail. He picked medicinal plants, analyzed and identified them.

I searched for pecan trees, the one native fruit tree in the heartland. The word "pecan," in fact, had come from the Shawnee-related Algonquin language. A century ago, Eagle Creekers would harvest the groves of pecans on the hillsides and sell them as far as Kentucky and Tennessee.

When Ernest Gates wrote his history of the Natives in the mid-1940s, he focused on Eagle Creek and other upland areas, such as Karbers Ridge, as being the centers of the Shawnee population. Given the mosquito-infested swamps and flooding along the rivers and lower creeks, he found most "camp grounds and burial sites also are located along the upper forks of the Saline River, and a favorite spot of the Shawnee was in front of the Eagle Mountains."

Most archaeologists agreed that there had even been a prehistoric shift to the hills for health, safety, and soil exhaustion in the lower river basin.

According to Gates, the last known living Shawnee was an older Shawnee woman who lived just a mile from here on Eagle Creek. "It is known that she lived alone in solitary squalor as late as 1875," Gates wrote, "but was so far neglected and unnoticed that she had disappeared for some considerable period of time before the farmers around realized that she no longer was among them."

In a romantic article written for the *St. Louis Globe-Democrat* in 1883, a reporter went in search of the "Sepulchre of the Shawnees," in this cave.

Gary pointed out that a metal gate prevented any entrance into the cave this season. The Forest Service had set up the frame to protect the endangered Indiana bat, which dwelled inside the massive confines of the cave. The endangered Indian and woodsman, alas, hadn't fared as well.

After taking a cool rest in front of the cave, Gary and I scrambled to a higher edge of the hill on the opposite side, searching for a clear view of the Eagle Creek Valley to the east. I could hear the faint rumble of a coal truck—I could always hear the faint beat of the bulldozers that had literally wiped out and depopulated the entire Eagle Creek basin to a righteous remnant of backwoods stowaways.

A hundred and fifty years before us, two other men had hiked up these same back hills to the cave in the summer of 1854. Unlike us, they had loaded their wagons with the finest surveying equipment. Both men came from patrician families of innovators. And while both set off with the same agenda of coal, each one made a discovery about the area's wealth of natural resources that would be overlooked in the rapacious schemes of the Gilded Age.

George Eschol Sellers saw Eagle Creek as the prologue of history; David D. Owen viewed the Shawnee range as a limitless inventory of minerals for the future.

It took another twenty years before Sellers became immortalized in Mark Twain's funny but unforgiving novel of the post–Civil War era of get-rich-quick schemes. In *The Gilded Age*, cowritten in jest with Hartford editor Charles Dudley Warner, Twain excoriates the endless machinations of a fictional Colonel Eschol Sellers, who never seems to exhaust himself of big ideas for ruinous inventions and property investments.

Historians are divided on whether Twain knew that George Eschol Sellers actually existed, but in truth he and his family held over a hundred patents for various inventions. By the time of his death in 1899, considered one of the most noted engineers in the country, Sellers held patents for a hill-climbing locomotive, and processes to convert steamboats to coal and remove brine from salt water. He had moved to southern Illinois, in fact, to work on a scheme to turn swamp cane into paper.

As the president of the fledgling Saline Coal and Manufacturing Company, the first such venture in the area, Sellers agreed to escort Owen on a geological survey of the hilly range surrounding Eagle Creek. Owen needed no introduction; he had carried out the first geological surveys of Indiana, Kentucky, and Arkansas. He was also the son of Robert Owen, the visionary social reformer from Scotland who had set up his utopian community across the Wabash River in New Harmony in 1825.

Owen could barely contain himself in reporting his findings. "It would be difficult to find a location in the United States where so many workable beds of coal are concentrated in a limited space." The quality of the coal surpassed anything he had seen from Pennsylvania to the Mississippi River. Eagle Creek was the priceless gem left behind by those who had stormed onto the California goldfields.

Sellers's Saline Coal and Manufacturing Company, in the process of seeking over one million dollars in start-up capital from eastern companies, couldn't have asked for a better analysis. In their charter of 1851, they laid claim to the largest venture in iron works and coal "in the world." In other words, as *Mining Magazine* reported, "with inexhaustible treasures of coal, iron, limestone, etc., and an immense and permanent demand for railroad iron pressing upon them, design to extend their capital to an amount about equal to that of the Pennsylvanian Coal Company, or the Delaware and Hudson Canal Company, whose stocks are among the most substantial securities in our markets."

Although their jaunt focused on the vast coal reserves in the area, a sea of prehistoric artifacts distracted Sellers's attention in the "broad and beautiful valley of Eagle Creek."

Sellers was obsessed with archaeology and indigenous Americans. It wasn't simply a hobby. He had perfected the art of chiseling arrowheads; he exhibited some of his findings in national museums in Philadelphia and Washington, DC. He wrote academic papers on prehistoric pottery and the largely overlooked complexities and advanced techniques of the prehistoric salt makers. With Owen, he had waded across so many acres and acres of pottery and fire pits along the nearby slopes of the Great Salt Spring that he believed the area had been a central base for an ancient culture. Burial mounds dotted the Eagle Creek valley and hills like trail markers. Noting the plethora of stone agricultural implements, such as chert and quartzite hoes and spades that littered their tracks, Sellers wrote that the entire Eagle Creek valley "was once cultivated by the prehistoric peoples that worked the salines."

The flurry of plows of pioneering farmers and axes of lumbermen would devastate the evidence of Sellers's discovery. The once dense virgin forests of hickory and oak had long been plundered—even before Sellers's first trip—and replaced by a new generation of pines. Outside of the immediate salt works area, the existence of the vast and sophisticated prehistoric population, like the hundred-foot-tall virgin forests, disappeared into lore.

Strangely enough, the Gilded Age never happened in Eagle Creek for Sellers. Although coal ventures would boom and bust around his company's large property interests for the next 150 years, his pioneering enterprise never went beyond Owen's survey. Until his death in 1898, he would blame Twain for defaming his character and driving away potential investors from the eastern seaboard. Threatening a $10,000 lawsuit, Sellers forced Twain to change the name of the deceitful Eschol Sellers character, which eventually took the stage in theatrical versions of *The Gilded Age* across the country. Twain apologized. Not that it helped. Though he changed the name to Mulberry or Beriah Sellers in subsequent stories, his literary imprint prefaced George E. Sellers's name for the rest of the century.

Owen stumbled on to another discovery in Eagle Creek that failed to resonate among the investors for coal and iron. At the Sulphur Spring he had casually collected a couple bottles of water. Back in his laboratory in Indiana, he found that the water contained "organic elements" of a tonic. In an offhand note, he remarked that the spring would "prove beneficial to invalids, especially to those debilitated by chronic ailments."

In his biography of Tecumseh, *God Gave Us This Country*, author Bil Gilbert recounted that the Ohio Shawnees planted prairie grasses over their cemeteries to hide any "traces of the grave of their fathers," as a last community act before their relocation in the 1830s. "They finally departed in mid-September but camped for several days at Greenville so as to drink for the last time from a spring whose waters were thought to be particularly healthful."

The spring that amazed Owen and the Shawnee on Eagle Mountain was dry now. And Sellers's coal camp headquarters across the valley in Bowlesville, like the "broad and beautiful valley of Eagle Creek" that he loved for its priceless archaeological and historical wealth, had also been strip-mined by the Peabody coal company, among other smaller companies.

It was all gone.

Barney once told me that a Shawnee legend recounted a herd of huge bison rampaging through the Ohio River Valley, laying waste to all in their path. To protect the tribe, a deity slew these great beasts with lightning bolts, finally chasing the last giant buffalo into exile across the Wabash River, never to trouble the Shawnee again.

It made me wonder if the beasts had simply transformed themselves into draglines and bulldozers and dump trucks.

Regardless, Barney and the Vinyard Indian Settlement were still here. He had prophesized in a poem:

> . . . for we know we are
> part of the shadows
> that sink deep into the
> lake after the sun
> has gone . . .

Cemetery in Pope County, IL. *(Photo by Charles F. Hammond.)*

◊

Chapter Three

BLACK DIAMONDS,
BLACK LIVES

The Entangled Roots of Slavery and Coal

On two former occasions, under a strong sense of duty, I urged the
gradual abolition of the remnant of slavery that still exists in violation of the fundamental laws of the state, and an amend of our
code in relation to free Negroes. I now emphatically and earnestly
press this recommendation. But, if the Legislature shall still think
proper to decline abolishing slavery, then I beseech the representatives of a people who love liberty, and have resolved that
their land shall be the land of the free, to adopt such measures
as will ultimately put an end to slavery. Let us at least cut the
entail, and not give what is wrong a legal descent, but fix the
time when slavery in Illinois shall cease.

—ILLINOIS GOVERNOR EDWARD COLES,
Farewell Address, 1826

I heard Ron Nelson before I ever met him. He was just finishing
up the Baptist morning hour on WEBQ AM radio, a Saturday ritual in the region, when the living tuned in to hear the readout obit-
uaries of the dead and thanked the Lord that they had been granted
another week.

WEBQ was launched more than a half century ago by a young man who lived in west Harrisburg near Liberty Baptist Church, who had learned about radios in the navy and then came home, fiddled with a receiver, and attached a wire to his mother's clothesline. It still crackled across the airways with that spirit of traditional country, real country, *the sound of radio like it used to be*. Spun the discs that made radio worth listening to in rural America: that Del Rio sound that gave us the Carter Family; those old country hits when "country" came from the churches, the hills, and the delta blues; when country told stories about hard times and keeping on the sunny side of life.

Ron wore a camouflage ball cap, a checkered shirt, old jeans held up by suspenders, and a pair of boots the first day we met, as if we were heading off to fish. He sported a nicely trimmed beard, though it had enough gray to betray the years and conflicts that had marked his life. He was ramrod in posture, with a slight middle-aged paunch. With a pair of oversized glasses, he reminded me of a retired country judge.

In his no-nonsense way Ron told me to get in the truck, while he placed a set of brass dowsing rods in the cab. He had first checked on his elderly mother, who lived in a modest bungalow in west Harrisburg. Nelson's concern for his mother was touching. He treated her with a gentleness that trained ministers had for the powerless and aged. He spoke in a comforting, nasal drawl that sounded pitch-perfect on a gospel music radio show in the darkest hour; that assured her that her main trial was long yet to come. During our first trip, he had set her up with a video of Alfred Hitchcock's *The Birds*.

Gary DeNeal begged off on this first meeting. He and Ron were old friends, and as long as I didn't talk politics or mention Bill Clinton's name, he assured me, Ron Nelson would be my friend. Gary looked sideways at me under his straw hat, the day before my meeting, as if to confirm that I had understood his point.

Ron Nelson was an ordained Baptist preacher, who tended to his flock on Sunday and ran a gun shop during the week.

There was some implication in Gary's words, of course, that my liberal politics might get in the way of my research. I was treading in a bastion of the conservative heartland. Gary had brought up this point many times. It always lingered as a warning of my outsider status, no matter how hard I tried to impress anyone with my family connection to the region.

"What about Paul Simon?" I once asked, referring to the legendary bow-tied U.S. senator, journalist, and liberal Democratic icon from southern Illinois in the 1980s and 1990s.

"He was an exception," Gary spat out. "Besides, you couldn't find a better friend of coal."

Far from politics, I found these red-state, blue-state distinctions tended to blur once the bread was broken, the catfish was served, and the family stories unfolded. They always had.

Funnily enough, the deeper I dug into Eagle Creek's history, the more I sought out and valued people whose politics seemingly contradicted mine, but also made me feel at home. There was a refusal to separate the legacy of the hills from the hill folk, whatever their foibles or triumphs may have been.

Was it because the only people left in Eagle Creek, or who cared about Eagle Creek, or were mule-skinned and fearless enough to take on the coal company's abuses were gun-toting evangelical hunters and ginseng gatherers who didn't like bureaucrats and politicians any more than I did? Perhaps.

In truth, coal politics completely derailed partisanship; the liberal Democrats in the Midwest were as beholden to the Big Coal lobby grip as any conservative Republican in Kentucky. In 2006, the junior senator from Illinois, Barack Obama, had cosponsored legislation to create an emissions-spewing and prohibitively expensive coal-to-liquid plant with Kentucky senator Jim Bunning, a conservative Republican, in an unusually misguided pander to the coal industry.

"Well, I never liked Clinton myself," I told Gary.

"Well, good, you and Ron should get along nicely," he quipped, in a singsong revival way. "And the lion shall sit down with the lamb one day."

Gary knew he was playing on this kind of stereotyping game, based on the rules of our views of the South. For we were in "the South," in many respects; the "southern" in southern Illinois had always distracted outsiders and local cultural brokers. It also lent itself to misperceptions that had hung like a fog over the region's more complex identity. Although the first wave of immigrants in the early 1800s, like my own family, had indeed come from the South, few critics had ever considered the reality that most—outside of a handful of Old Dominion gentry and the salt well operators—were nonslaveholders, fleeing the slave-based economy for a reason: They didn't agree with the tradition of bondage. Nonetheless, for decades, provincial politicians and revisionist historians preferred to pigeonhole the region as the last surrendered outpost of the defeated South, as if it were an unhinged piece of Appalachia or the Ozarks that had floated down the river and left a backwash of ignorance, backwardness, and violence.

This couldn't have been further from the truth—for Appalachia, the Ozarks, or southern Illinois. Historically, the confluence of the two great rivers—Ohio and Mississippi—had made southern Illinois a crossroads of cultures, a burning ground of industrial conflict, and the pioneering front lines for social change. Far from any landlocked hollow that had enjoyed a couple hundred years of solitude, the region had always flourished in debate as a borderland of overlapping beliefs, straddling the political and social hinges of the North and South with its own brand of populism.

Wasn't William Jennings Bryan, the "Great Commoner" from Salem, southern Illinois's gift to American populism in the nineteenth century?

If anything, the region's unique place in the American heartland assured it a history of paradoxes; of frightening episodes of enslavement and kidnappings; and inspiring stories of resistance and enlightenment. You had radical abolitionists and Johnny Rebs here, but somehow the uniqueness of the Johnny Rebs in the land of Lincoln had gotten the best of the storytellers' imaginations. Outside of the murder of Elijah Lovejoy, the crusading abolitionist journalist in Alton, Illinois's anti-slavery past in the southern part of the region had always been left out of the story.

En route to Eagle Creek, I cringed every time I drove by a Confederate flag staked in front of a farmhouse south of Harrisburg, in a community near Mitchellsville. Didn't they know that the namesake Dr. Mitchell had defied a racist gaggle and allowed two black families to farm on his property after the Civil War?

Not that those very farms were still here. They had been strip-mined.

Not that southern Illinois efforts hadn't resoundingly debunked these prejudices and outside Confederate assumptions. In this so-called heartland of copperheads that still lingered in tall tales, especially for anyone in Chicago or the Springfield capital, the historical truth was that southern Illinois provided a staging ground for General Ulysses Grant and his Union forces, and a tipping point in the Civil War. When the legendary General John "Black Jack" Logan led his Third Division of southern Illinois Union troops into victory at Vicksburg, Mississippi, and then was promoted to lead the army at the Battle of Atlanta, the region's role on the front lines of the Civil War could not have been more dramatic.

Our southern Illinois boys, including my ancestors in Eagle Creek (which had enrolled en masse for the Union), trounced the Confederates.

Hadn't the first graduating class at Southern Illinois University in Carbondale in the 1860s included two black students?

Hadn't the first black major filmmaker in America, Oscar Micheaux, drawn on his childhood in the southern Illinois town of Metropolis for his first novel, *The Conquest*, and made a singular film response to the Klan classic, "Birth of a Nation"?

On the other hand, didn't it take until 1972 for the integration of lunch counters at Cairo, Illinois?

All of these contradictions actually led back to Ron Nelson.

He may have started preaching in local Baptist churches and revivals in his teens, been ordained at the age of twenty, and taken up the oldest profession in southern Illinois—gunsmithing—but his true vocation was that of a grassroots historian. He had written, edited, and published untold volumes of stories, memoirs, and church notes. At one point, after attending the seminary, he had enrolled at Southern Illinois University for a masters degree in history, but he dropped out because he lacked computer skills. The memory still rankled Nelson. His ground-level historical research in the Shawnee Hills, and among early Baptist records, had few peers in academia.

In truth, Ron's tedious work in combing the archives and searching through cobwebbed church attics was the foundation on which other historians climbed the ladder. No one had done more to chronicle two fundamental areas of regional development that others had relegated to the historical back burners in Illinois: Baptist history and slavery.

For all of the fallout over supposed Confederate sympathy in southern Illinois, and the shamefulness of the belated civil rights movement, Ron knew a more startling fact had been silenced in the Illinois and American history books: Before Lincoln and the Civil War, Illinois had been a slave state. Moreover, a loophole in the state's constitution of 1818 had specifically allowed legal slavery near Eagle Creek.

Not only did slavery take place in Illinois, its horrific practice had been sanctioned by the political powers until the mid-nineteenth century for one reason: Tax revenues from the salt wells near Eagle Creek, supplemented by coal mining, overruled the legislature's sense of humanity. Its demise didn't occur until a monumental battle with courageous anti-slavery crusaders living in its very midst.

Why did we have slavery in Illinois in the first place?

"Hold tight," Ron said, pulling out of his mother's driveway. "I want to take you to a cemetery."

With Ron, that line would be repeated many times.

◊ ◊ ◊

"WHEN PATRICK HENRY was declaring, 'Give me liberty or give me death,'" Ron was telling me in the truck, his voice becoming increasingly more cranky, "the Baptists understood what he was talking about."

He hadn't taken a breath since he turned the ignition of the truck. With one hand on the steering wheel, and the other in the air, Ron often shot a look over at me, as if concerned I might be hedging in the pew during his historical sermon. He was referring, of course, to the great patriot's speech at the House of Burgesses in 1775.

"I mean, haven't you read the Parson's Cause?" Ron asked, and then he followed up before I could answer. "Already, by 1763, Patrick Henry was chastising the established Church of England, the Anglicans, and talking about the beating of Baptist preachers."

Ron almost looked offended by the thought of the Anglicans. Henry's cause, of course, became the great crusade for religious freedom. As the first postcolonial governor of Virginia in 1776, one of Henry's first acts was to insert a clause for religious freedom in the state constitution. Most readers of history, though, in Ron's mind, often glossed over the role of Henry in defending imprisoned and persecuted Baptist preachers, many of whom served in the front lines of the Revolutionary dissenters.

In Ron's eyes, there was a reason so many pioneering Baptists had blazed the trails across the Appalachians, the Ohio River Valley, and arrived as the first American settlers in southern Illinois. In a word: liberty. After so many generations of preaching through the gates of prison, obliged to pay taxes to support the corrupt Church of England clergy, and bearing the brunt of violent mobs, the Northwest Ordinance of 1787 was like a clarion call:

"No person, demeaning himself in a peaceable and orderly manner, shall ever be molested on account of his mode of worship or religious sentiments. . . . "

The Ordinance, which included Illinois, also issued another clause:

"There shall be neither slavery nor involuntary servitude in the said territory, otherwise than in the punishment of crimes, whereof the party shall have been duly convicted."

Pulling up to a gate, just west of Harrisburg, Ron hopped out of the truck, unlatched the lock, and then stepped back into his seat, in midsentence.

"For many Baptists, the two were connected." He was referring to the ordinance, of course, but somehow our attention had already strayed to the dirt lane that snaked like a trench through an abandoned minefield. "This is private property, the mine owns it," he went on. "But we have a right to cross. This is one cemetery we managed to save."

The Williford cemetery appeared more forsaken than saved. It huddled in a tiny acre of woods, like a farmer's retirement plot, untended and overgrown. Ron walked me to the edge of the cemetery, where a few foundation stones sat as if they had been strewn from a bulldozer in no apparent order.

There was an important historical clue in this rubble.

Back in the 1960s and 1970s, the colossus Chicago-owned Sahara Coal Company, which fueled the Commonwealth Edison electricity plants in the Windy City, had strip-mined the area of Liberty all the way to the blacktop. Laws prevented the desecration of the cemetery—as long as it had been marked and repeatedly guarded.

"Important details there," Ron noted. "Marked and guarded," as if the dead needed more than the Grim Reaper to defend them.

He explained how the first Liberty Baptist Church, a log cabin hewn from the forest west of Harrisburg, had most likely been founded by Elder Eli Barbre in 1832. Barbre's footnote in history took place in Indiana a few years prior, when he had pastored the same church attended by a young Abraham Lincoln and his family. Ron relished that detail, but it was secondary to Barbre's other role at Liberty: The Baptist church had been established as part of the Friends of Humanity, a fervent anti-slavery organization that had divided the Baptist loyalties since the first prayers had been offered on Illinois soil.

There was more in these broken and abandoned stones. In 1853, the pioneers in the area had gathered at the Liberty log cabin church and devised a plan to create a new town. This had not simply been a planning meeting; it was a political maneuver to shift the county seat of Saline County to the hillside once called Crusoe's Island, which eventually became the coal-mining town of Harrisburg.

While Harrisburg's destiny played out in coal, some of its founders from that Liberty church meeting didn't fare as well. John Cain, who had served as a sort of elder statesmen for the crowd, lived nearby. His own Cain community—as well as his historic role as one of the four founders of Harrisburg—was strip-mined and eliminated during that same period in the 1970s, when the 65-cubic-yard shovels and monstrous draglines made a clean sweep of the area and dug up nearly 30 million tons of coal.

The Williford cemetery looked like a trauma survivor: in pieces, all coherence gone.

But Ron wanted to tell me about the cemetery that didn't get protected. He snorted, spat out some phlegm, and then returned to the American Revolution.

"Wilson Henderson served as a scout with Francis Marion, the famous 'Swamp Fox' in South Carolina that evaded the British forces," he went on. The nearby coal-mining town of Marion, in fact, had been named after the legendary American patriot. Henderson had been a teenager. After the Revolution, he immigrated like many Southerner patriots, hopscotching his way through brief periods of settlement in Tennessee and Kentucky, before he landed in the nearby area of Bankston's Fork in 1818. As one of the pioneer Baptist preachers, Henderson went on to found several churches and Baptist associations, though not without considerable controversy. Henderson had taken part in the long-brewing battle over church doctrine that had divided the Baptists into two main camps, based on issues of grace, general atonement, predestination, and the employment of missionaries. As part of the Friends of Humanity, he had also sided with the anti-slavery Baptists who would play a key role in Illinois politics in 1824, when the state voters barely turned down a referendum to transform Illinois into a full-fledged slave state.

Unfortunately, the Sahara Coal Company got to Henderson before the history books. Henderson's burial ground under his beloved orchard was strip-mined into oblivion in 1947. Years later, one bulldozer operator privately confessed that he saw skulls and bones rolling onto his shovel. To be fair, the shamed Sahara Coal Company put up a marker honoring Henderson at the old Bankston's Fork.

Then came Amax, an Indiana-based coal company, in the 1970s. In a preliminary report, as required by law, on the "selected demographic, social, economic and cultural characteristics of the people" at the designated site, the report researcher borrowed from a modern philosopher of geography when considering the impact of strip mining on the local communities:

"Under all—the land, but on the land—the people, what of the people? Land will be taken out of agricultural productions, homes will be destroyed, and families will be relocated. . . . The goal for AMAX is to get the coal as expeditiously as possible. In so doing AMAX has created serious problems for the people affected and, in the long run, for their community and for the county."

Without any authorization from the church or family, the coal company moved the preacher's marker to the newly built and relocated Bankston's Fork Baptist Church and cemetery, and then strip-mined Henderson's second burial spot. A can of coal dust was placed at his new tombstone. In 1983, Ron took part in a special ceremony for Henderson, whose giant role in the Baptist history still lingered over the church like a beacon of light.

"Here lies Wilson Henderson, and over here he lies, and over here he lies," Ron mused, climbing back into the truck. His voice had taken on that solemn tone of the Baptist hour. "Ash to ash, coal dust to coal dust. A Revolutionary War veteran and Baptist preacher who couldn't keep out of the way of the coal shovel."

◊ ◊ ◊

MOST HISTORY BOOKS would agree: A wealthy aristocracy that ruled over the South's low country for centuries rose on the backs of slave labor in the cotton and rice fields.

A less known historical fact: Slave labor also gave birth to the coal industry and its future barons.

Thomas Jefferson's Old Dominion dipped into its coal pits a half century before the American Revolution with African-gripped picks and shovels. As early as 1765, ads in the *New York Mercury* newspaper appeared for coal sales from slave-operated mines in Chesterfield County in Virginia. Still, in 1770, the American colonies relied on and imported thousands of tons of coal from Britain; an irritation, for sure, but it did not generate any great rivalry, as much as it festered as an incipient resentment of dependence.

The "mineral fuel economy" booming out the industrial revolution that so inspired Jefferson in late-eighteenth-century England may have been a secondary source of incentive for the budding American coal prospectors and patriots. Their first concern was within their own sights: The once vast woodlands along the eastern seaboard and piedmont were quickly vanishing. As early as 1790, an observer noted in a Philadelphia newspaper: "The increasing scarcity and dearness of firewood indicates the absolute necessity of attending in the future to the coal mines of this country."

Either way, as retreating Hessian solders in the American Revolution forces noted in their diaries, in Virginia in the 1780s, black slaves had been laboring in the trenches of coal pits for decades.

By the time French aristocrat the duke de La Rochefoucauld visited the Dover Pit coal mine near Richmond in 1796, en route to Jefferson's home, slave labor had become a key component in Virginia's coal trade. The Frenchman counted over five hundred black slaves toiling in a single underground mine. The primitive conditions of the mines horrified him. Despite the incredible dangers, including frequent cave-ins, methane gas explosions and fires, and flooding, the slaves had no choice. Anyone who refused to work was whipped. The death toll in these mines was unfathomable.

By 1837, as one writer noted in the *Farmers Journal*, coal companies in Virginia relied entirely not only on slave labor, but also on the expertise of slave engineers, who served as superintendents and directed the mining operations. "And they, only," the editor concluded, "knew anything of the condition of the coal."

While historian Ronald L. Lewis estimated that a minimum of forty coal-mining companies operated in the Richmond basin between the American Revolution and the Civil War, the real Virginia boom in coal took place in the early 1800s in the western part of the state along the Ohio River Valley.

With the discovery of salt in the Kanawha River Valley, coal quickly replaced wood as a fuel to boil and crystallize the salt. In fact, across the river in Scioto, Ohio, coal-powered furnaces at the labor-intensive salt works dominated wood for fuel as early as 1807. Within a few years, steamboats plied down the Ohio River with coal-laden barges.

As a writer in the *New York Columbian* newspaper responded to a member of the British parliament a year before the War of 1812, few discoveries united the United States like coal. He admonished: "Our dependence upon your country has been carried so far, that the sea-ports of the United States expected their regular quotas from Ireland, Scotland and England. . . . Is there anything that can more effectually fasten and dove tail the union? Our resources are so abundant, that we shall be happier in procuring fuels from our own mines, than deriving it from yours. . . . Moreover, our domestic coal will be brought to the consumer cheaper than yours. And you know, where fuel is cheap, all the arts are carried on with a corresponding thriftiness and ease."

There was one catch in cheap coal: It required slaves. And it took a lot of lives.

In the spring of 1838, over forty black slaves and their two foremen were buried alive seven hundred feet below the earth, when an explosion devastated the Black Heath coal pit in Virginia. Undaunted, the president of a nearby coal mine took out an ad in a newspaper for more laborers. He appealed directly to slave owners to hire out their slaves. "There is no better place in this country where slave labor commands as much, where their general health is better, and where the treatment and contentment of the slaves are surpassed. It is true that within the last few years several disastrous accidents have occurred, but from the scientific and practical skill attracted to the mines, these accidents will be of rare occurrence, it is to be hoped."

Whether that hopeful occurrence rarely came or not, the brutal nature of the labor, without proper ventilation or safety, resulted in a deadly atmosphere. At the Dover Pit in Virginia in 1837, one visitor noted that slaves literally worked as mules to transport the coal to the main entry. He wrote: "Each man has a chain fastened by straps around his breast, which he hooks to the corve, and thus harnessed, and in a stooping posture, he drags his heavy load over the floor of rock."

Lacking the engineering technologies from Britain, the sheer force of the slave labor to function as human bulldozers stunned a visiting Scottish coal engineer. "At the will of their master," he wrote in a letter, slaves at the coal mines in Virginia "could be seen removing as high as thirty feet of cover to obtain four feet of coal."

By the 1850s, over 3,000 slaves worked in the combined coal and salt productions in the Kanawha River Valley alone, in modern-day West Virginia—including Booker T. Washington, who rose out of slavery to become one of the most important African American figures in the late nineteenth century. Slaves also served as the backbone of the first coal mines in Alabama.

To some observers, such as the Pottsville *Miners' Journal* in 1865, the coal trade in the Kanawha River Valley had been "cursed and controlled by the slave masters who 'like the dog in the manger' have for fifty years denied it to enterprise, and knew not how to profit for its immense mineral wealth."

That curse came to an end in the spring of 1865. When Union forces advanced into Confederate territory in Virginia, slaves climbed out of the coal pits at Dover in total desertion and fled for Richmond, bringing this ignominious first chapter of the coal industry to an end.

◊ ◊ ◊

NORTH OF THE Mason-Dixon Line, the entangled destiny of the ancient salt and coal basins shared the modern schemes of slavery.

In fact, black slaves arrived in the coal mines in the Illinois country nearly half a century before their counterparts dug the first pits in Virginia. During the Shawnee period, over five hundred black slaves from Haiti floated up the Mississippi River and disembarked on the Illinois shores at Fort Chartres in 1722. Sanctioned by the French Crown, mining engineer Phillipe Renault arrived with the ruthless aims of the Company of the Indies to extract as much of the mineral wealth as possible in the new territory.

While Renault launched some coal operations, he quickly turned his sights to lead, mainly based in Missouri. Two decades later, he returned to his country a wealthy man. His slaves, among those who survived, remained as part of the French American colonies in Illinois and Missouri.

The anti-slavery clause in the Northwest Ordinance of 1787 notwithstanding, by the time Lewis and Clark observed blacksmiths and gunsmiths employing coal in their work along the riverbeds in southern Illinois in 1803, slavery had become an entrenched part of the trading economy in the region. Slave-owning settlers simply interpreted the law to be applicable to new immigrants; the French, as well as the pioneering Americans, kept their slaves or servants, and actually paid taxes on them.

In 1803, however, this policy changed in language, but not practice. As part of the Indiana Territory, residents in Illinois could engage in "voluntary" indenture contracts. Voluntary was an illusory term, of course. Residents were allowed to travel across the Ohio River and into slave states, such as Kentucky and Tennessee, return with a slave, who was then offered an indentured contract of typically thirty to fifty years—many "voluntary" indenture contracts were drawn up to ninety-nine years—or be sold back into slavery on the other side of the river. Young slaves fared even worse; those under fifteen were automatically indentured for twenty years, whereupon they could "voluntarily" indenture themselves for the rest of their lives. In the meantime, the masters were allowed to sell and trade their servants like property; most servants simply lived out the rest of their lives with the inheritors of their contracts.

In truth, despite the laws, the entry and purchasing of slaves continued for decades.

The year of 1803 also marked the handover of the Great Salt Spring from Native control to the Americans. By that fall, a slave-owning Kentucky salt operator had earned the first lease from the government to produce 120,000 bushels of salt. He didn't last long. Over the next few years, a series of lessees would take control of the wells, increasing the ranks of slaves.

The Illinois Territory adopted the indenture laws of Indiana, which had been updated over the course of six years, when it was established in 1809. The slave owners, in fact, demanded more. No one, more so, than the salt well operators near Eagle Creek.

If anything, history has immortalized the act of slavery in name alone: The Great Salt Spring quickly became known as Nigger Well or Nigger Furnace. It stills remains the Negro Spring today. A second spring, Half Moon Lick, was located closer to the town of Equality.

By 1810, an estimated thousand black slaves had toiled in the forested area as woodcutters and salt kettle attendants. Some had been temporarily brought over from Kentucky and Tennessee. Salt operators complained that only the black slaves were capable of the grueling work; that, in fact, many hired hands—such as my first Colbert ancestors, who had migrated to the salt well frontier in 1805—had actually abandoned the area for their own farms as squatters. The slaves hauled the lumber and water, tended the fires for scores of 60- to 100-gallon cast-iron kettles used to boil the brine into crystals, scraped the draining pans and boards, and loaded the bushels of salt into the storage sheds or onto boats at the Saline River. As the forest receded from the confines of the salt wells, even more slaves were required to cut and haul timber from miles away, and then develop a wooden pipe system that provided water to the furnaces. An estimated one hundred miles of augured logs—massive trees hollowed out for a four-inch pipe—stretched across the hills and valleys. Over 130,000 bushels of salt were loaded and sold that year, effectively breaking any monopoly in Kentucky and supplying the region from Indiana to Missouri and as far south as Tennessee.

According to one traveler, the living conditions among the laborers were appalling. Living in makeshift hovels, with very little food, most languished in some sort of stage of ill health.

Not that this garnered the attention of the landlords, our government in Washington. The rapid deforestation around the salt wells brought more concern. Albert Gallatin, the Swiss-born secretary of the Treasury, had already envisioned the use of coal as part of a national system of roads and canals development. In 1809, he instructed the governor of Illinois to introduce conditions to "effectually prevent the waste of timber, and to encourage the use of coal" at the salt furnaces, to which lessees would pay less rent. A year later, lessee Captain H. Butler wrote the governor of his experiment with an "air furnace to reduce the amount of fuel used." Seeking government payments for improvements to the salt wells—the state of Ohio already granted rebates for the use of coal in their salt furnaces—Butler wrote that he had found a way to manufacture the salt with coal.

While coal slowly began to be implemented at the salt furnaces, dug out from nearby banks by slaves, the turnover in lessees held back any dramatic shift. In 1812, however, two developments took place that would accelerate the demand for coal. With the strain of the war with Britain, the federal government altered its original intent of leasing out the salt wells—to provide cheap salt to as many people as possible. In need of revenue, the government allowed the salt operators to nearly double their rates, resulting in more rent revenues. In the meantime, the government set aside a six-mile tract of land—nearly 100,000 acres—as the United States Saline Reservation, arguably one of the first federally designated forests in the nation. This would not only provide more access to timber, including the northern hills of Eagle Creek, it also opened up more territory for private salt interests, as opposed to general settlement. As an additional element to the new leases, the government granted the unlimited use of "stone coal" on the premises.

Two years later, surveyors found the reservation possessed great quantities of coal, "which may be transmitted to the works by water, or the water may be conveyed by pipes to the coal banks."

To accommodate the labor demands of the salt operators, the Illinois territorial government passed a law in 1814 that allowed slaves to be imported from outside the state for one-year contracts. The legislators declared that the lucrative salt trade "could not be successfully carried on by white laborers." A year earlier, Illinois had also become the only free state or territory to deny the entry of free black immigrants. The Kentucky border, of course, was less than fifteen miles away at the riverside. The slaves could literally gather at the river, touch their toes to the water, and be returned to the coal-stoked furnaces within an hour.

The Illinois governor at the time, Ninian Edwards, owned a considerable number of slaves himself. In 1815, he put an ad in an Illinois newspaper to sell twenty-two slaves, "among them several of both sexes, between the ages of 10 to 17." The same ad also offered a full-blooded stud horse and a large English bull for sale.

To the dismay of emancipationists around the country, Illinois ratified its state constitution in 1818 with two jarring clauses. No slavery or involuntary servitude would be allowed—though, unlike

Indiana's constitution, previously enslaved and indentured servants remained in their same status.

More important, the constitution had one exception: Legal slavery would be allowed "within the tract reserved for the salt works near Shawneetown" until 1825. Those same salt works employed the same slaves to dig out the coal for the furnaces. Recognizing that more than one-third of the state's tax revenues came from the salt wells, the anti-slavery advocates capitulated to the demands of the slave-owning companies. In essence, the inalienable rights of man in other free states came in a distant second to the power of the tax revenues for Illinois's emancipationists.

Even more troubling, of course, was the fact that the U.S. Congress accepted this constitution with its slave-owning loophole.

A year later in 1819, the Illinois legislature passed the Black Codes, which called "for whipping lazy blacks or mulattoes who are servants or slaves," and stipulated that "blacks and mulattoes found without certificates of freedom could be arrested, advertised and sold."

In the meantime, over a thousand black slaves became the residents of the Eagle Creek and Great Salt Spring area over the next decade.

◊   ◊   ◊

"THE COAL AND LEAD MINES will, when protected by the arm of authority," John Kinzie, the governor of the Michigan territory, declared in 1815, "become very important to the frontier."

Kinzie had his eyes on Illinois. In 1810, a black slave named Peter Boon had shoveled and loaded the outcroppings of coal along the south bank of the Big Muddy River in Jackson County, Illinois. Pushing off toward the Mississippi River in their flatboat, William Boon, a captain in the mounted rangers, and his slave Peter transported the first commercial barge of coal in the heartland.

Despite Peter Boon's presence on the slave schedules, virtually every history book and modern news report of this historic event failed to recognize his enslavement, or the fact that William Boon purchased a "voluntarily indentured" servant as late as 1822. One text geared toward children referred to Peter as Boon's African American friend. As a former lead miner from Kentucky and Missouri, Boon engineered the first commercial slope mine in Illinois. He and his slave embarked on six epic voyages down the Mississippi to New Orleans, where they were paid in European currency for coal and loads of forest and farm products.

Boon's efforts attracted attention. As the first state legislator from southwestern Illinois, he also played a role in shaping the laws that allowed for slave labor to assist his work. He would also set the precedent for the entrepreneurial coal foundations in government office—effectively, the first coal lobby in cahoots with the statewide government.

In 1822, Joseph Duncan, also a senator from Jackson County, who later served as governor of Illinois during the volatile 1830s, loaded several barges of coal north of Tower destined for New Orleans; the cargo included the first sales attributed to a foreign buyer. In 1836, John Reynolds, a future governor and former slave-owner who had once advertised to collect his runaway slave in Cahokia, built the first railroad in the Mississippi River Valley to transport the vast reserves of coal on his land to a depot across from St. Louis. Over 150,000 bushels of coal had been mined in Reynold's St. Clair County.

By then, coal had increasingly replaced wood as the main fuel at the salt furnaces around Eagle Creek. Over 8,000 bushels of coal were mined at a single shaft near one salt well in 1824. In an 1828 petition to the U.S. Congress, asking for the right to sell off from the Saline Reservation lands, the Illinois legislature had excitedly proclaimed the discovery of an "inexhaustible quantity of stone coal" that made the woodland reserve useless in the manufacturing of salt. Coal slowly began to replace salt as the industrial fortune to be mined in the area.

By the time John Crenshaw became the great salt king in the Eagle Creek area, coal-fired furnaces burned throughout the hills and valleys like lighthouses to a future fossil-fueled economy.

A year earlier, back on the coal banks of Boon's Big Muddy, the Mount Carbon Coal Company emerged from the fledging efforts and issued stock for $200,000 in value. Ads appeared in newspapers in New York, Philadelphia, and Cincinnati for investors. Noting that the mine had been worked on a limited scale for years, the ad declared: "Coal must ere long, be generally adopted for the use of steam-boats, and sugar plantations, on the Mississippi, and for foundries, steam-mills, sugar refineries, cotton presses, and other works at New Orleans; there would, besides, if this coal were in the market, be a large demand for the outward bound shipping from that port, and as ballast for those in the Havana and South American trade, indeed the demand may be considered almost unlimited."

The slave-holding South was not far away. The prime investor behind the Mount Carbon Coal Company also ran a coal mine operation with slaves in Richmond, Virginia.

◊ ◊ ◊

"I'M NOT ANTI-MINING," Ron Nelson was telling me on another trip. "Mining is important. It's been the backbone of our economy down here. So, don't get me wrong."

The truck bumped along the back roads on the western side of Eagle Mountain. It was a lovely fall day. The narrow road gave way to ruts in many places. No one but hunters or hikers ever took the western route over the mountain.

"But there's a morality in this," he went on. Ron often looked pained at what he was discussing. "I teach ethics. If you're not taught to have respect for the land, to understand the history of the land, then you'll destroy it. It bothers me when people destroy historical sites. When they don't show respect."

He pointed toward the northern ridge of Horseshoe. Perhaps the oldest upheaval in the heartland, dating back to the formation of the Appalachian and Ozark mountains, the craggy Horseshoe ridge and its series of bluffs and hollows looked southeast into Eagle Creek.

"I remember a lot of log cabins out there as a boy and wondered who lived in them," he said. "There were once fifty cabins on the road into Horseshoe. They're all gone now."

As a squirrel-hunter as a kid, Ron and his cousins had ranged across the mountain slopes and knew every hollow. One of his ancestors, John Estes, an anti-slavery advocate, had been murdered on a horse trail to Horseshoe.

"Sometimes we're living right in the midst of history and we don't even know it."

Ron dated much of his historical pilgrimage back to a casual meeting at the home of one of his fellow pastors. At the time, in the 1970s, Ron had been the pastor of the First Baptist Church in Elizabethtown on the Ohio River. He had served other churches in Peoria, Illinois, and at a mission for Native Americans in Dallas, Texas. There in his friend's living room, Ron had an awakening, of sorts.

"He started talking about the Friends of Humanity, anti-slavery societies," he went on, his hand gripping the steering wheel as we bumped over the dirt road. His voice rose, as if still amazed by the discovery. "I had never heard anything like that. I didn't know what it meant."

So, Ron started digging. He wanted to understand why these emancipationist Baptists emerged and how their early ministries had shaped their lives. There was a yearning about Nelson that somehow reflected a larger personal struggle with his religious and historical mission. You could tell that he had confronted a certain amount of resistance.

"Folks in the congregation were like, who cares? What do you think you're doing, Nelson?"

Dating back to 1794, when Baptist elder Josiah Dodge cut the ice in Fountain Creek and baptized James Lemen in southwestern Illinois on a cold winter day, the emancipation spirit had been planted in the first American community in the state. These anti-slavery advocates, however, were not northern Yankees; Dodge was a Kentuckian, another leader came from Georgia, and the Lemen family and their five preaching sons had immigrated from Virginia. In 1809, the Lemens drew a line in the sand for Baptists: They declared no fellowship for slaveholders, nor "for those who fellowship them." They founded the Baptist Church of Christ, Friends of Humanity movement, which soon swept across congregations in the southern Illinois range. It also bitterly divided the congregations.

After we had driven over the rocky Eagle Mountain road, heading east through the dark cover of a forest, Ron suddenly halted the truck at the side of the ridge. We were now overlooking the Eagle Creek valley. I immediately saw a huge oak tree several feet away, surrounded by a stand of smaller pines and underbrush. If there had ever been a mustering oak, or a landmark tree in the Eagle Creek area, this was it.

"The founder of the First Baptist Church in Elizabethtown, where I was pastor," Ron spoke up, "was Stephen Stilley. It was originally called the Big Creek Baptist Church. It was founded in 1806."

Although by 1806 the exploits of river pirates and a criminal syndicate along Elizabethtown's shores carried currency in the earliest chronicles, an Irish travel writer had a different experience near the infamous Cave-in-Rock haunt on the Ohio River. Sauntering along the current in his boat, Thomas Ashe heard an anthem swell to a great pitch and then waft across the river. He paddled closer to the mouth of another cave, where choral music "melted like the notes of an Eolian harp," and there he saw forty people on their knees. They were worshipping in the riverside cavern. There was a transport in the mysterious and simple music that stunned the Irishman, and "without wasting time of frigid speculation of so sublime a spectacle," he raced in and threw himself to the dust "in an effusion of praise to God."

Stephen Stilley's congregation watched in silence at the spectacle, though they must have been delighted in its fervor.

"Watch your step," Ron said, hopping out of the truck. Walking ahead of me in the high grass, he looked over his shoulder and pointed out a wobbly metal fence around the perimeter of the area. "It just galled them that they couldn't get this one last little acre of coal."

I was walking in the footsteps of my first ancestors on our private version of Jerusalem Ridge. And those footsteps had nearly been erased from the earth.

"We cleared the land as far as we could on the ridge," Ron recounted, as we stood at the entrance of the Stilley cemetery, which jutted off the eastern ridge on the Eagle Mountains. "There were so many copperheads, folks were scared. But I pushed them to keep going. And we kept finding graves, tombstones. At least thirty of them." Under the canopy of the huge oak tree, its trunk too wide for two men to wrap their arms around and touch, a plaque stood like an official government marker: "Elder Stephen Stilley, 1765–1841, born in Somerset County, Maryland, he came west as a pioneer Baptist preacher." Ron pointed at an error on the plaque; Stilley had been incorrectly named as a veteran of the War of 1812. His nephew, most likely, another Stephen Stilley from the neighboring county had served in the war.

"I was furious when I saw that error," he went on, shaking his head. "But we were in a hurry then. They had just about stripped up the ridge, and I wanted to protect as much of the cemetery as possible."

Nelson's passion for Elder Stephen Stilley, our shared ancestor, linked us as distantly related cousins. In the early 1980s, as the Brown Mining Company stripped the coal along Rose Creek, a tributary off Eagle Creek, and began to wind up the eastern ridges of the Eagle Mountains, Ron alone recognized the historical significance of Stilley's grave. There was just one problem: He had to find it. Located on private land, buried in the thick underbrush where copperheads held sway, Nelson managed to enlist an army of Baptists to join him in the search. The old oak tree served as their point of reference. With the permission of the landowner, Ron and his crew cleared the area until the tombstones emerged like signposts. He cleared as much as possible, maintained grass-cutting crews for years, placed a fence around the cemetery (again with the landlord's permission), and then held the public unveiling of the plaque in the middle of the forest, if only to draw attention to the preservation of the area and its heritage.

Born along the Nanticoke River in Somerset County, Maryland, Stilley came from a prominent family of Swedish immigrants, who had been a part of the New Sweden settlements in Delaware and Maryland in the 1640s. The original Swedish immigrant had been a fugitive from the island of Solo, who had escaped a death sentence over a land dispute. Stephen Stilley and his family migrated to Craven County, North Carolina, before the American Revolution, branded as dissenters by the British authorities. He married a Baptist minister's daughter in 1791 and then joined the waves of frontier parties that took to the Wilderness Road to eastern Tennessee. He served as a missionary to the Cherokees and woodlands communities. By 1805, Stilley had become a Baptist circuit rider in Kentucky and soon crossed the Ohio River into Illinois to found the first church in the southeastern part of the state.

Although Stilley had purchased this 160-acre mountain farm in 1819, we assumed he had actually homesteaded the area several years before. He had actually been preaching in the New Madrid, Missouri, area during the earthquake of 1811 and returned to Eagle Creek soon after.

"It was a beautiful October day in 1983," Ron recalled, describing the ceremony for the cemetery. "The goldenrods were yellow, and the evergreens looked polished by the rain." He pulled some of the weeds as he walked around. The Illinois Baptist Association and American Legion had joined for a formal celebration of Stilley's life. The ruts of mud kept any cars from making it up the mountain road, so men and women in their Sunday best climbed onto bales of straw in the back of a four-wheel-drive pickup truck and bounced their way over the ridge.

Roy Reynolds, married to one of our distantly related cousins and a Baptist minister, sang "Wayfaring Stranger" with such a high, lonesome intensity that it still remained in Ron's memory like a haunting harbinger. Roy's own family farm near Mitchellsville had been strip-mined a few years before; his father had been injured in an underground mining accident. When he reached the lines "But beauteous fields lie just beyond me, where souls redeemed their vigil keep," everyone looked out at the Eagle Creek valley and wondered.

In the hallowed silence after the song, after the command had been given and twenty-one guns were drawn and fired, and after the bugler had played the final taps, only the faint grind of the draglines and bulldozers strip-mining the valley could be heard.

"See down there," Ron said, walking toward the edge of the ridge.

A huge gash rolled across the valley like a spread of lava from Pompeii. These were the ruins of the strip mines from the 1930s, and then the 1950s and 1980s. And now they had been reopened like scar tissue that would never heal. A new strip mine launched by the Illinois Fuel Company, a Kentucky-based corporation that had specialized in devastating mountaintop removal operations in Appalachia, had begun to strip away at the hillsides. A few miles up the valley, like a lonely ship at sea amid the wrath of the mines, stood the Jones cemetery and the Mount Pleasant Social Brethren Church.

The Jones cemetery represented more than a few gravestones. The Mount Pleasant church, in fact, was the birthplace of the Social Brethren sect in the 1860s, which had since spiraled into congregations around the Midwest. For Ron, however, the history went deeper. The Jones cemetery had been the original place of the anti-slavery Eagle Creek Friends of Humanity Baptist Church.

In 1838, various members of our extended Stilley family helped to found the Eagle Creek Baptist Church, as a Friends of Humanity sanctuary. William Mills, the young barrel maker from eastern Tennessee who had built our family's Oval Hill Farm and homestead, served as one of the church messengers. He had married Stephen Stilley's daughter, Haeland, in the 1820s. They made the first down payment of $20 for the homestead on our knoll at Eagle Creek. In the summer of 1849, a sect of anti-slavery Baptist woodsmen from around Eagle Creek came together to help them raise the walls and roof of our family's original log cabin on the Oval Hill Farm.

While my grandfather would not hack out the first large window of the cabin for nearly another hundred years, William Mills and Haeland Stilley laid the sandstone foundations of the homeplace at Eagle Creek in the volatile decade before the Civil War. They mounted stones from the lower creek for a chimney. Hewn oak logs, trimmed of their rough bark and flattened on either side to form square timber, stretched across the walls, ceiling, and puncheon floors. They didn't possess nails but interlocked the corners of the logs by fitting them together in alternating tiers of saddle notches.

Mills lived in the old cabin on the hill until his nineties. He survived two outbreaks of cholera in Eagle Creek, yellow and scarlet fever, the "cold plague," and malaria. He lost his sons in the Civil War.

Yet, it took the strip mine to erase Mills's legacy from the valley.

Mills had eventually donated part of his land for the Bethel Baptist Church, which had also been destroyed in the final stripping of our land, and was rebuilt across from our family's Colbert cemetery.

It was not the historic nature of the anti-slavery church, though, that claimed Ron's attention. You could tell by his tense nature that something else bothered him.

To be anti-slavery in Eagle Creek in that period required not only a conscience but an extraordinary amount of courage. Outside marauders from Kentucky and elsewhere had terrorized the valley's black ranks at the salt wells and coal mines, and transformed the backwoods into an arena of kidnapping, enslavement, and slave-trading. That was for starters. Our anti-slavery ancestors at the Oval Hill Farm had literally been on the front lines of slavery; they shared their property line with the region's most dreaded and powerful slave owner and salt trader.

"The mine stopped at the Stilley cemetery property," Ron said, walking back to the truck. "But it's what they stripped below in your valley that really matters."

◊ ◊ ◊

IN EXAMINING the slave past of Haiti, historian Michel-Rolph Trouillot discussed the role of narratives in "unearthing the silences." In Haiti's case, Trouillot found a deliberate suppression of any acknowledgment by French and other Western historians of the island's earlier slave rebellion that eventually led to independence in 1804. The idea of a successful slave revolt was simply unthinkable to a Western audience. Therefore, it wasn't reported; the facts were "too unlikely," the news had to be false.

According to Trouillot, the subsequent historical narrative of the events took on two trends: erasure and trivialization. The custodians of history literally silenced the past.

In this respect, the past is a *position* and does not exist independently of the present.

Erasure and trivialization are two powerful accusations. The concept of silencing the past also treads a line of criminal intent, an act not simply of denial but of violent repression.

Over the past twenty-five years in our country, state and federal laws have been passed to ensure the protection of historic archaeological sites. These are not just ruins, but evidence of our historical memory. For example, before any strip-mining permits are issued, coal companies are required to contract with an independent company for an archaeological survey of the area, whose work is regulated by the state's historic preservation agency. In many respects, these laws have created a cottage industry of archaeologists and anthropologists, many of whom rely on the same coal companies for work over a period of several decades. Without a doubt, this makes for a potentially compromising relationship: the coal operators want to expedite the lengthy permit process; the archaeological companies want to maintain their business. Typically, according to one longtime archaeologist I met in Eagle Creek, a hired archaeologist in a coal mine survey would spend two or three days at a particular site, with some additional examination of the historical documents and records. Most archaeologists logged one hundred hours of work on their reports for a particular mine.

For virtually every archaeological survey conducted in the immediate Eagle Creek area over the past two decades, archaeologists filed surveys of topography, soils, and conducted shovel tests and visual inspections of the land for cultural and historic artifacts. Historical plats and maps were consulted, though rarely a single document before 1876.

No oral histories, genealogies, church or county histories, or published narratives were typically reviewed.

There was a certain checklist of items that replicated itself on the survey forms for years—decades—that seemed unduly uniform.

Finally, the hired archaeologist would make a recommendation for project clearance or eligibility for the National Register of Historic Places.

According to a historic archaeological report for one of our Colbert family homesteads sites that lay within the Shawnee National Forest boundaries, "All of the 19th and 20th century rural farmstead sites within the Shawnee National Forest represent cultural properties that potentially meet the eligibility criteria for the National Register of Historic Places." Yet, not a single site in Eagle Creek was ever recommended for National Register eligibility.

To my knowledge and review of the public records, every single archaeological survey short report was accepted for project clearance—in this case, a strip mine—by the Illinois Historic Preservation Agency, the government entity in charge of reviewing such processes.

Cemeteries, as Ron pointed out, remained the last resort to unearth the silences.

◊ ◊ ◊

THE FIRST TIME I spoke with Harlan Booten, the octogenarian farmer was chopping wood. He still possessed the muscular build of a lumberjack; he stood straight as a hickory tree, dressed in overalls and a work coat and a baseball cap.

Harlan loved baseball. In the 1940s, his fastball terrorized every batter within the region's baseball leagues. When a scout appeared from the Detroit Tigers in a swanky automobile, quietly observed Harlan from the stands in the town of Equality, and then offered him a chance to play on one of Detroit's minor league farm teams, Harlan made the hardest decision of his life. He had been offered $15 a baseball game.

"But I couldn't leave Daddy with the harvest coming up," Harlan said.

He returned to the farm. They planted by the moon; they dropped the potatoes and corn seeds during Libra. He fended off the wolves from his cattle, and a phantom cougar that ranged these hills at night like an invisible but cunning threat.

The hard-throwing pitcher never got the chance to play professional baseball again. His only other dream was to play against Earl Bumpus, the legendary Negro league southpaw pitcher, who even drew the praise of the St. Louis Cardinals' Dizzy Dean. When Harlan finally made it across the river to a Negro league game in Kentucky, Bumpus had already moved on to a famed career with the Kansas City Monarchs.

Harlan lived on the county line, just across the Eagle Creek valley, on a hillside farm that had been originally settled by the Giles Taylor family in 1818. Taylor had been a Revolutionary soldier, but maimed somehow, so he functioned as the first schoolteacher in the backwoods in 1823 and maintained a business interest in the salt wells. His son, Edmund Dick Taylor, rose from a low-level horse driver at the salt works to become one of the richest men in Chicago, a confidant of both Abraham Lincoln and Stephen Douglas, and the president of one of the largest coal companies in northern Illinois.

"I'd never work in a coal mine." Harlan laughed, taking a seat by the woodstove in his living room. "I'm too big."

It made me think of my grandfather, a similarly towering man who worked the five-foot rooms with a crooked back and bent-over head for eight hours.

Not that Harlan had stayed away from coal. Just down the road, one local farmer had his own coal mine for local use. Whenever his family's coal bucket got low, Harlan would take the wagon down to Tom Osborn's mine, trundle the trolley car back into the mine, load up his own take, and then cart it home. The coal trade almost functioned on the honor system. In fact, one evening, Harlan's father had set off the dynamite, slept in the wagon, and retrieved the coal himself in the morning.

"That was good coal, high Btu's" Harlan recalled, shaking his head. "It burned good. Red, yellow, and all peacocky."

But the strip mines kept creeping closer. Nearly twenty years ago, an explosion from a Peabody coal blast shattered Harlan's well and ruptured his aquifer. He had to truck in his water ever since.

"I gave them a piece of my mind," he laughed. "But that was some of the finest water you would have ever tasted. What a shame."

In keeping with an ancient tradition that dated back to medieval times, a water witch, equipped with dowsing rods, had located the position of the well.

When a *Chicago Tribune* reporter appeared at Harlan's home right before Christmas in 2002, a new chapter in the strip mines was finally revealed. Harlan agreed to lease part of his ridge to a coal company, though he had first issued a warning.

"All my life I've been told there's a Negro cemetery out there," he told the *Tribune* reporter. "Them people's got a soul, just like you and me."

Walking with Booten to the hillside, where a clearing gave way to sandstone blocks and shallow grave depressions, the *Tribune* reporter hailed it the oldest African American cemetery in Illinois.

The graves were attributed to the nearby salt wells; the Taylors' property, in fact, was just outside the reservation boundaries.

The survey of the archaeological firm hired by the coal company, Illinois Fuel, considered the graves a "local legend." The site was deemed ineligible for historic preservation status. Nor had it been registered with the Illinois Comptroller's office under the Cemetery Care Act—therefore, the coal operators were free to bulldoze the site.

Strangely enough, perhaps for the first time, or perhaps because the *Tribune* article was syndicated to newspapers across the country, the coal company decided against the interpretation of the archaeologists and refused to mine.

But the real story for Ron Nelson, and fellow Crenshaw rascal Jon Musgrave, did not appear in the *Tribune* article. Musgrave wrote a book, *Slaves, Salt, Sex and Mr. Crenshaw*, which examined the overlooked story of slavery in the area. When Musgrave, in the reporter's company, had asked Booten about where the black community had lived, the older farmer confidently responded, "Across from the old Bethel Church," the fields that had adjoined our family's and Crenshaw's property on Eagle Creek.

Another octogenarian from Eagle Creek simply told me, without wanting to be named: "We all knew colored folks had originally lived near the creek. We just didn't talk about it, because they were long gone by the time our families moved in."

In 1858, after the original Eagle Creek Baptist Church had either burned down or collapsed, remnants of the congregation and another church on the west side of the Eagle Mountains decided to form the new Bethel Church branch at Eagle Creek. Our ancestors who lived up on the Oval Hill Farm, William Mills and his daughter, donated the land from their original homestead. As part of the kinship that determined the social relations and politics of the area, the church was essentially an extension of our family branches.

Bethel, of course, was a common church name, meaning "the house of god." It was also the name of a nearby Primitive Baptist church, which took its name from the landowner, Chester Bethel. But for Ron, a more symbolic air resonated with the name; the Bethel Church had been the first Lemen parish to launch the anti-slavery Friends of Humanity movement in southern Illinois.

It wasn't a matter of happenstance for Ron. Like the first Eagle Creek Baptist Church up the road, the Bethel Church sat directly to the side of the farm of John Crenshaw, the infamous salt well operator, slave kidnapper, and future Old Slave House owner.

Dating back to 1818, if not earlier, our cluster of families had settled as the first pioneers along the Eagle Creek valley. They raised the first mill in the area. They built their farms. The Crenshaws, who had arrived from Missouri, actually purchased part of their land from my Colbert family; one of their other neighbors was a land speculator from Louisville, Kentucky, an unusually wealthy Irish merchant and slave owner, who bankrolled part of the salt works.

While John Crenshaw ostensibly worked his way up the ladder at the salt wells, his real investment capital came from another enterprise. Ron had uncovered documents that proved Crenshaw had eventually purchased a farm in Tennessee, where he operated as a slave trader and kidnapper of free African Americans. In 1829, Crenshaw paradoxically filed a suit to obtain damages for the loss of a slave when a boat capsized in the Ohio River—a brazen admission of slave owning when it had been outlawed. Over the course of the next two decades, Crenshaw would be embroiled in several lawsuits and indictments.

In a period when the bounties for wolf scalps and "the kidnapping of free Negroes" in the backwoods of Eagle Creek remained "exceedingly profitable," according to a late-nineteenth-century historical account, Crenshaw flourished. In truth, the lucrative trade of salt had been devastated by the discovery of the salt wells on the Kanawha River Valley, where the wholesale use of slaves and coal soon overtook the Illinois traders' monopoly. By 1830, the Kanawha River Valley dominated the salt trade. By the time Crenshaw amassed his large holdings, most of his sales were local. According to James Harrison Wilson, a legendary Civil War commander from nearby Shawneetown, the demise of Crenshaw's salt and coal works had "let loose a large number of rough operatives." The kidnapping and transaction of free African Americans—including a former maid for the Wilson family—became "common."

While all of the attention has historically been focused on Crenshaw's lurid Old Slave House, which had been built in 1838 as a crowning achievement of his role as the salt king, the most despicable and dangerous period of his reign actually took place at Eagle Creek.

In 1824, the eyes of the nation shifted to Illinois, when the salt and coal traders engineered a scheme to call for a new constitutional convention. As George Flower, an English settler in the Albion commune north of Shawneetown explained, the Eagle Creek villain and his cohort's plan was exceedingly clear: "The lessees of the salines— Granger [Crenshaw's other name, which had been used on various slave records], and others . . . made a bold stroke to perpetuate their system of servile labor, not by asking for an extension of time for hiring hands to work the saline, but they sought so to change the constitution as to make the whole of Illinois a slave-state."

Three players emerged in the anti-slavery movement in Illinois, which suddenly found itself within a hair of becoming the first free state to turn pro-slavery: Governor Edward Coles, the erudite aristocrat from Virginia, who had served as a special ambassador to Russia and freed his own inherited slaves when he moved to Illinois; Flower and Morris Birkbeck and their English followers in the Albion commune along the Wabash River; and the Friends of

Humanity movement in the Baptist churches in southern Illinois. When Illinois voters turned down the convention vote in the summer of 1824, a sigh of relief was released across the nation and in the American heartland. If Illinois had passed this convention vote, other states like Indiana would have easily followed.

The unsung credit, in Ron's mind, went to the backwoods Baptists, who bravely confronted Crenshaw and the salt works operators in their own backyard. It was a volatile and violent period. Armed vigilantes roamed the area. It was one thing for Cole to stand on the porch of his mansion on the far flanks of the Mississippi and hail the joys of freedom, or the patrician English pioneers to write stirring letters to the Shawneetown newspaper from their tight-knit Albion commune. It took another level of courage from the backwoods Baptists to take the fight directly to slave-owning salt and coal traders in the forests of Eagle Creek.

"I first walked around the area in 1977, with your mother's uncles, Ralph and Henry Stilley," Ron told me, as we arrived at the wasteland strip mines along Eagle Creek.

Our denuded hills now stretched across the valley with a haunting vacancy. It felt strange to be standing alone in an area where a dynamic community—the first settlement in the area—once thrived for two centuries. There was an air of an emptied field: of death, not life, despite the verdant spread of grass across strange ruts and broken slopes. The area looked abandoned. There was no wildlife. No people. No homes. No barns. No horses. No trees. As part of the so-called reclamation laws, the coal company had replanted a type of grass, which grew in clumps like weeds. Not a single tree had been planted on our ancestral property.

Eagle Creek suddenly loomed in my mind like my own private Gettysburg battlefield. Bulldozers, instead of the mourning wagons, had dragged off the bones of the dead and then turned around on their machines and covered up the wreckage of the past with an eight-foot layer of clay and topsoil. This included Crenshaw's property; the graves of his own parents had been destroyed. The disgraceful memory of his family's presence in the valley had been erased.

We stood by the clearing where the Bethel Church had once been blessed on the land donated by our family. "Upon this rock I will build my church," went the scripture; and upon this rock explosives fractured it into pieces. With the agreement of the dwindling congregation, the church had been demolished and a new building built across the road from our Colbert cemetery. Whether the coal company's blasting had been the tipping point of despair, or the congregation had dissipated to a righteous remnant that could no longer support a weekly meeting, the new church doors rarely opened now.

The covenant of the church had been removed. The people of Eagle Creek had literally been removed, as well.

"I came back here in 1996, while I was studying John Crenshaw and the Old Slave House," Ron went on. "We identified John Crenshaw's homeplace as directly west of the Bethel Church. Gary and I visited the Crenshaw property and noticed several graves on the west side of the road. I used my brass dowsing rods and surveyed around the property and then noticed the field just east of the Crenshaw property. This property was located just north of the Bethel Church. Gary and I surveyed a large cemetery containing hundreds of graves, possible three to four hundred graves. There were no stones standing, but evidence of broken ones. No names were discernable and all I could find were fragments. This field at that time was in soybean stubble. This cemetery is gone now, though, as well as the Crenshaw property and their graves, which were destroyed by the strip mining."

One older Eagle Creek resident told me, not wanting to be identified: "I remember them saying how they had to move so many grave stones in that field, how they knew there were graves there."

These were some of the graves of the thousands of black slaves from the salt works and earliest coal pits that Harlan Booten and all of the old-timers secretly knew about at Eagle Creek. Ron had appealed to the offices of the city and county clerks, the forest service, and other state agencies to intervene and at least carry out a more extensive archaeological survey. He published his findings in the 150th anniversary edition of *The History of Saline County* before a single explosive was detonated. He had photos of the staked-out graves. Other texts cited his work.

"Everyone knew there was a black cemetery down there," one older resident told me. "And I think a lot of people were just as happy for it to go away, so we didn't have to think about that sad part of our history anymore."

In the archaeological survey commissioned by the coal company, no cemetery was noted, none of Nelson's published writings was cited, and no maps were filed, outside of the generic 1876 atlas. No local resident was interviewed.

If anything, the archaeologists would have mocked Ron's method of research. He had used dowsing rods to find the graves and church foundations, just as German coal engineers had done for centuries to detect minerals, water, and displaced earth. The ancient process of dowsing for water—water witching—used the same rods, which crossed on their own regard when passing over moved earth. To be sure, many consider the art of dowsing a complete sham. Other scientists shrug their shoulders and can't explain the accuracy. After using this method on cemeteries and historic building foundations for the past twenty-five years, and accurately discovering several historic building sites and lost cemeteries, Ron had no doubts about his method of research. The broken tombstones spoke for themselves.

Not that it mattered anymore. The graves and tombstones in Eagle Creek were churned into bits of dust; the last voices of the slaves had been buried with mining waste. Their silences would remain unearthed.

As we stood for the last time in the area of the Oval Hill Farm, or at least in a place that might have been near, the landmarks and contours of the land completely destroyed, I was reminded how our old farm would have been a lookout point for both emancipationists and slaves. In defiance of their neighbor John Crenshaw and his slave-trading cohorts at the salt wells and coal mines, our ancestors' homeplace had been a sanctuary of liberty.

◊ ◊ ◊

"YOU KNOW, like when I'm out fishing," Nelson chattered one day, as we drove to another cemetery in Saline County. "Every Monday I'm out there, on my boat, and I'm wondering about John Bunyan and the Pilgrim's Progress."

Nelson explained the late-seventeenth-century Christian allegory, written by a jailed Baptist minister who had held services outside the purview of the Church of England. In the story, the Christian pilgrim journeys from the City of Destruction and, arriving at the Hill of Difficulty, he stays with a congregation. He has to prepare himself for the battle in the Valley of Humiliation.

Ron pointed out the truck window at the Eagle Creek valley.

"'Yea, though I walk through the valley of the shadow of death, I will fear no evil: for thou art with me; thy rod and thy staff they comfort me.'"

I didn't say anything, but I felt little comfort driving through the valley of strip mines, this modern City of Destruction.

CERTIFICATE No. 2323

STATE OF

ILLINOIS

DEPARTMENT OF MINES AND MINERALS

State Miners' Examining Board

Certificate of Competency of Coal Miner

To Whom It May Concern:

This Is to Certify, That ****** ROBERT FOLLOWELL ******

of 11 E. W. Raymond, Harrisburg , County of Saline , State of Illinois,

whose description is set forth below, having made oath, and given satisfactory evidence, that he has worked in Coal Mines for not less than two years, and having answered intelligently and correctly, the questions required by law and the Rules of this Board and having produced satisfactory evidence to the Board that he has successfully completed the course in First Aid to the Injured prescribed by the Department of Mines and Minerals of Illinois and being found duly qualified, is hereby granted this **Certificate of Competency**, and is entitled and authorized to seek and accept employment as a Coal Miner in the Mines of the State of Illinois.

Birthplace Illinois ; date of birth June 5, 1901 ; age 46 ; height 6 feet — inches;

weight 193 ; color of hair Gray ; color of eyes Blue ; nationality American ;

None ; years of experience 4 .

DONE BY authority of the State Miners' Examining Board, this 11th day

of March 19 48 , in proof of which we hereby affix our seal and attach

our signatures.

[SEAL]

Robert R. Lause

Director

Robert Followell's coal miner certificate. *(Courtesy of the author.)*

◊

Chapter Four

WHO KILLED THE MINERS?

The Anatomy of Denial

He's had more hard luck than most men could stand
The mines were his first love, but never his friend
He's lived a hard life, and hard he'll die.
Black lung's done got him, his time is nigh.

—HAZEL DICKENS, *"Black Lung"*

H ovie Stunson spoke with the rapid-fire confidence of a true believer. He loved to talk about coal mining. He could talk in tongues about coal mining. If the Illinois Coal Association ever needed a natural-born representative, Hovie Stunson was the man.

To be sure, though, he was hardly some flack for the coal industry. Hovie's encyclopedic knowledge of coal mining unfolded with the lure of a passionate museum guide who didn't want the tour to end. He knew how to whip up an incredible story with the most obscure statistics and mining references in a single breath, while somehow translating every bit of coal jargon into layman's speak as he inhaled for the next round.

Hovie may have been in his forties, but I came to see him as an ancient storyteller trapped in a young man's body. He spoke in that matter-of-fact way as if he had gone through every episode of history himself, back in the nineteenth century. *Ah, boy, that was something*. Thin as a railroad tie, Hovie had a way of shaping himself into a sinewy force of nature, his hands afloat, his head swaying his wavy hair, his astonished eyes tucked behind large glasses as if he couldn't fathom what he was recounting either. And he always wore a long, youthful smile that stretched down to his pointy chin with a contentedness that was inspiring.

"Check out the men's room in the basement," Hovie told me, the first time we met at the Harrisburg Public Library, where he headed the maintenance team and oversaw the genealogy room.

That long smile nearly dragged on the floor. Men's room? I walked down and opened the door. With bamboo-paneled walls, hanging plants, and a series of oceanside photos, the restroom looked more like an overflow room in some Margaritaville bar.

"Hawaii actually," Hovie chimed in, and then he pointed out the geographic references of the photos, the plants, and even the bamboo that had some sort of relation to the island.

This sort of attention to detail punctuated every conversation with Hovie. He didn't do anything halfway. As a young man, he dominated the bowling alleys in the region, winning more trophies than he could stack in a warehouse. He even bowled on the Peabody coal company team. He had offers to bowl professionally. On one fateful evening, he threw the ball with too much glamour on the last frame, ripping the pins with a chorus of thunder. The 10 pin didn't fall. Hovie ended up with a phenomenal 299 score—a breath away from a perfect score. Burned out after thirteen years of playing several nights a week, crisscrossing the state in tournaments, he quit and looked for another passion.

He turned his energy toward collections. He developed a passion for trains. He collected Civil War memorabilia—Confederate, in homage to his mother's Tennessee past. He collected miniature stock cars—in homage to his love of Nascar racing.

Nothing surpassed his love for coal mining.

This was in homage to his father, Rusty Stunson, a legendary mining superintendent for the Peabody coal company, whose expertise in opening and operating underground mines took him around the world. Even under it: He worked in Peabody's large operations in Australia, as well. This included the Eagle No. 1 mine on the eastern edge of Eagle Creek. A smoker of three packs of cigarettes a day, he died from lung cancer while Hovie was still a young man.

"My Dad loved coal mining," Hovie recounted. "He talked about coal mining all day long. Talked about it in his sleep."

And that is how his son began to absorb the stories, the blueprints, the spreadsheets, the maps, and the vernacular of the trade. His father's openness made all the difference to Hovie.

"Most miners keep it all inside," Hovie told me, as if speaking from experience. "They get home and don't talk, and no one asks them anything. So, their life underground remains among them and other miners."

Hovie's mother was different. She insisted her husband recount his daily affairs in detail, if only to loosen the pressure valve of his intense job. He was not only responsible for the highly competitive production levels; he had to watch out for everyone's life. If he wasn't on site, the mine called him before they called an ambulance. So, he sat at the dinner table and ate his pork chops and potatoes, talked about the workers and their habits, their errors, who did what to whom, the problems, the breakdowns, the strikes, and the accidents.

As an adolescent, Hovie didn't even think about using the phone when his father came back from work. The line always had to be free in case of an emergency. Instead, Hovie listened to his father. Listened to every detail of every story.

"My dad swore all the time." Hovie laughed. "But his swearing was like poetry."

"I was probably eight or nine the first time I was in a mine," Hovie told me and then quickly corrected himself. "I mean, I was probably a baby the first time I visited a mine. But when I was a little older, I'd go with my dad to work, like over at the Eagle mine, and learn about every inch of the business."

"Rusty's kid is here," someone would announce. A private tour was arranged. He hopped on the elevator or conveyor, lowered into the deepest rooms of the mine, and then scampered about as if he owned the place. The employees either begrudgingly or happily took the kid around; most likely, his big-eyed passion for the business entertained them, allowed them a few free moments. He operated the continuous miner machines before he could drive the streets of Harrisburg. He knew the underground passages like the back warrens of his town.

"Coal gets so pretty," Hovie said, his eyes widening, describing the continuous miner machines that shaved the seams of coal. "Like a wall of diamonds."

Throwing out his hands, squatting on his knees, Hovie walked me through the process of drilling the holes, placing in the explosives, and bringing down the face of coal in the old days.

"Couldn't get away with that now." Hovie laughed. "Those inspectors mark down a violation for a speck of dirt on a toilet seat nowadays."

On his deathbed, Hovie's father asked him to do something other than go into the mines. His hand was missing a finger, crushed between trains like many miners working the trip rider. Their family had known enough death and disaster; uncles and grandfathers and cousins had done their time in the mines. Hovie's cousin had been electrocuted in a mine. It was time for Hovie to move on.

But that didn't stop Hovie. After he graduated from high school, he took an associate degree in technical coal-mining studies at the local community college. When Kerr-McGee, the industrial chemical, uranium, and petroleum giant, announced in 1981 that it would be opening up one of the largest coal mines in the region, in nearby Galatia, Hovie couldn't wait to get underground.

He turned in his application. He took an entrance exam. At the first interview, the Kerr-McGee representative was so overwhelmed by Hovie's technical knowledge and his effusive raillery that he declared the young man should take a supervising position, not an entry-level job. He shook hands and told Hovie to expect a call for work.

That call never came.

Although Hovie's father may have been a superintendent, and taken a role in management, he had been a member of the United Mine Workers in his earlier capacity as a coal miner. As had Hovie's grandfather and uncles. Like virtually every other coal miner in Illinois at that point.

Illinois had always been the heartland of the union.

Hovie wasn't hired at the Kerr-McGee mine. Nor were any local miners who had been connected to the union's front ranks. The shaft suddenly swelled with out-of-state nonunion miners to break any union attempt at the mine. When he returned to talk to the company representative who had gushed about his test scores and knowledge, Hovie heard an incoherent excuse about waiting lists and long lines. He saw his file get placed into a large folder.

A new age in coal mining was about to begin in southern Illinois. And Hovie Stunson, its native son and most conversant coal authority, had not been invited to take part. Despite the rejection, Hovie didn't flinch. He moved on.

Hovie turned to harness racing, working the standardbreds with his cousins. They produced plenty of winners and trophies, like everything else Hovie did.

Illinois's greatest coal supporter would never work a day in the mines.

◊ ◊ ◊

ON THAT FATEFUL DAY in 1950, my grandpa rolled his Chevy down to Uncle Alfred's house; his brother-in-law watched him load his pail, helmet, and lamp into the backseat, and then the two miners bumped down the hill in silence until the road spun west. They both had a wad of tobacco lodged in their cheeks before the sun rose. Bob was happy with his new Chevy. In the old days in Eagle Creek, they had never made it going forward with the old Model T. He'd have to stall the car at the foot of a hill, turn it around, and then back up the steep hills and bends for a couple of miles, driving in reverse to keep the engine's slipknot of fuel connected to the gas line. No fuel pumps in those days.

From a distance, the coal mines always appeared like the edges of a war zone. Unfinished and transient high rises of buildings, tipples, conveyor belts, trucks, squadrons of dirty and injured men aside wrecks and piles of metal. Barriers and barbed wire. Gob piles emanated the quiet hum of energy. Black dust caked the walls and roads and faces of anything and anyone who went underground to make a living.

War was not a remote metaphor for these mines. It was not uncommon for mines to maintain Gatling guns on their premises. The National Guard had been called out to occupy the mining property and nearby town of Harrisburg in the mid-1930s, when an actual armed conflict between rival unions took the lives of twenty-one miners and bystanders, including women and children, and made national headlines. Bombs had been set off; bridges had been destroyed. Drive-by shootings took place. Saline County's blood-soaked legacy rivaled neighboring Williamson County, which spent the better part of a century shaking its legacy from a labor conflict in 1922 that turned into a tragic slaughter of revenge. Historian Paul Angle called the "Herrin massacre," as it was known, the "worst episode in the history of American industrial warfare."

But Herrin was another story.

Bob was a peaceful man. He quit his hard drinking once his kids were born. He didn't even like to hunt. As a country boy, he understood the laws of nature, the laws of men, and the laws of the mining culture. He never crossed a picket line; held his kids to that law of the union. Nor would he have allowed any man—any scab, that is—to cross it to take his job.

Like most miners at the Dering No. 2 mine and in Saline County, Bob had always been a member of the renegade Progressive Miners union, despite the retribution of John L. Lewis's legendary forty-year grip over the United Mine Workers. Like every other member of the rebellious Progressive Mine Workers of America, he also knew that Mother Jones had insisted on being buried in southern Illinois. His union guarded her grave.

If Eagle Creek was considered a bastion of independent thinking, it didn't take much for an Eagle Creeker to resist the dictatorial ways of a corrupt union boss.

Bob bent his back like a sapling that morning and crawled into the cage that would transport him from the fall of 1950 to the lower Pennsylvania bedrock of coal formed out of the crushed floor of ancient forests and plants 300 million years ago.

They lit their lamps. They submerged 456 feet deep and then two and half miles away from the hoisting shaft. They coughed and cleared their throats. The cage arrived and they scattered to their posts. In the past, caged canaries had served as sentries; the first to go when the oxygen levels diminished or gas was tapped. Crooked in these scratched back corridors, Bob leaned over in the five-foot floor for hours, setting the explosives into the walls of thick seams of coal, hurrying to a safe corner, forever aware of the destructive power in his hands. He liked the job. He respected its role. He could make white magic with the load in his hands.

One blast didn't go off in the late morning. Bob looked around at the crew awaiting his initiative. It was his job to check and see if his explosive was a dud. He fixed the lamp on his helmet, took a wheeze of air cankered by coal dust and sulfur, spat out a black gob of phlegm; then he approached his explosive lodged into the ancient seam of coal and stepped forward and touched his pack of explosives. It was too late. It wasn't a dud. The blast went off. A wall of coal encased him, masking his face in coal.

The doctor couldn't understand how Bob Followell had survived the explosion. The miner considered it an act of God. As a young rambler, Bob had once waited on a mountain in the Colorado Rockies with a group of religious folk convinced that the rapture was coming. As the doctor picked out the coal from the miner's face until tedium set in, Bob now wondered if the rapture would sound not from the trumpets of Gabriel but from the hiss and boom of a set of explosives. The doctor threw his hands up and sent Bob back home. Blue lesions dotted his face, as if he had been branded by coal for life, just like outlaws had been branded for their sins in the early days. Pieces of coal remained embedded in his forehead and cheeks until he was buried years later and the coal was placed back into the earth.

There was coal in his blood. His lungs were already blackened like the seams he had worked.

◊ ◊ ◊

"ALL COAL MINING safety laws were written in miners' blood," he was saying.

In the late summer of 2007, I sat in the living room of my mom's cousin who had lost the Oval Hill Farm. His new house sat off the old highway between Harrisburg and Shawneetown. We attempted to chat, but our eyes and minds were transfixed on the giant TV screen. No one understood what was truly transpiring with more fear than my mom's cousin, whose son-in-law had been killed in a nearby underground mine.

Six coal miners had been trapped in a collapsed shaft in the Crandall Canyon coal mine in Utah for a week. Four days after that accident, three construction workers in southwestern Indiana fell to their deaths in a coal mine air shaft. As the round-the-clock news coverage of the coal-mining tragedy in Utah unfolded with an enduring if dwindling hope—intercut with the disquieting persona of Robert E. Murray, the CEO of Murray Energy and co-owner of the Crandall Canyon mine who held regular press conferences—our nation was reminded that a crisis is never a crisis in the public's eye until it is validated by disaster.

No one knew this better than the coal miners and the community in Sago, West Virginia, where twelve miners lost their lives in January 2006. They were some of the recent ones, joining the legions of nameless across the country, who had lost so many of their own over the decades.

In the last century, an estimated 104,000 Americans and immigrants died in coal-mining accidents in our country.

I sat and watched the huge TV screen and thought about my grandfather, who barely survived an explosion.

But my grandfather was lucky. Just one year later, at the New Orient Coal Mine in West Frankfort, Illinois, just up the road, 119 miners died in an explosion when an electric spark triggered a pocket of methane gas. That mining accident prompted the Federal Coal Mine Safety Act of 1952, which called for annual inspections in underground coal mines, and charged the Bureau of Mines to issue citations and imminent-danger withdrawal orders. According to the U.S. Department of Labor's Mine Safety and Health Administration (MSHA), the act also "authorized the assessment of civil penalties against mine operators for noncompliance with withdrawal orders or for refusing to give inspectors access to mine property."

The penalties never seemed to amount to much. A half century later, the legacy of those coal miners in southern Illinois seemed all but forgotten. Take the Murray-owned mine in Crandall Canyon, Utah; its parent company, American Coal Company, also owned the former Kerr-McGee Galatia mine in southern Illinois (less than twenty miles from where my grandfather nearly lost his life), which had received 869 citations for violations at the mine in 2007. Digging deeper into the Mine Safety and Health Administration records, the *Salt Lake Tribune* reported that Murray's mine in Galatia had racked up 2,787 violations since 2005. More than 660 of the violations ranked as substantial enough to possibly "result in an injury or illness of a reasonably serious nature." Murray's response to the violations was to challenge them in a prolonged court battle.

As one of the largest independent operators in the country, Murray had bought that mine in Galatia from Kerr-McGee in 1998. Bob Murray, the sixty-seven-year-old company president, seemed like a character out of the nineteenth-century coal days; he dominated the TV news reports with defiant, melodramatic, and increasingly impatient statements about the Crandall Canyon disaster.

Murray's bluster carried on the longtime tradition of the coal company boss at the scene of the crime, coal-dusted face and all. Historically, they seemed to come from two molds; either the privileged-son-turned-social-entrepreneur who manipulated his political connections to reap a fortune; or the rags-to-riches-bare-knuckled-operator who defied the odds and muscled his way through the market with a string of fleetingly profitable mines.

Murray was the latter. In light of the Crandall Canyon crisis, his story had become legendary. He was the coal miner's son who had donned a helmet and gone underground to fend for his family, after his father had been paralyzed in an accident in Ohio. Murray worked his way up the ladder, attended university, and then went into management until his gruff style cost him his job. So, he mortgaged his house and started his own company. He ran a tight ship; he tolerated very little questioning. He turned his company into a multimillion-dollar enterprise.

Murray seemed to delight in clashing with the opposition. His attack-dog testimonies on Capitol Hill were famous for their invective against the East and West coast "elites." He railed against unions. But as the fingers of blame for the Crandall Canyon disaster pointed directly at Murray's use of retreat mining, the dangerous process of knocking the pillars in the deep mines and jeopardizing the safety of the miners, Murray went back on the offensive. He blamed the disaster on an earthquake. He even invoked one of his favorite topics: denying global warming.

He lectured reporters hovering around Crandall Canyon: "Without coal to manufacture our electricity, our products will not compete in the global marketplace against foreign countries because our manufacturers depend on coal for low-cost electricity, and people on fixed incomes will not be able to pay for their electric bills. Every one of these global warming bills that has been introduced in Congress today will eliminate the coal industry and increase your electric rates four to fivefold."

By the fall of 2008, the Mining Safety and Health Administration slapped Murray with a $1.46 million fine for "flagrant violations" at the Galatia mine. Murray called it trivial—a no-toilet-paper-in-the-bathroom situation. He accused MSHA officials, who had taken it on the chin for their own negligence in the Crandall Canyon disaster, of trying to "rehabilitate its own public image at the expense of mining companies and business."

Murray was right about one thing: MSHA's image was in the sewer. But not only for its incompetence. During the George W. Bush administration, MSHA's mining safety staff had been gutted to its lowest levels in four decades, and the budget slashed by 18 percent, when adjusted for inflation. In the spring of 2008, MSHA officials admitted that they had failed to assess fines for more than 4,000 violations over that same period.

Murray's nonunion mine in southern Illinois, of course, had more than a toilet paper problem. A public health researcher identified nearly 200 serious violations for combustible material, electrical-system problems, and poor roof and rib control in 2008. Galatia was an accident waiting to happen.

Galatia was not only the mine that refused to hire Hovie; this was the mine that served as the precursor to Sago and Crandall Canyon and broke the back of the United Mine Workers in Illinois.

Crandall Canyon—nonunion. Sago, West Virginia—nonunion. The truth was that the great majority of accidents took place in nonunion mines.

As we watched the drama unfolding in Utah, I understood how coal miners and their communities continued to pay the highest personal price for our energy consumption.

A few days later, three more men in a rescue team were crushed to death in the Crandall Canyon mine when another part of the mine caved-in.

The rescue was eventually abandoned. The company sealed the mine entrances. The miners were entombed like soldiers from an unnamed war. A year later, Murray was fined $1.3 million by MSHA for disregarding earlier warnings and citations for mining violations.

More penalties. More coal. More deaths.

What was a miner's life worth? Limited by worker compensation insurance, death benefits topped at $8,000 for miners with no dependents, and roughly $176,000 (paid over the first six years) for those with dependents. Litigation, of course, soon followed on both sides and didn't reach a settlement for another two years.

Sure, coal was cheap. A miner's life was treated the same. It always had been.

The cruel irony of the Crandall Canyon and Sago disasters was that coal mining had never been safer. A record low in mining deaths—twenty-two—took place in 2005.

That had not always been the case.

◊ ◊ ◊

NO ONE QUITE UNDERSTOOD what business an Oklahoma chemical company like Kerr-McGee had in sinking a coal mine a few miles northwest of Harrisburg in southern Illinois in 1981. The company had made its name for striking oil in Oklahoma during World War II; it soon shifted to mining uranium on Navajo land in the 1950s. After the OPEC crisis in the mid-1970s turned the tables on the oil markets, Kerr-McGee set its sights on another energy source: coal.

An incident in the mid-1970s forever cemented the company's reputation. When Karen Silkwood, a whistle-blowing lab technician and union activist at the Kerr-McGee Cimarron River plutonium plant in Oklahoma, was killed in a mysterious car accident as she traveled to a meeting with a member of the Atomic Energy Commission and a *New York Times* reporter, her case became a rallying cause for antinuclear activists. Silkwood had suffered radiation exposure and was prepared to divulge information on the company's cover-up of plant accidents and the mishandling of hazardous waste.

That last detail never went unnoticed. "Sure, in the back of our minds," as one retired coal miner near Harrisburg once told me, his own home threatened by underground longwall mining, "if you spoke up, you often wondered who was going to be the Silkwood in the coal industry."

In August 1981, 99 percent of the coal miners in Illinois were unionized. The union-busting era of the Reagan administration, however, which set the standard during the breaking of the air traffic controllers' strike in 1981, had begun to bloom in full force. Nowhere was it as devastating as in the coalfields.

Within a year of sinking its first southern Illinois mine, Kerr-McGee rebuilt its operation, sank one of the largest deep underground mines in the region, and hired seven hundred nonunion miners.

Not without a battle, though.

A coal miner from Harrisburg, who preferred to remain anonymous, described the scene to me like this: "The media was waiting for blood that summer of 1981. And we aimed to give it to them. But then, somehow, after the protest was all said and done, we went away, and Kerr-McGee came back and sank their mine."

Kerr-McGee's decision to launch a nonunion operation in Galatia, Illinois, was not simply an aberration. Only a few miles away from where United Miner Workers had won a bitter battle for recognition nearly a century before, the union miners viewed it as a declaration of war on their jobs.

"We got the day off from the other mines to join the protest that day in August," another Harrisburg coal miner told me. He was referring to his union job in another mine. Eventually, over 14,500 coal miners in the state would walk out of the pits that summer in solidarity with the southern Illinois union members.

Time magazine, like most media outlets, had rushed to the scene of the Galatia protest in 1981, in anticipation of much violence and bloodshed. The media had always thrived on accounts of the coal mining "wars." The two words almost seem inexorably connected:

coal wars. The Illinois coalfields would be no exception. Virden riot. Herrin massacre. Bloody Williamson. The Illinois mine wars.

The media correspondents were not disappointed. Thousands of demonstrators stormed the Kerr-McGee compound. The resentment against the union-busting operations quickly exploded.

"We ripped down the chain-link fence," the Harrisburg coal miner went on, describing the fence that surrounded the 1,300-acre site. The security guards and police were showered with Molotov cocktails and rocks. The protesters set the Kerr-McGee offices on fire, burning them to the ground. They torched the construction equipment, as well.

"I saw a truck driver jump out of his cab and run into the woods," the coal miner laughed.

Before the melee was over, the National Guard and state troopers had called in reinforcements. Helicopters dropped tear-gas bombs to break up the protests.

The tear gas did more than break up the protests; in effect, it shattered the resolve of the union miners, who returned to their mines, while the Kerr-McGee nonunion operation was quietly rebuilt and put into play as one of the largest underground mines in the heartland. The union protest—and its ultimate defeat— signaled the beginning of the end of union control over the mines in the region.

Within a decade, as mines in Illinois shut down from the plunging demand triggered by the Clean Air Act, many of those who had ripped down the Kerr-McGee fence found themselves drifting back to the state's largest mine that had managed to remain open.

"Yeah, it was bitter," the Harrisburg coal miner told me. When his own unionized mine closed in the early 1990s, the coal miner in Harrisburg found himself applying for a nonunion job at the Galatia mine. He was now retired from the mines. "But Galatia was the only game in town for a while. I'm a roof bolter. There are no other jobs around here. We tried to organize but it was impossible." He held up his finger and described marking the letters "UMWA" into the coal dust in various rooms and passages as a silent protest.

The struggle to maintain a union in the southern Illinois coal mines only worsened when Bob Murray took over the Galatia mine in the late 1990s.

As Murray lashed out at the media and United Mine Workers during the Crandall Canyon disaster, the nation was reminded again of anti-union antics. He accused the United Mine Workers, who had sent rescue teams to the Utah mine, of seeking to exploit the tragedy for union recruitment. Looking back at Murray's longtime battles with the union in Ohio and Pennsylvania, the *Militant*, a union newspaper, reprinted a 2002 article by former miner worker Frank Forrestal:

"For several years, union miners have been locked in battle with Murray. In the fall of 1999, the union struck Maple Creek for three days over antiunion moves by the company. In December 2000 the Maple Creek local rejected a proposed contract by a vote of 335 to 10. The contract proposed an annual 30-cent-an-hour wage increase. Miners demanded that they be paid the same as Bituminous Coal Operators Association miners.

"Last summer the union called 'Memorial Days' to protest Murray's opening of a nonunion mine in Ohio and his 'abuse of hundreds of coal miners who have accepted frozen wages and made other sacrifices to keep the company's operations afloat,' according to a UMWA press release.

"Many skirmishes have occurred over health and safety issues, violations of work rules, and unjust firings. Almost every day the company is hit with state and federal violations. Several times the mine, or sections of it, have been ordered shut down. There have been several dangerous incidents of unacceptable levels of methane gas reported in the mine. Maple Creek has one of the highest lost-time injury rates in the industry.

"Workers were also fed up with the so-called company 'awareness' meetings. In these bathhouse meetings, it was common for Murray to insult miners to their faces, as well as to hear countless slanders against the union. Murray's unbecoming behavior has become widely known. The Pennsylvania regional office of the NLRB issued a formal complaint last October against Murray and Maple Creek president D. Lynn Shank for 'threatening and vilifying Maple Creek miners' representative, the United Mine Workers of America (UMWA) and its officers.'

"On top of this, Murray has filed numerous defamation lawsuits with the National Labor Relations Board (NLRB) against the union and leading union officials. Most have been dismissed by the courts. Last fall the NLRB ruled against Murray who charged that the 'Memorial Days' taken by miners were illegal."

During the initial union clash in Galatia in 1981, *Time* magazine had declared "the Ghost of John L. Lewis" hovered about the township.

The ghost of the tyrannical president of the United Mine Workers, who ruled his district branches from the 1920s until 1960 as the most powerful union advocate in the nation, was still a presence in Galatia today. But not the only one. A quarter century later, the cited negligence underlining the death of miners at the sister mine in Crandall Canyon should have provided a wakeup call to nonunion miners. It most certainly granted a glimpse into the bloody past—and the bloody future—of mines without union leadership and protection.

By the time of the Crandall Canyon disaster in 2007, an estimated one out of every four coal miners in the nation was a card-carrying union member.

In truth, much older ghosts and many other labor legends haunted that mine. And a lot of blood.

◊   ◊   ◊

"WHEN MINING BEGAN," noted a U.S. Coal Commission report in the 1920s, examining the conditions before the union movement in 1897, "it was upon a ruinously competitive basis. Profit was the sole object; the life and health of employees was of no moment. Men worked in water half-way up to their knees, in gas-filled rooms, in unventilated mines where the air was so foul that no man could work long without seriously impairing his health. There was no workmen's compensation law, accidents were frequent. . . . The average daily wage of the miner was from $1.25 to $2.00."

There were no such things, of course, as workplace safety laws or mining inspections. In fact, the late-nineteenth-century boom in coal mining had generated a rash of so many unskilled and ill-prepared small operations that those mines functioned as certain death traps.

Miners not only lived and worked in deplorable conditions, they were subjected to the whims of the market, often out of work for the long summer months and forced to migrate for poorly paid day labor. Displaced and unorganized, the miners faced a situation of extreme vulnerability. They often lived in company-owned houses, held in debt, compelled to patronize company-owned shops, and were paid in a company script only valid at company businesses.

To address this miserable situation, the United Mine Workers of America called for a general strike across the nation in 1897. Founded in Columbus, Ohio, in 1890, they counted less than four hundred members in Illinois. Little did the district leaders know that a flamboyant thirty-one-year-old miner in southern Illinois, a veteran of hunger marches on the nation's Capitol in Washington,

DC, in 1894, would don a silk top hat, a Prince Albert topcoat, and an umbrella and declare himself "General" Alexander Bradley.

Born in England and raised in Collinsville, Illinois, Bradley had first entered the mines at the age of nine. Over the years, he had listened to his coal-mining father's stories about the need to "stand up and face the mine-owner and insist on fair treatment and a wage sufficient to permit him to live like a human being."

Calling for secret meetings in the woods outside of Mount Olive, Bradley took the lead in organizing miners into the nascent stages of the movement. The mines in their area were not the largest, however, so they devised a plan; they began to march from mine to mine in southern Illinois, in a crusade to unionize the workers. Thousands of miners swept across the coalfields, attentive to Bradley's spellbinding speeches and flashy attire, assisting in setting up a union vote.

In what could have been an explosive situation, Bradley managed to march his band of brothers with an astonishing level of calm and levity. He somehow found the funds to feed his army. He forbade any violence. And the mines unionized.

By the end of 1897, the union ranks grew from 400 to over 30,000. With the backing of the militant southern Illinois contingent, the United Mine Workers ironed out a deal with coal operators for an eight-hour day, a six-day week, and major concessions for better working conditions. And a 30 percent increase in wages. They also agreed to a statewide scale of forty cents per ton.

Bradley's rank and file, though, and the United Mine Workers nationwide, were tested later that year. While the "General" and the UMWA had successfully bridged ethnic differences among various European and non-English-speaking miners, the Chicago-based company for a mine in Virden, Illinois, looked south of the Mason-Dixon Line for an old tactic of division. Recognizing that black

laborers had been used in the mines in Alabama and Tennessee—
many in a decades-long scandal of convict labor, or rather, laborers
who had been framed for minor offenses and sent to the coal prison
labor camps—the Chicago company sent a recruiter to Birming-
ham, Alabama, to hire nonunion black coal miners and break
Bradley's strike.

Offered thirty cents per ton, the black coal miners were mis-
takenly told that the regular miners had left their jobs to serve in
the Spanish-American War. They boarded the trains. So did their
armed escorts, Thiel Detective Service agents out of St. Louis.

The governor of Illinois called on the Chicago-Virden Coal
Company to halt their plans. "If you bring in this imported labor
you do so, according to your own message, with the full knowledge
that you will provoke riot and bloodshed."

The Chicago-based president of the company responded: "We
are going to operate our mines and we absolutely decline to assume
any of the responsibility that the laws of Illinois place upon the
executive."

Their intentions were clear; they planned to test the mettle of
the striking union, and the resolve of the governor. In the coal company's mind, the lives of the strikebreakers were as expendable as
the miners.

When the escorted strikebreakers arrived at an armed stockade
set up near the train station in Virden around midday on October 12,
1898, a shootout erupted. It lasted ten minutes. The company gunmen overpowered the strikers with their modern Winchester rifles;
the striking miners returned fire with shotguns and hunting rifles.
Twelve men were killed; seven were miners, five were armed
guards. Forty strikers were wounded. None of the black strikebreakers was wounded.

The National Guard arrived several hours later. The governor's
inaction was ultimately denounced across the country.

While some of the strikebreakers stayed and found work in the mine or joined the union, Bradley's defiance and protest against Virden rang out across the country as a bellwether of the union movement's resolve. They had held the line. Within seven years, the holdout Carterville coal operator declared bankruptcy and negotiated with the union.

The absentee coal operatives also played this divisive race card in nearby Pana and Carterville. The United Mine Workers had been founded as an integrated union—one of the few in the nation at the time. And although African Americans eventually took leadership roles in southern Illinois and accounted for nearly 15 percent of the union ranks by 1900, the overall effect of the deceitful racial ploy and subsequent infusions of outside Klan operatives would have repercussions for decades to come.

In her memoirs, civil rights activist and educator Helen Bass Williams, who grew up in the segregated black coal camps of Dewmaine and Colp near Carterville, recounted the constant attacks by racist mobs when African American miners joined the union. Houses were burned to the ground; whole families hid in the woods. Williams's maternal grandfather had escaped the convict-leasing system of slavery in Coal Creek, Tennessee, after coal miners went on strike in 1891. Her father ended up serving as the secretary of the local office of the United Mine Workers in southern Illinois.

Alexander Bradley died in 1918 from suspected black lung disease, having returned to the mines as a front loader. His role in building the United Mine Workers disappeared from most history texts. But the militant southern Illinois mine workers had become the most powerful vanguard in the union movement.

◊ ◊ ◊

MOTHER JONES. The very name of the miner's angel conjures up an image of fearlessness for most union and progressive activists.

That diminutive frosty-haired old woman with a flat cap, round glasses, a long black dress that forever dragged in the dust of marches, and a broken Irish grin that placed her resiliency over ruthlessness and defied men—always men—to resist.

Her motto was simple: Pray for the dead, and fight like hell for the living.

Mary "Mother" Jones had prayed for a lot of the dead. At the age of thirty-seven, she lost her four young children and husband to a yellow fever epidemic. Four years later, she lost her entire life belongings to the Great Fire in Chicago in 1871. She took her despair and grief and placed it in the labor movement, living as a seamstress for Chicago's wealthiest families during the day, and a member of the Knights of Labor during the nights. She once reflected on what she saw between the chasm of the rich and poor, and how it changed her life: "Often while sewing for the lords and barons who lived in magnificent houses on the Lake Shore Drive, I would look out of the plate glass windows and see the poor, shivering wretches, jobless and hungry, walking alongside the frozen lake front. . . . The contrast of their condition with that of the tropical comfort of the people for whom I sewed was painful to me. My employers seemed neither to notice nor to care."

The barons on Lake Shore Drive included the growing coal dealers and coal operators, like Samuel Insull and Francis Peabody, among others. By 1890, at the age of sixty, Mother Jones turned to a peripatetic life as a labor organizer for coal miners, often on the payroll of the United Mine Workers or more radical unions. She became the "miner's angel," unafraid to confront the most violent hired guns. Over the next twenty-five years, she roamed from the coal-mining battles in Colorado, to the brutal clashes in the company-locked-down West Virginia coalfields. At the age of eighty-three, after leading a coal miners' march in West Virginia, she was convicted for conspiracy of murder and sentenced to twenty years in prison. The sentence was so outrageous that the West Virginia governor commuted the sentence.

In 1922, the nonagenarian left the United Mine Workers; she considered John L. Lewis, whose bellows for mining justice in the corridors of power would ring from the First World War until the civil rights movement, to be a wrong choice to lead a truly democratic union.

The southern Illinois coalfields, in her mind, represented the heartland of the independent rank-and-file coal miner—not the cowed dominion of labor leaders like John L. Lewis. As novelist John Griswold noted in his portrait of the Herrin mining conflict, *The Democracy of Ghosts*, the southern Illinois coalfields were the "heart of the most radical community in America of its time."

Mother Jones died in the fall of 1930, at the reported age of one hundred. Some historians dispute her age, not that it matters. Her body was placed on a train that followed Abraham Lincoln's same journey back to Illinois, where huge crowds lined the tracks to pay their last respects to "the Mother."

At her request, the nation's coal miners buried Mother Jones at Mount Olive in the south-central Illinois coalfields—the burning ground of unionism—at the only Union Miners' Cemetery in the nation. It had been established after the Virden battle, when a Mount Olive church refused to inter the bodies of the seven strikers. A local coal miner raised the money to buy the plots, which soon spread across the fields; an arching gate declared it the terrain of union miners.

"When the last call comes for me to take my final rest," Mother Jones had written, "will the miners see that I get a resting place in the same clay that shelters the miners who gave up their lives on the hills of Virden, Illinois. . . . They are responsible for Illinois being

the best organized labor state in America. I hope it will be my consolation when I pass away to feel I sleep under the clay with those
brave boys."

The hallowed hills and southern Illinois miners not only gave
birth to the coal-mining union movement, but also gave their lives
to defend it. The first national coal miners' union, in fact, was
formed in Belleville, Illinois, in 1861, by a cadre of largely English
miners. The American Miners' Association, however, failed to expand into an effective nationwide movement when the economic
turmoil of the 1870s disrupted the markets. Failing market demands gutted any cohesive attempts to organize miners.

Mother Jones joined General Bradley at his graveside. Other
rebels in the Progressive union movement, including one of our
family's distant cousins from Eagle Creek, soon joined them.

◊ ◊ ◊

INTO THIS SUBTERRANEAN and volatile world entered a clean
twenty-four-year-old Yale graduate and son of a wealthy Chicago
lawyer, who had borrowed $100, bought a wagon and two mules,
and started his career as a coal hauler. By 1895, Francis S. Peabody
sank his first mine in southern Illinois, just across our county line
near Marion. This was Peabody Mine No. 1. The thick coal seams
of southern Illinois launched Peabody into an energy market that
would explode within a decade, and eventually place him in the
forefront as the exclusive contractor to provide coal to Chicago's legendary baron of electric utilities, Samuel Insull.

"I was running a small coal operation—cheerfully and happily—
in the southern end of the state," Peabody once remarked, before the
unions came. "I was paying my men 25 cents a box for hand mining
and for loading coal. The box contained anywhere from 2,000 to 2,500
or 2,600 pounds."

Not everyone was cheerful and happy, especially the scores of child laborers who worked twelve hours a day in the mines.

Nonetheless, Peabody became a very, very wealthy tycoon, a powerbroker in the Democratic Party, and a brand name for the coal industry.

Chicago, the "world's largest market of coal," needed coal to heat homes and businesses, to fuel growing factories and steelyards, and power the trains. Southern Illinois had it. By the time Peabody's men hoisted his first ton of coal in Williamson County, seven major rail lines had been tracked across the Midwest to shuttle southern Illinois's huge reserves of coal to Chicago and St. Louis. Writing in the *Chicago Herald* in 1890, Paul Hull, who had married into a southern Illinois family, reminded his financial readers of what David Owen had determined a half century before in Eagle Creek: "Harrisburg lies at the door of the richest coal and mineral regions east of the Rocky Mountains. This is rather strong, but it is true. Seven miles southeast of here are the mountains of Illinois. How many Chicago people know that there is a mountain range in this state? It is part of the upheaval or mountain chain, which extends through Virginia, Kentucky, Illinois, and ends with the Iron Mountain in Missouri."

Those mountains were our Eagle Mountain range, of course. But Hull was not interested in beauty of the hills and hollers.

"There is enough coal in Illinois south of Centralia to give the whole world fuel for the next thousand years. There lies under the fair bosom of Illinois 27,000 square miles of coal, the aggregate beds being twenty feet thick. No similar area of land on the face of the earth has so much coal beneath it. Illinois has as much coal as Pennsylvania, and yet Illinois is celebrated for corn. The riches on the surface of this great state are a beggar's fling compared to what lies beneath."

Peabody seized on Hull's prescient, though admittedly romantic, writings. So did the many others in Chicago.

In 1905, the great land grab took place. The bulk of the mineral rights in the three main coal counties in southern Illinois—Saline, Franklin, and Williamson—were purchased by a dozen absentee corporations based in Chicago, New York, Boston, and St. Louis within two years. These included some of the nation's largest corporations, including U.S. Steel and New York Central Railroad. Two companies shipped directly to the steel mills in Chicago; most companies mainly served the coal dealers in Chicago and St. Louis. Four companies dealt directly with the demands of the railroads; by the late 1920s, over 70 percent of all coal consumed by the American railroads came from the Illinois Basin.

In effect, the coalfields of southern Illinois, and its residents, became a vassal colony to Chicago and the whims of a handful of absentee operators.

The disparity between the two worlds inevitably set them at odds; it determined who would pay the true price for "cheap" coal. Although Samuel Insull, a former colleague of Thomas Edison in New York, brought the bright lights to the Lake Shore mansions in the big city of Chicago with southern Illinois coal in the late 1890s, Eagle Creek and its outsourced miners would not flip the electrical switch in their own homes until 1950.

In 1912, testifying at the U.S. Commission on Industrial Relations, a deliberate Mr. Peabody didn't pull any punches in his public persona. It came down to a choice, he declared, between our desire for cheap coal or our desire for sustainability: "The conservation of the resources of the earth can not be successfully carried on when the owner of the property is compelled to produce his product as cheaply as it can be produced." For his part, Mr. Peabody understood what side he stood on.

"I believe the survival of the fittest—meaning the fittest from geological conditions, the quality of the coal, and the amount of money that a man can earn in working in the thicker veins—should make those mines having the geological, geographical, and the economical advantages—meaning the quality of the coal—the mines that should be operated, while those that have not those advantages should be abandoned until economic conditions have either so increased the demand for the product of coal that then can be worked economically or that the thicker veins have been exhausted."

By 1955, Peabody's son and grandsons understood that the market laws that determined the survival of the fittest still favored our coveting of cheap coal. Their company collapsed into the depths of failure. Unable to compete using their old underground mine operations, Peabody was purchased by Sinclair Coal Company and moved to St. Louis. Sinclair, though, kept the famous Peabody name. But it took a new, cheap path in mining coal.

The Peabody Energy company became the leader in strip mining—the least costly, but the dirtiest and most ruthless way to obtain coal. Their decision worked successfully, at least for their stockholders. Today, Peabody Energy is the world's largest coal provider, producing over 250 million tons of coal a year; it announced a record eightfold profit for its last quarter of 2008.

In the 1990s, a real estate developer bought Francis Peabody's Mayslake estate and Tudor mansion outside of Chicago, which had been sold to a community of the Franciscan order as a retreat center after his death in 1922. The real estate developer planned to raze the buildings and forests, including a historic indigenous Potawatomi settlement, and build a subdivision of luxury houses. Outraged by the proposal, local citizens passed a referendum that allowed the Du-Page County Forest Preserve District to purchase the property and turn it into an environmental and cultural education center.

Eagle Creek, of course, had another destiny.

◊   ◊   ◊

IF PEABODY NEEDED a colorful counterpart in southern Illinois, the scrappy Thomas O'Gara could have played the role. In contrast to Peabody's patrician intrigues among the Chicago elite, O'Gara had arrived in the Windy City from Ireland with little but ambition and a beguiling personality. To be sure, O'Gara did not immigrate to the States as a victim of the potato famine; he had attended the university in Ireland and headed to America with a vision of taking advantage of its growing industrial might in the 1880s. Like Peabody, O'Gara launched himself as a coal peddler in Chicago and then established his own firm in 1897 as a wholesale dealer to factories and plants.

On the heels of the 1903 coal famine and winter despair in the northern cities—which brought in a windfall of profit for O'Gara and Peabody, as well as most coal dealers—the O'Gara Coal Company emerged out of the Marquette Building in Chicago with over $6 million in capital to invest. Focusing at first on Saline County, O'Gara quickly bought up over a dozen deep-shaft and shipping mines from the local investors and gained a virtual monopoly on the county's coal industry.

Over the next two decades, more than 30,000 workers—including large waves of immigrants from Eastern Europe and Italy—found work in the three main southern Illinois counties. O'Gara reportedly had 6,000 coal miners on his own payroll by 1910 and churned out 7 million tons of coal.

The coal boom generated a level of newfound giddiness for the bankers, real estate jobbers, and merchants. In less than a generation, southern Illinois shifted its identity from a self-proclaimed southern backwoods farm culture to a chain of coal towns and camps peopled with immigrants, southern blacks, and migratory workers from around the South and Midwest.

The optimism soared to new heights: One newspaper declared that southern Illinois had enough coal until AD 9279. (That's not a typo.) A published history of the region declared in 1910 that O'Gara's fortune would shine like a rainbow over the county for the next fifty years.

Indeed, by the First World War, southern Illinois was the top-producing coal region west of the Appalachian Mountains and ranked third in the nation.

No attempt was made to attract any other industries or invest in a diversified economy. The bankers would have laughed at the concept; even the most conservative observers calculated that southern Illinois had at least 1,500 years of coal to mine.

While the coal barons, bankers, and merchants were celebrating record profits, a new phenomenon shook the coalfields: They became known as the killing fields.

Between 1883 and 1962, according to historian Philip Kalisch, nearly forty coal-mining disasters—defined by the Bureau of Mines as more than five deaths—turned the Illinois coalfields into a veritable graveyard. At times, it would have been safer to be on the combat front during the Spanish-American or First World wars, than serve in an Illinois mine. And the majority of the accidents took place in southern Illinois.

The term "accident" would be a generous statement. The majority of the mining disasters were a result of gross oversight and criminal negligence by the coal companies in haste to profit from the coal boom.

In his memoirs, mine inspector and superintendent Oscar Cartlidge referred to this era as the "period of disasters." The main cause, in his opinion, was a "rivalry between the operators to see which could get out a maximum tonnage in the shortest time. This high pressure on the superintendents caused them to take chances which otherwise they might not have taken."

As an aside, he admitted his own ignorance about the growing mining operations. "None of us had much knowledge of the properties and actions of gases and coal dust, and there were not a few who argued strenuously that coal dust would not explode."

They learned the opposite. Or rather, the coal miners learned and paid with their lives.

A typical disaster took place in Zeigler in 1905. Half of the one-hundred-man crew died in an explosion of ignited methane gas after a foreman insisted on stopping the ventilation fans for four days. The company was cited for violations. The widows received no compensation.

In those days, the state released an annual report on coal, detailing every fatality. (Strangely, this practice ended after the war years; names, ages, and accident details are no longer listed, only statistics.) It was a shame, because the morbid breakdown of deaths somehow humanized the whole coal-mining crisis:

July 14, 1906, Harvey Dunning, miner, aged twenty-four years, single, employed at the O'Gara Coal Company's mine No. 6, was killed by falling rock in room No. 4.

August 29, 1906, Anglo Correll, miner, aged thirty-two years, married, employed by the Carterville District Coal Company, was instantly killed. The cager had his usual number of men on the cage and rang for the engineer to hoist; just as the cage was leaving the bottom, the deceased came running past those who were waiting for the next cage to come out and leaped on the cage and was caught between the cage and the casing of the shaft, crushing his head. He leaves a widow and three children.

September 6, 1906, Harry Hall, miner, aged thirty-nine, married, employed by Lake Creek Coal Company, was fatally burned.

He was burned so severely that he died three days afterward. He leaves a widow and two children.

November 14, 1906, Richard Lee, trapper, aged sixteen years, single, employed by the Big Muddy Coal and Iron Company, was killed while coming up on a cage. He lost his balance and fell from the cage to the bottom of the shaft.

December 17, 1906, Claude Miler, miner, aged seventeen years, single, employed by National Mining Company, was killed instantly by falling slate at the face of his room, fractured his skull over the right eye.

December 22, 1906, John Willis, trapper, aged sixty-six years, married, employed at the Peabody Coal Company, stepped into the middle of the track and the three cars that had been uncoupled struck him, the first one ran over him and he was found dead under the second car. He leaves a widow and five children.

In 1909, the nation was stunned when 259 coal miners died in a fire at the Cherry Mine in upstate Illinois. Outraged by the lack of inspection and mining safety, legislators in Washington, DC, created the first U.S. Bureau of Mines. The act, however well meaning, lacked any real teeth. In truth, the agency was not granted any authority to enforce any of the laws, only promote health and safety.

The accidents from coal dust and methane gas, the explosions, the fires—these all continued on an alarming scale as production and poorly run operations boomed.

At the same time, another glitch was developing with the coal boom: The growth of production suddenly leaped ahead of the growth of capacity. In essence, the avarice of the coal barons was leading to too much mined coal, and this resulted in a "cutthroat competition" to sell coal below the cost of production. In the end, miners found themselves only working 220 days a year, and without a stipend for nearly a third of the calendar. In the process, competition from nonunion coal in Appalachia added to further uncertainty in the highly organized Illinois Basin.

Nonetheless, celebrated historian George Smith, whose *History of Southern Illinois* is considered one of the great classics, couldn't hide his enthusiasm for O'Gara and the coal barons:

"One of the greatest corporations engaged in this work is the O'Gara Coal Company, which in its comparatively brief existence has accomplished wonders and whose methods towards employees and in all its commercial dealings are most admirable. It is indeed a pleasure to the publishers of a work of this nature to accord recognition to an industry which has proved as much a blessing to a great section of country and given it such worldwide prestige."

A few months after the history book's publication in 1912, Francis Peabody shook his head at the U.S. Commission on Industrial Relations. He couldn't understand how one of the largest producers of coal in the state—in the country, no less—could have gone bankrupt so quickly. Indicted for fraud and taking kickbacks from railroad companies, O'Gara's company was declared "hopelessly insolvent."

O'Gara disappeared to New York, while miners lost work, wages, and property, and the company reorganized. As Peabody said in his blunt manner: "The miners can move. We see continually all over the world abandoned cities and abandoned towns and abandoned neighborhoods. Political economy has taught us that that comes from the survival of the fittest. I mean by that the men that can produce cheapest and best must take the market first."

The end of the boom was not too far off in the distance.

◊ ◊ ◊

IN 1958, SOCIOLOGISTS from Southern Illinois University released what was hailed as a breakthrough study, *People of Coal Town*.

Armed with their charts and questionnaires, the buttoned-down academics had toured the coalfields, identified a representative town, and examined coal-mining communities as a distinct "people."

They came to three conclusions: Coal miners were characterized by violence, resignation, and superstition. And they were racist, too.

In many respects, this study perpetuated the backward-hillbilly stereotype that had already been branded on the pioneers and woodsmen, and simply shifted it to various ethnicities that had migrated into the coal towns.

It made Ben Brinkley laugh. On his front lawn in Harrisburg, he sat by a pond with various types of tropical fish, attempting to strike a match for his cigarette. At the age of eighty-five, Ben shook a little, his demeanor almost wistful, but still managed to light the end of his cigarette. He didn't really have enough breath, though, to keep the cigarette burning. It didn't matter. He'd smash it to the ground and light up another one.

Since the age of twelve, Ben had promised himself to read two books a week. He didn't have much choice. Though his ancestors had lived in the Eagle Creek hollers since the 1780s, he had grown up in the coal camp of Muddy, a township a few miles north of Harrisburg. As a student, he found himself borrowing armloads of books from the school library. With the mines and railroads functioning well during his youth, Muddy turned its high tax revenues toward education. Every kid was provided notebooks, books, pens, and pencils; the school library rivaled any found in a midwestern town twice its size.

"My dad was a coal miner," Ben told me. "He only went through the eighth grade, but he had a tremendous respect for education."

His father, like other coal miners, served on the school board. He pushed Ben into obtaining a college degree in English. Ben ended up returning to Harrisburg, taught English in the local high school, and then shifted toward a career as a union organizer for teachers. His poems had been published in various anthologies and won regional awards.

For a region branded as superstitious and resigned, Ben's agnostic views would not have been particularly at odds with the "Great Agnostic," Colonel Robert G. Ingersoll. Ingersoll also taught school in the area, tended to a brief legal career a few miles from Muddy in the town of Raleigh, and then went on to become one of the most revered and reviled humanist thinkers and admired orators in the nation in the nineteenth century. His lectures packed the largest auditoriums of the day. He railed against the "Mistakes of Moses," invoked the mythos of "The Gods," and drew the hatred of virtually every major religious community of the day for his spellbinding address on "Why I Am an Agnostic."

A rusting sign in Ingersoll's honor rested on the narrow road to the Galatia mine. According to the venerable southern Illinois historian John Allen, Ingersoll's first speech was delivered at a school in Bowlesville, a mining encampment that had been strip-mined into oblivion on the eastern edge of Eagle Creek.

Ben relished his role in town as a gadfly; his front lawn posted the first BARACK OBAMA FOR PRESIDENT sign in the county. He served on the board of a domestic-violence center that created a stir of controversy for naming itself after a pioneer midwife.

"No, superstitious and resigned, I don't think so," he said, trying to light a new cigarette.

He did see a parallel between a battered wife and a single-economy region that had succumbed to the demands of ruthless coal companies. The abuse never ended.

Ben lost his father in 1950, when a rock dislodged from the roof in an underground mine and killed him instantly.

Ben never visited his grave.

For the one hundredth anniversary program for Saline County, a page was dedicated to those who had lost their lives serving in a foreign war. An equally long page listed the names of those who had died in the mines.

◊ ◊ ◊

THE FAMILY OF Jackson K. Dering, the namesake of the Dering No. 2 underground coal mine that employed my grandfather, probably never worried about their estate being strip-mined. In fact, the year before my mom and her family returned to Eagle Creek, the Illinois Department of Natural Resources purchased the Dering estate north of Chicago and turned it into a training school for game wardens and conservationists.

Born in Wisconsin in 1870, as a young man Dering found work in Chicago as a sales agent for the Consolidated Coal Company and the Rivertown Coal Company. He started his own J. K. Dering venture in 1897 and never looked back. By 1906, hailed by one national business magazine as the "ruler of the coal industry in Illinois and Indiana," he became actively involved in one of the largest coal and railroad mergers in American history. He had been a longtime advocate of consolidation, in an attempt to limit competition. Like Peabody and O'Gara, Dering reaped a tremendous profit from the "great coal famine" in 1903, when nationwide strikes reduced supply and triggered government intervention during a harsh winter. Looking to expand his coal supplies, Dering also marched down to the southern Illinois coalfields for new investments.

After its bankruptcy, Dering eventually became the executive of the reorganized O'Gara Company, which continued its monopoly on the deep underground shaft mines in the county.

History contained a bitter irony for this sudden takeover of the southern Illinois economy by Chicago corporations. In the 1820s, bankers from Chicago had beseeched the First Bank of Illinois in

Shawneetown for a loan. Loaded with salt mine revenues, which would collapse in less than twenty years, the Shawneetown bankers refused the Chicago loan request. Without access to a river, the financiers in southern Illinois didn't believe any enterprise in Chicago could ever flourish.

This historical cycle in the boom-and-bust industries, however, did not seem to make an impression on the Chicago entrepreneurs.

The Dering No. 2 mine, where my grandfather worked, opened as a shaft mine in 1918, during the heyday of the coal industry. In fact, from 1906 until the early 1920s, driven by the demands of the railroads, the steel mills, and the booming chemical industry, nearly 100,000 coal miners found work in the Illinois mines. Coal production in the state reached an all-time high in 1925 of over 100 million tons.

A new age of mechanization—loading machines in underground shaft mines—was now being introduced to drastically reduce labor needs.

The initial crack in the industry began with the post–World War I depression in 1921. The next year, a nationwide strike spiraled out of control in the neighboring county, leading to the deaths of at least twenty strikebreakers, company employees, and miners. The incident, infamously known as the Herrin massacre, would mark the beginning of the end of the short, swift time of prosperity of coal in that era. It would also brand the culture of the inhabitants from the area as a seedbed for natural-born killers.

◊ ◊ ◊

WHEN THE MORE SENSATIONAL elements of the Herrin massacre of 1922 are set aside, one emerging phenomenon with historical importance has been overlooked: the controversial role of strip mining by an absentee landlord and its devastating impact on coal miners and their communities. In 1921, a company from Cleveland,

Ohio, transported a 95-ton steam shovel, the legendary Bucyrus that had carved the Panama Canal from 1904 to 1908, to their strip mine in Williamson County. Although commercial strip mining got its start in Illinois in 1866, it had not progressed much beyond plows and scrapers. The Bucyrus was a veritable monster that would make the earth tremble.

The earth did shake in 1922, but for other reasons. When union mine workers went on strike across the nation, the Cleveland company ignored the demands and hired strikebreakers from Skid Row in Chicago. Incensed strikers converged on the strip mine one hot summer day. From his comfort zone, John L. Lewis had referred to the strip miners as "outlaws." An armed battle broke out among the company employees, the bewildered scabs (many of whom had no idea of the ensuing conflict), and the union members. To make matters worse, the company superintendent had prided himself on breaking unions in Kansas; he had armed the company with Gatling guns and the bravado of Fort Knox. Unfortunately, he was not familiar with the history of mine workers in southern Illinois. After three striking miners were murdered, an angry mob dynamited the draglines and steam shovel equipment and eventually executed at least twenty strikebreakers and company employees in the woods near Herrin.

Although none of the charged miners was convicted, the nightmare essentially placed the tombstone on the coal industry in southern Illinois for the next generation.

Within a decade, southern Illinois ranked as one of the most impoverished regions in the entire country. A government report gave an overview in late 1930:

"Today, the southern Illinois coalfield presents a picture, almost unrelieved, of utter economic devastation. The years since 1923 have seen the community lose three out of every four of its mines. They have seen a half-dozen once lively coal centers gradually sink to ghost towns. They have seen the building-and-loan bubble burst in every coal town and every bank throughout the greater part of the coalfield driven into bankruptcy. They have seen employment shrink until two out of every five workers were 'surplus' at the busiest season of the year, while the public-assistance load climbed until it included more than half the entire population of the three counties (Saline, Franklin, and Williamson). They have seen the coal boom subside and give way to hopeless poverty."

The report went on: "A total of 34 coal-town banks collapsed within 2 years, and 7 million dollars in savings were swept away. The building and loan associations, to whom a large part of the population was debtor, found themselves unable to collect high interest on property that had suddenly become almost worthless. There followed score upon score of repossessions, and hundreds of building-and-loan houses were razed for secondhand lumber. Little businessmen by the dozens closed their doors. The tax structure collapsed."

J. K. Dering died suddenly in 1925, though his mining operations continued in the region. In 1934, while southern Illinois possessed one of the highest infant and adult morality rates in the nation, J. K. Dering Jr. and his mother decided to cast off these dreary times and go on an adventure, so they organized a luxury cruise to South America, departing from their plantation in Los Mochis, Mexico.

It didn't go quite as planned. A few of the joining tourists sued Dering for fraud.

Back home, as the nation slowly sank into the Great Depression, facing the drastic reductions of the labor ranks from mechanization, lower demand, and the increasing role of the nonunion coal in Appalachia, John L. Lewis attempted to pull off a compromise, agreeing to a pay cut in a period of compounding poverty. The holdout, however, came from the union miners in Illinois, especially in the depressed areas in the southern and south-central parts of the state, where fertile farmland was rare, and no other economy had ever developed.

When ballots for the vote on the new accord disappeared in Illinois, throwing the union into disarray, Lewis invoked his authority and signed the agreement. The coal miners in southern Illinois felt betrayed. An anti-Lewis movement had been brewing for years. Within days, an interunion battle erupted, resulting in the founding of the Progressive Miners of America movement in 1932.

Lewis and his United Mine Workers, of course, didn't sit back without a fight. Within days, Joe Colbert, a distant relative of my family's Eagle Creek pioneers and an active organizer for the Progressives, was gunned down near the New Orient Mine in West Frankfort. He was buried near Mother Jones's grave in the Union Miners' Cemetery.

Hailed by historian John Fenoli as the "darkest chapter" in the history of coal mining in Illinois, the most tragic "war" was not between the miners and the coal companies, but between the miners themselves. By the time the "war" had ended a year later, more miners and innocent bystanders were killed and wounded than in the Herrin massacre.

Following in the tradition of General Bradley, the Progressive miners began to march—or drive their cars and trucks in a caravan this time. They met UMWA resistance every step of the away. Roofing nails lined the road, derailing the convey of vehicles en route to striking miners. Bombs and stacks of dynamite were detonated.

What distinguished the Progressive movement, however, from other labor conflicts was the role of women. Led by Agnes Burns Wieck, a coal miner's daughter from Spillertown in southern Illinois, the Women's Auxiliary of the Progressive Miners of America barnstormed the state on behalf of their coal miner sons, fathers, and husbands. Declaring that "we are not ladies, we are women," Wieck rallied in the spirit of both Mother Jones and Bradley. On the anniversary of the Virden conflict, Wieck spoke at the annual event at the miners' cemetery in Mount Olive and recalled the battle of Virden as the foundation for the Progressive movement. "The Virden martyrs will forever be in the hearts and minds of Illinois miners. Their bones may be dust, but their deeds will never be forgotten. Let the memory of their courage inspire us. Miners and miners' wives and children may find the courage to carry on, forever if need be, the fight for right and justice."

Months earlier, over 10,000 women had converged on the capitol steps in Springfield, Illinois, and pushed their way into a meeting with the governor. According to one sheriff, the "women are tougher than the men."

Near Harrisburg, the conflict focused on the Peabody No. 47 mine, where five hundred Progressive coal miners went on strike. In October 1933, when Peabody attempted to circumvent the Progressive union and imported United Mine Workers members from other counties, the coal company set off a season of violence that would terrorize the region. Within days, the National Guard had occupied Harrisburg, bayonets fixed on their rifles, forbidding any public gatherings on the streets.

The action, of course, was taking place at the mine. Progressive gunmen managed to hold off any scabs or trap intruding members of the United Mine Workers. On one day alone in October, over 5,000 rounds of ammunition were fired into the Peabody mine. Outside of a short period in November, when a judged allowed miners to have their rifles for hunting season—a very reasonable move during a period of near starvation—any efforts by the National Guard and police to disarm the miners did not prevent the fighting from spreading.

Appearing in Harrisburg that fall, Wieck drew a huge crowd of women and coal miners. She appealed to the conscience of the coal companies and the United Mine Workers bosses and then blasted the governor and federal officials for squandering scarce resources on the protection of the coal company's mines, instead of dealing directly with the problem. "It is a crime against the underfed children of the Saline County miners to spend thousands of dollars to maintain troops in their midst. The mothers of these children are asking themselves if this is the New Deal for miners. The courthouse square and streets of Harrisburg have taken on the appearance of Taylorville, a county seat whose name has been dragged into the dust by the Peabody Coal Company. Last night when I walked out of a meeting of Progressive miners' wives, and saw the gleam of the bayonets, the words 'New Deal' seemed like a mockery."

Wieck went on. "We women warned the federal government, in our recent message to President Roosevelt, that there could be no peace in the coal fields, as long as hunger stalks and hatred of John Lewis goads more and more men into rebellion against his dictatorship of the coal fields. . . . Now we find the troops moving south and Saline County becomes a military zone. Where will it all end?

"Frankly, the patience of our women is exhausted. Anything may happen. When a mother at mealtime goes out into the yard, pretending she is not hungry to let the children eat what little is on the table, in that mother's heart there is a bitterness that may result in anything. We women refuse to see our children starve in the midst of plenty and we will not see our men go back into slavery under the Lewis regime."

The rest of the nation took notice of what was taking place in the coalfields in that long summer of 1933. In an editorial from a Washington correspondent that ran in the Harrisburg *Daily Register*, Burton Kline wrote:

"Coal is the canned and preserved heat of the sun. Your life depends upon it—your life, your business and everybody else's business. It runs the country. It runs the world. And for 50 years, the mining of coal in the United States has been a chaos and a scandal. We have prided ourselves on scientific management in every other industry. This scientific management has made our nation a marvel among all the others. Other nations have sent delegations here to learn how we did it all. Only coal, the fundamental industry of all, has been backward—half a century behind the rest.

"All the greed that one kind of humanity could be guilty of, all the misery that another kind could suffer, have been the outcome of coal in the past fifty years. While miners starved on bottom wages, the operators themselves went bankrupt from cutting each other's throats—always, incidentally, cutting wages lower and lower. . . . The railroads, heaviest users of coal, were the heaviest offenders. Maybe they had to do it. They had to have coal at the lowest cost. To get it they forced competing operators to bid. That meant cut prices, cut wages, long hours, the closing of mines, the closing of whole mining towns and their trade life. And these towns had supplied the railroads themselves with profitable freight. What more idiotic course could be imagined! It was nose cutting with a vengeance, to spite the face of the nation."

Wieck and her brigades of women pressed on with their striking men.

An East St. Louis newspaper marveled at Wieck's role in galvanizing the spirit of the women to challenge their men and the dilemmas of past mining strikes:

"In the old days, women of the mine areas were a hazard to the success of any strike. The men knew that a complaining woman at home could drive the most militant union man back to the pits without victory. Now the women, organized under the auxiliary, glory in the privations they suffer. They would not let the men go back if they wanted to go, unless the return was a distinct victory. That, says Mrs. Wieck, is why there never can be a compromise between the Progressives and the U.M.W.A. in Illinois.

"The second factor is that as an organization the women have taken an important role in the actual hostilities. They have picketed and they have marched in demonstrations. They have held meetings in the face of orders forbidding meetings. Where they might have starved singly, they have learned through organization to raise money for food, clothing, and strike expenses."

Hailed as the "great coal field hell-raiser," a modern-day Mother Jones from southern Illinois, Wieck lived to see the Progressive Miners recognized as the elected union at the Peabody and Dering mines in Saline County. Wrecked by internal dissension and the relentless power of Lewis, however, the Progressive Miners failed to ever expand beyond the region and ultimately dissipated into a secondary role by the 1950s.

◊ ◊ ◊

THE HERRIN MASSACRE is generally held up as the defining act of savagery among coal miners in southern Illinois—or the nation, for that matter. The *St. Louis Globe-Democrat* called it "the most brutal and horrifying crime that has ever stained the garments of organized labor."

For James Ballowe, the nationally acclaimed poet who grew up in Herrin, and whose coal miner grandfather had quietly participated in the mob rule, a "strategy of silence" was invoked about his history. Years later, Ballowe saw his grandfather as "one of those who could commit incomprehensible deeds to preserve their painfully acquired humanity."

In a tribute to his family's coal-mining past, he wrote:

> The holes you made
> like yourselves
> are collapsing
> inward. Whole towns
> rest within
> the grave you dug.

Strangely, though, the nation has fallen into a similar strategy of silence about the culpability of coal operators in allowing unsafe conditions for mining accidents. Even the most gruesome mining disasters rarely evoke more than a state of sadness when we consider the tens of thousands of coal miners—over 104,000 actually—who have died in the mines from accidents. Between 1903 and 1930—the same period of the Herrin massacre—over 5,000 coal miners in Illinois alone lost their lives.

Many, if not a majority of those "accidents" should not be considered mishaps, but acts of negligent homicide.

In the spring of 1946, a group of UMWA miners from Centralia, Illinois, outraged by the political machinations in the Department of Mines and Minerals, wrote a letter urging the governor to take action on clearly dangerous buildups of coal dust. The letter described the mine's situation, the politics, and then made a desperate request for intervention:

"In fact, Governor Green, this is a plea to you, to please save our lives, to please make the Department of Mines and Minerals enforce the laws at No. 5 mine of the Centralia Coal Company at Centralia, Illinois, at which mine we are employed, before we have a dust explosion at this mine like just happened in Kentucky and West Virginia."

Despite numerous inspections, recommendations, and noted violations, the mine owners did not consider the dust situation to be an imminent danger.

On March 25, 1947, an explosion ripped through the Centralia mine and killed 111 miners. Half of them died from carbon monoxide poisoning. Three of the four men who had written the governor also died in the explosion.

As the *St. Louis Post-Dispatch* pointed out, a crime was committed at Centralia. Just like modern operators, the Centralia Coal Company had made it a habitual practice to violate mining safety laws and simply pay the fines.

Coal was cheap in this fashion.

A subsequent investigation found that the Department of Mines and Minerals, staffed with many former coal industry officials, had not only dismissed the danger warnings, but also had taken contributions from coal companies to downplay any safety concerns.

The massacres didn't end in southern Illinois.

At the New Orient No. 2 mine between Benton and West Frankfort, at one time the largest shaft mine in the world, federal inspectors found numerous violations in the summer of 1951. Their main concern was with the buildup of methane gas, inadequate ventilation, and a noticeable lack of rock dusting—the very same issues that had dogged virtually every mine in southern Illinois for a half century. A month later, the UMWA warned the coal company that the mine was "extremely hazardous."

Less than five months later, on a Friday night at the West Frankfort high school basketball game, an announcement rang out that silenced the crowd. It was December 21; Christmas decorations adorned the school gym. The voice screamed, "Dr. Barnett, Dr. Andy Barnett, please report to No. 4 portal at New Orient Mine at once—there has been a catastrophe."

An explosion had taken the lives of 119 miners this time.

Days later, the community still in shock, John L. Lewis took it on himself to rain down a bit of the righteous anger that every coal miner in America felt:

"The mining industry continues to be a mortician's paradise. I just watched 119 funerals in two days. Can you imagine anything more heart-rending? One hundred nineteen funerals in that little community in two days!

"They went to work, the last shift before Christmas. And many of them were brought home to their loved ones in rubber sacks— rubber sacks! Because they were mangled, and shattered, and blown apart, and cooked with gas, until they no longer resembled human beings. All the best morticians could do was to put them in long rubber sacks with a zipper. For a Christmas present in Franklin County 119 families could look at rubber sacks in lieu of their loved ones."

A ballad from the Welsh coalfields, often sung by folksinger Pete Seeger, echoed Lewis's words:

Oh what will you give me, say the sad bells of Rhymney
Is there hope for the future, say the brown bells of Merthyr
Who made the mine owners, say the black bells of Rhondda
And who killed the miners, say the grim bells of Blaenau. . . .

◊ ◊ ◊

RIGHT AFTER CHRISTMAS in 1973, my grandfather received the largest check in his life, $8,347, as part of his settlement for denied payments for black lung disability from the Federal Coal Mine Health and Safety Act of 1969. It took a subsequent Black Lung Benefits Act of 1972 to actually dislodge the proper funds for ailing coal miners.

Denial had always been part of the miner's fate and the mine owner's ways.

In 1831, a doctor in Edinburgh, Scotland, made the first autopsy and diagnosis of an afflicted coal miner who died from breathlessness, coughing, and chest pains. The doctor opened up his patient and found lungs of "black carbonaceous colour." He recognized that the illness derived from "the habitual inhalation of a quantity of coal dust with which the atmosphere of a coal-mine must be constantly charged."

Nearly a century later, despite the mounting death toll from "miner's lung," coal companies, and the governmental agencies under their thumbs, still denied the existence of black lung and went so far as to have their company doctors declare that the inhalation of coal dust made a miner "immune to tuberculosis."

In 1919, during a nationwide strike, the United Mine Workers called for protection from coal dust and its black lung counterpart, and noted that the need for a shorter workday was actually the result of "miner's asthma." Nonetheless, the health hazard of coal dust went unnoticed for decades.

In fact, despite various state initiatives for examinations and medical care, it took an aggressive campaign by the United Mine Workers in the late 1960s for the issue to be recognized on a federal level. Even then, it wasn't until a mining disaster in West Virginia, which took seventy-eight lives, that President Richard Nixon begrudgingly signed the Coal Mine Health and Safety Act, which included the Black Lung Benefits Program, into law.

An estimated 250,000 coal miners have died from black lung disease; a National Institute for Occupational Safety and Health study found that 10,000 miners have died from black lung in the last decade. Three times as many suffered an agonizing fate of respiratory problems throughout their lives.

The miners gave their lives; the taxpayers, not the coal companies, picked up the bill. Over the past four decades, the Black Lung Benefits Program has cost more than $40 billion. Although the law mandated the program to be funded by the coal industry, a report by the Environmental Affairs Board at the University of California in Santa Barbara found that the mining companies had "borrowed $8.7 billion from the federal Treasury since the program's inception. This taxpayer-funded shortage is expected to increase to $68 billion by 2040." The reported concluded: "Black lung compensation, a cost associated directly with the operation of the coal industry, is a serious expense borne by the public. This expense does not show up on the utility bill, but is paid for by consumers nonetheless."

◊   ◊   ◊

ONE SATURDAY MORNING, I saw Hovie standing by a fold-up metal table at the grounds of the Saline County pioneer village museum in Harrisburg. A sizeable crowd had gathered for one of those classic rural Americana summer festivals, where nostalgia for an arcadian woodlands past reigned supreme. Local actors sweated happily in nineteenth-century wool clothing on a muggy day. Children and their grandparents wandered from demonstrations of pioneer lifestyles, from the weaver on the loom, to the competing woodcutters, to the firing of the muskets.

An old cabin from Eagle Creek anchored the museum grounds like a transplanted mustering oak. Various branches of my extended family had lived in this cabin, including members of the Aydelott family. In fact, the first Aydelott who had hewn the logs was the brother-in-law of the builder of our old homeplace that had been destroyed. This cabin stood like a monument to a celebrated pioneer past, lovingly renovated and maintained, and stocked with extraordinary attention to the household items of the day.

I wondered if anyone knew what had happened to Eagle Creek since the cabin had been removed; that our past had not simply been transplanted to a local park in Harrisburg, but the grounds under its foundations had been wiped out by the strip miners.

Hovie held down the fort at the front entrance. A gaggle of children loitered at his side, looking at the various coal-mining pictures, touching the pieces of coal, a coal miner's lamp and iconic lunch pail, and other bits of mining heritage that weighed down the table like a load from an abandoned mine. With a ball cap, tight jeans, and a checkered shirt, Hovie's wiry body shifted from left to right, hastily responding to as many questions as he could answer in a single breath.

But, it wasn't only children who looked on his table with fascination. Slowly, retired coal miners approached the table, quietly thanked Hovie for his father's role in securing them a job, not firing them on a bad day, making sure they always had bread on their table. And then a steady line of wives and daughters lingered around the table with seeming hesitation.

A question would be asked: "What is a roof bolter? That's what my husband did for ten years."

Hovie, as the extraordinary conduit to the coal mines, answered the question the coal miner had never been asked by his wife.

In the late 1990s, Hovie and his mother joined the United Mine Workers and hopped a bus to Washington, DC. They took part in a demonstration for better enforcement of black lung laws.

Even today, three coal miners die daily from a disease that was diagnosed in 1831. Despite a recent spike in black lung cases, the Mine Safety and Health Administration under the Bush administration announced in the months after the Crandall Canyon disaster that the agency was too busy "to tackle respirable dust."

"I don't think they understand how important the union has been," Hovie told me during a lull in the action by his table. He flipped through the pages of the mine photos, as if flipping through a family album, dropping details about each mine under his breath.

After the Sago, West Virginia, tragedy in 2006, historian Noah Leavitt analyzed the impact of the union movement on mining safety. Writing in *Slate* magazine, he stated: "In the 30-year period prior to enactment of these safety statutes, more than 19,000 miners were killed in the nation's coal mines. Whereas in the 30-year period following enactment of the 1969 Mine Act, there were 86 percent fewer coal-mining deaths." Leavitt added: "An almost 50 percent decrease in coal-mining fatality rates between 1971 and 1975." In testimony before Congress in 2000, a UMWA spokesperson called this law "one of the most effective pieces of worker health and safety legislation in the history of this country."

After surveying the 25,000 federal health records for nonunion underground coal mines in neighboring Kentucky, the *Louisville Courier-Journal* newspaper concluded: "Small, non-union mines generally pay less, cheat more on dust tests and don't have union stewards demanding compliance with costly safety regulations."

Months after the Sago mining disaster, and only months before his own death-ridden operation at Crandall Canyon, Murray adamantly fought any new updates to the mine safety laws, calling the modern measures for wireless communication and other innovations "extremely misguided." For Big Coal, little had changed since Peabody's views in 1912: Any governmental interference for mine safety was simply an act of "playing politics" that cost him time and money.

Three months after the Crandall Canyon tragedy, Governor Rod Blagojevich announced special taxpayer subsidies totaling in the millions to Murray and the International Coal Company, the owners of the Sago, West Virginia, mine, to expand their mining operations.

In proud coal-mining towns like Harrisburg or Galatia, there were no monuments to coal miners. No union memorials. No plaques. No statues. No cemetery plots. No banners. No coal miner festivals or parades or special days. Only Hovie had put together a small room on coal-mining history in a building at the Pioneer Museum that had once been designated the "poor house."

And only Hovie Stunson continued to unfold his table for coal miner souvenirs and photos and tell those who would listen about the extraordinary heritage of his beloved coal miners.

Vintage "Visit Shawnee Hills" postcard. *(Courtesy of the author.)*

◊

Chapter Five

BLACK WATERS, BLACK WATERS

The Murder of Little Egypt

By the cool rushing waterfall the wildflowers dream
And through every green valley, there runs a clear stream
Now there's scenes of destruction on every hand
And only black waters run down through my land

—JEAN RITCHIE, *"Black Waters"*

Rick Abbey sauntered around his hometown of Eldorado, just northeast of Harrisburg, with an amused but diffident grin. He kept his hair trimmed, giving him a boyish look in his late forties. He was short and stocky.

"I need to check on the trails," Rick told me one day, referring to the stretches of the Shawnee National Forest that wound around the rim of Eagle Creek valley until the Garden of the Gods. As a member of the River to River Trail association, which had been founded by John O'Dell as a celebration of the Shawnee upland range that essentially bridged the Ohio River to the banks of the Mississippi, Rick was responsible for maintaining the paths and blazes etched on the trees in the Garden of the Gods Wilderness

183

section. He spoke with a passion about the hiking club, almost with the commitment of a union member. In fact, Rick had been a member of the Sierra Club for years.

That was his volunteer day job. During the evening, he sank hundreds of feet underground into a coal mine, where he worked in various capacities as a roof bolter or machine operator.

For Rick, the mine was another forest to explore. Fern leaves and fossils were common in the mines, of course. In fact, in 1996, coal miners at two Peabody mines in eastern Illinois stumbled onto an intact 300-million-year-old Pennsylvanian rain forest that had been fossilized in the roof of the mine. It stretched for four acres— as large as the city of San Francisco. By 2004, paleobotanists from around the world descended into the mines and were astonished to see hundred-foot trees, club mosses, and tree-size horsetails "that looked like giant asparagus." Draping ferns were encased along the mine walls from an ancient swamp. They concluded that the forest had been preserved along a fault line estuary that sank dramatically during an earthquake.

"I mean, if you think about it," Rick told me, "coal is just a bunch of trees and plants turned to peat, which formed into carbon deposits of coal." He smiled. "Just takes a few million years."

Though his grandfather and uncles had been coal miners, Rick had never grown up with the idea of making his living underground. On a whim, he and two buddies applied for jobs at the Sahara mine outside of Harrisburg in the 1970s; they were still in their teens. They did it on a lark. And to their surprise, they were hired, signed up with the Progressive Miners union, and began to work their way up the coal-mining ladder. Rick moved to other mines, transferred to the United Mine Workers, but when the Illinois coal industry hit the skids in the late 1980s, he found himself out of work. He turned to truck driving, but the lonely roads and absence from his family tugged at his conscience. In the mid-1990s, he took a nonunion job at the Galatia mine, which was less than a half-hour drive west of Eldorado.

Over the next fifteen years, he continued to hopscotch mine jobs, essentially going where the best-paying action took place. Once a thriving coal-mining town in the pre–World War II days, Eldorado now struggled like most of southern Illinois with a boarded up Main Street, a handful of fast-food restaurants off a stretch of the state highway, and a perennial unemployment rate of 15 to 20 percent that rivaled the despair of the Rust Belt.

"Not much of a coal-mining culture left," Rick said one evening, as he took me to a back alley in Eldorado, where a huge mural stretched across the brick walls with a history of coal mining in the area. The union halls stood empty. Miners commuted from faraway towns; Eldorado itself had closed its last mine a half century ago. In the old days, over a few thousand miners could walk to ten large mines, carting their lunch pails in unison, discussing the number of loaded trains during their daily march. Their wives and children were always within listening distance of the siren—that ring of fire that signaled an accident. The town was unified somehow by the shared misery of coal dust and the sour smell of smoke.

Spring, wrote one Eldorado miner, never really came to a coal town. A film of gray coated the lens of daily life, in whatever season.

The mural had emerged in the last years like a nostalgic reminder of a time when coal stoked the furnaces of our imaginations. As in 1946, when one of the social realist paintings of miners by Eldorado artist Vachel Davis was selected as a stamp by the U.S. Postal Service for the two hundredth anniversary of the coal-mining industry. The politicians in the Springfield capital even dedicated a similar statue based on Davis's acclaimed work.

No such statue stood today in Eldorado, strangely enough.

Pointing at the various panels, Rick walked me through the stages of mechanization, depicted in the simple strokes of realism: the pick and shovels; the mule trains; the continuous miner; the tipple, the trains, and then the coal-fired plants.

I stood back with Rick, and we fell into a lull of silence, looking at the miners staring back at us from the brick walls. There was a yearning for an American pastoral of industry in this mural; but, that yearning seemed so at odds, so out of place in the idyllic scenes. The irony was that pastoral image had more to do with the nearby Shawnee forests in the background, not the confines of a coal town that couldn't sustain itself.

In fact, the coal miners almost appeared like fossils embedded in the walls, frozen in poses, captured in a fault of ancient geography.

◊ ◊ ◊

THIS STRANGE DICHOTOMY of natural resources—coal versus the forest—had always been at play in the Shawnee woodlands in southern Illinois. And it had always been entangled in the competing interests of the first pioneers.

At the World's Columbian Exposition in Chicago in 1893, southern Illinois promoted two particular displays, among others: 150 species of native hardwoods were proudly featured as symbols of the region's unusually diverse forests; and a 10-ton chunk of coal, measuring more than nine-by-five feet, was hailed as one of the largest single pieces ever carted out of a mine.

That wasn't the only coal-related exhibit. As Jeff Goodell pointed out in his book *Big Coal: The Dirty Secret Behind America's Energy Future*, after 22 million fairgoers at the Chicago World's Fair in 1893 "got a glimpse of the futuristic all-dream electric Dream City, electricity became an instant icon. In cities across America, from Akron to San Francisco, local citizens banded together to bring electric lights to their Main Streets."

As early as 1819, a year after the Illinois constitution was ratified and the state came into existence, the Agricultural Society of Illinois formed to discourage the backwoods farmers from cutting down the dense hardwood forests that originally covered over 40 percent of Illinois. A lush swamp woodlands camped across the valleys and hills of the lower third of the state like a detached range of the Cumberlands.

Since the late 1790s, the first Baptists and early pioneers had referred to this lower third of Illinois as "Egypt," marking the confluence of the Ohio and Mississippi rivers. Egyptian names abounded; Cairo, of course, at the tip, Thebes, Carmi, Karnak, Goshen, Dongola. The name stuck; legends emerged with biblical connotations. More important, Egypt defined the region as distinct from the rest of Illinois, and with that distinction came the shades of darkness and mystery that still lurked among the backwoods people.

Down in Egypt. This common phrase had an ominous ring of gloom to the dwellers filling the prairies and rising heartland cities.

One of the first rules of the Agricultural Society stated: "We must call attention to the inhabitants to the substituting as a fuel in the place of wood, stone coal, which seems to have been bountifully provided for us."

Illinois governor Edward Coles, a patrician Virginian who had been an active abolitionist and Agricultural Society member, went one step further. In 1821, he lambasted the Egyptian woodsmen for their tradition of "exterminating the forests" and called on the pioneers to approach the new state with a different way of living.

"I think it is to be deplored as an evil to the state, the predilection of many of our settlers for building and making improvements in their forests," Coles wrote. Deforestation, in his view, was leading to miasmic swamps and unproductive landscapes. Examining the "destruction of timber" on the nearly 100,000 acres set aside for the reservation of the Saline Reservation near Eagle Creek, and the impact of the ax-wielding wave of settlers pouring in from the southeastern states, Coles found this "predilection for destruction" came from "old and deep rooted habits" that needed to change.

The answer to deforestation, according to Coles and fellow Agricultural Society member Morris Birkbeck, the English pioneer who helped to found the Albion community in southeastern Illinois, was to turn to coal. The outcroppings of the black diamond, in their minds, gave Illinois a chance to save its woodlands and fuel the ambitions of its new towns.

However, for Birkbeck and his Albion followers, coming from coal-fired industrial England with the strict regimen of productivity, and for Coles, who had been raised among the aristocracy in Virginia's Tidewater region and served as a special envoy for President James Madison in Russia and France, there was an enduring obstacle to the enlightened new coal state of Illinois: the mores of the backwoodsmen who had carved out the first communities in places like Eagle Creek.

In modern terms, they didn't know what to do with my family of border-fighting woodsmen now that the daunting forests had been penetrated, the Indian wars had been won, the first industries of salt and coal had been launched, and the "civilized" settlers had arrived to lay out their farms and towns.

In essence, the woodsman became an impediment to industrial and agricultural progress.

All they want to do is hunt, Birkbeck lamented. All they desire are forests.

Birkbeck, and his fellow English pioneer George Flower, questioned why these frontiersmen and their families even wanted to live in the "dreary wilderness." They saw the backwoodsman as "incarcerated" and "shut from the common air" because he had chosen to live in the forests like the Indians.

The term "backwoodsman" itself emerged from a biased connotation. For those who still regarded England as the focal point of progress, the "backwoods" referred to the Appalachian range "behind" the eastern seaboard. On the other hand, for those who viewed the frontier as the new America, the woods served as the front line of change and the future. "Frontiersman," seemingly, was the positive counterpart.

Either way, the woodsman, like my Eagle Creek ancestors, had paradoxically removed the Indian, only to be subjected to the increasing pressures of removal by a new type of immigrant. In his *Sketches of History, Life, and Manners in the West*, author James Hall, who briefly edited one of the first newspapers in Shawneetown and then a literary magazine in the Illinois territorial capital of Vandalia, captured that conundrum for the first pioneers in the 1820s.

Hall wrote: "Our pioneers have been born and reared on the frontier, and have, from generation to generation, by successive removals, remained in the same relative situation in respect to the Indians and our own government." Hall found that the woodsman's delight to "rove uncontrolled in the woods," like the Indian, doomed him to the same sense of invasion of his "ancient heritage." Ultimately, it would also force the woodsman to defend himself from removal.

For the woodsmen, the American pastoral was not one of cleared and tidy farms, but the wealth of the forests and its wildlife; the openness of the hills and hollows; the freedom of not seeing the smoke rise from the chimney of a neighbor; the wilderness and its natural ways that had been denied to the peasantry in Europe's conquered dominions.

"You English are very industrious," Birkbeck quoted his woodsman neighbors, "but we have freedom."

For my ancestors, the great American pastoral sat on the wooded hills of Eagle Creek, not the cleared prairies.

We tend to forget that the freedom of religion and expression that so formed our early American experience was also wedded to the freedom of open spaces, unencumbered by the encroachment of lords or government agencies or high priests.

The only thing my ancestors had been allowed to hunt in the Old World were fellow border fighters on the opposing fields of the warring lairds.

William Henry Harrison, who pounded Thomas Jefferson's hammer at the famed Tippecanoe battle with the Shawnee, and determined the first Indian removal policy as governor of Indiana, certainly understood this historical dynamic of the woodsman. The aristocratic Harrison, the son of a powerful Virginia plantation family, manipulated the lore of the backwoodsmen in his 1840 campaign for presidency. When a newspaper mocked the voters as country rubes—"Give him a barrel of hard cider, and settle a pension of two thousand a year on him . . . he will sit by the side of a 'sea coal' fire and study moral philosophy"—Harrison held up the log cabin and the coonskin-capped voting woodsman as his campaign symbols. Funny enough, touring on behalf of Harrison's Whigs, a young Abraham Lincoln visited the northern edge of Eagle Creek in the nearby town of Equality for the first time in 1840.

Harrison's exploitation of the backwoodsman worked wonders. He was elected president. But the woodsman mystique didn't last long. Harrison died of pneumonia within the first month of his presidency in Washington, DC.

Freedom notwithstanding, leading settlers like the patrician English pioneer Birkbeck had not accepted Harrison's log cabin campaign or this concept of wilderness living. He continually referred to it as "indolence" and was offended by the lack of productivity. He couldn't fathom this desire to live in the woods and not shape a new town. He declared the plagues of Egypt simply needed to be charmed by Aaron's rod.

Either that, or the backwoodsmen needed to move on and let the new immigrants settle the Illinois country, and dig its coal.

◊　◊　◊

THE ELDERLY REPRESENTATIVE of the coal company that strip-mined our old homeplace once told me something on the phone that stayed in my mind for years: "You know how those country people want to get out of the hills and into town. So we helped your cousin out."

His gruff old voice sounded so sincere, and yet we both knew the truth was otherwise. That our cousin had just renovated the old homeplace and had planned for his daughter to become the eighth generation to inhabit the historic log cabin. That they had been harassed and blasted and covered with coal dust and fly rock for years to the point of desperation. That their well and sole source of drinking water had been shattered into a black pool of muck. That they had been removed—compensated, of course, and most likely compensated well. But removed.

Those country people didn't want to get out of the hills. There was a reason—that same sense of freedom and love of the land that Birkbeck mocked—why they had chosen to live in Eagle Creek for two hundred years.

The coal company executive laughed at the indolence of "country people" today. They were in his way—our nation's way of producing energy. At least, coal-extracted energy.

Birkbeck could not have done a better job of removing the backwoodsman in the name of progress.

I always wanted to ask the coal operator, who had declared his commitment to the area and people, if he would have strip-mined his own well-tended family farm had the same rich coal seams been found underneath its surface. But I never did. I knew the answer.

◊ ◊ ◊

IN 1975, in one of the first articles he ever wrote for *Outdoor Illinois*—a magazine edited in the nearby southern Illinois town of Benton by Dan Malkovich (a coal miner's son, also known as actor John Malkovich's father)—Gary DeNeal recounted the moonshine culture in the "fabled terrain of Eagle Creek." For Gary, having grown up on the "other side of the mountain," Eagle Creek rivaled the Appalachian moonshine havens depicted in nineteenth-century novels like *The Trail of the Lonesome Pine* by John Fox Jr.

"Eagle Creek was as much an attitude as a particular geographical location," Gary wrote. "In its devotion to moonshining, fighting and protracted revivals, it was all too typical of many isolated hill regions."

As a boy, Gary's uncle Earl regaled him with Eagle Creek stories in which he snuck over the mountain and fiddled at the dances, and "Eagle Creekers turned out to be as rowdy as rumor painted them though generous to a fault if they liked you."

How Eagle Creek went from being one of the first pioneer and progressive abolitionist communities in Illinois—in the heartland of the nation—to a depraved haven for gun-toting Bible-beating moonshine-drinking feuding hillbillies had more to do with the kind of lore that seeped into romance novels and true-crime rags than any real truth.

Given its placement on the earliest travel routes to the Great Salt Spring and its sanitary mountain slopes in a century of swamp-related diseases, Eagle Creek had historically been a community of exchange, innovation, and progress, despite its backwoods location. It had spawned the first gristmill in the region. Within a generation, it churned out the first doctor, and a pottery operation that exported its ceramic goods back to Germany. It stood in the forefront of the anti-slavery movement. It gave birth to a new Protestant denomination—the Social Brethren—and it even maintained an active Odd Fellows charity club until the Great Depression.

As farmers, like my extended family, Eagle Creekers were renowned for their sorghum molasses–making for a century. In an economically depressed region like southern Illinois, sorghum was one of the few delights in an otherwise bitter diet.

But 'shine, the wondrous brew of white lightning that tantalized and scandalized and socialized a nation, gave Eagle Creek its reputation.

Not that moonshine was a bad thing. Every culture, including our ancestors in the British and Irish isles and Nordic forests, had perfected their own mind-altering brew and migrated with it. Every grandmother in the hollers knew the medicinal effect of a toddy to revive a sick one; a little moonshine stirred into warm milk. Every house had a nip of mountain scotch available for those cold nights when the wind howled, and visitors arrived like frozen ghosts needing a jolt of fire. Even the 50-gallon Baptists partook, spending the better part of their Sunday meetings apologizing for their Saturday parties.

After the glorious Volstead Act went into law in 1920, prohibiting the sale of alcohol, the farmers along the Eagle Mountains and nearby winding creeks took advantage of the famed springs that every mining surveyor had noted for over a hundred years—if anything, good moonshine needed clean water, and the best moonshine cookers needed the seasoned hardwoods of ash and hickory. Protected by the craggy hills and narrow hollows, and a single wagon road that wound through the gap in a slow creep of ruts, moonshiners flourished in a sustainable economy for the first time in their lives. They didn't have to rely on their meager corn, sorghum sales, and livestock. It gave farmhands a chance to get

beyond their $1-a-day stipends; for a lucky few, making and ped-
dling moonshine made for a preferable option to the deadly underground mines.

"Coal mine, moonshine, or move it down the line" went the
expression.

This is the truth: All righteousness aside, the rest of the region
relied on Eagle Creek to get through the long dry days.

Those were the golden years. The Eagle Creekers supplied the
drinking needs of the mining communities throughout southeastern Illinois. An estimated three stills dotted every Eagle Creek
holler; one out of three men had their own operation going. Smoke
signals rose in broad daylight from the barrel cookers like billows of
clouds from a factory. One census taker in the 1920s claimed he
found so many men working at the stills in the Eagle Creek area
that he veered from walking to the remote houses and made his tal-
lies from still to still.

Long before Prohibition, however, moonshine had become a
hallowed tradition in Eagle Creek—and virtually everywhere in
backwoods America. Alexander Hamilton triggered a whiskey rebellion in Pennsylvania after the American Revolution because he
recognized the tax value in liquor to pay down the national debt.
He didn't realize that insurrection was a powerful chaser for offended whiskey makers.

Moonshine, on the other hand, generated the legends and lore
of shadowy dealings in the dark hills that fueled the imaginations
of generations of writers. Eagle Creek became a code word for
lawlessness.

In a memoir about his circuit riding, self-proclaimed "celebrated divine healer" Willis M. Brown recalled a religious meeting
in the 1890s in the "roughest place in the state of Illinois, on Eagle
Creek. There were a number of drunkards, gamblers, infidels and
outlaws there."

Storyteller and historian Elihu Hall, from the neighboring Hardin County, went further in his rhapsodic prose poem about Eagle Creek, in *Anna's War*. He wrote:

"The community which gained the widest notoriety and helped most to make the Ozarks of Illinois and Kentucky famous for their pioneer 'free for alls of fist and skull' was Eagle Creek on the slopes of the mountains in Gallatin County. However it appears that the settlement along that famous creek and branch of the Saline very early on their own accord abandoned horse-thieving, though drinking, gambling, carousing and fighting ran rife to their zenith of terror on Eagle Creek for many years. They habitually formed horse-back raids, traveling unbelievable distances to whip out the greatest gatherings they could hear of, called together by schools, churches, chivaries, log-rollings, house-raisings or what not; till raids of Eagle Creekers became dreaded in Ozark regions almost equal to those of Black Hawk Indians on the Northern Plains."

Even the *New York Times* couldn't resist the Eagle Creek lore. A small news article ran in 1895 that described a moonshine-soaked brawl that broke out at a church Christmas party on Eagle Creek. Despite the extraordinary history and regional conflicts, that ridiculous bit of news would be the only story ever written about the area in the famed New York newspaper.

"Everyone in Eagle Creek has an outlaw in the woodpile of family lore," my uncle reminded me. His great-uncle, our beloved walrus-mustached Uncle Thomas Womack, who befriended my grandfather and took him under his wing to the northern California forests as a young man, left behind a buried chest of loot in the Eagle Mountains that he had robbed from a bank in Shawneetown. Uncle Thomas never made it back to Eagle Creek.

When I told this to an old Eagle Creek farmer once, he nodded, amused by the violent yarns that underlined the moonshine stories.

"I knew one of the big moonshine families," he said. "They worked their tails off with my daddy to build a barn. They didn't leave until it was finished, knowing he wouldn't pay them anymore. And yet, a single incident with a distant cousin dishonored their family name for generations. That's what happened."

Why were the moonshiners so vilified when they served the needs of those godly religious folks in town?

He shrugged his shoulders. He added, funny how no one ever mentioned that when the largely mainstream townsfolk made up the Ku Klux Klan and operated with impunity in southern Illinois in the 1920s, one area defied them: Eagle Creek. He recalled a famous Klan encounter not found in history books, outside of personal narratives in the nearby Lamb community. When the Klan made a raid on Eagle Creek, clad in their white robes and pointy hats, the moonshiners stood their ground and opened fire.

"This was indeed a surprise and a shock to the Klan," wrote one participant, in *The Stories of the Lamb Community*. "This first and only volley took all the patriotism out of the Klan raiders—they scattered like a flock of quails."

The Klan, which terrorized the coal-mining towns in southern Illinois for years, never dared to enter Eagle Creek again. Nor did its leader ever bother to return to pick up his pointy hat, which remained on display at an Eagle Creek farmhouse, not far from where a wolf had been slain and strung up for view.

Either way, the old farmer explained, a well-planted story, more than smoking rifles, managed to keep the revenuers and snooping mining surveyors out of Eagle Creek for half a century. Eagle Creek's reputation alone functioned as a bulwark of defense. The goal: They were left alone.

As long as the creeks ran clean and the forest thrived, moonshine continued to roll down like righteous streams. That environmental detail, though, became the hardest element in the back-woods to protect.

◊ ◊ ◊

DON WEST'S ADMONITION in Appalachia in the 1980s could not have been more true in southern Illinois: "The abuse of the land has always gone hand in hand with the abuse of the miner or woods-man. It's easy to take and strip mine someone's land if we have con-vinced the world that its inhabitants are disposable, poor white trash. Bunch of hillbillies."

The criminal lore of southern Illinois had a shadowy counter-part: It somehow covered up the contemporary crime of strip min-ing with a quilt of caricatures that turned the backwoods people into disposal relics of the past. I learned this on a journey into the region's criminal past one day.

I crossed over to Egypt from Kentucky on a flatbed car ferry, a whisper of fog hovering on the banks of the Ohio. The ferry was one of the oldest still operating on the river, a throwback to the days when pioneers mounted flatboats with their life possessions and placed their fate in the water's flow. There wasn't as much as a wrin-kle in the water's surface that morning. As the ferry pushed off the Kentucky landing, I stepped out of my car, felt a chill in the air, and scanned the bluffs along the Illinois shore. A fogbow hovered at the eastern end of the valley; a distant barge loaded with coal headed toward the confluence of the Ohio and Mississippi rivers. Straight ahead, mists moved along the trees on the outcroppings.

Gary stood waiting on the other side of the river like an accom-plice to the crime. Part of his mission at *Springhouse* magazine had been to sort fact from fiction in the seams of criminal exploits that had provided a treasury of outrageous stories about the region for writers, journalists, and filmmakers. The stories dated back to the 1790s, when

Samuel Mason posted a sign above a cave along the river with the ruse WILSON'S LIQUOR VAULT AND HOUSE OF ENTERTAINMENT.

Even before I landed, I could make out the dark caverns along the Illinois banks of the river that had sheltered what one historian called the "criminally audacious." Not far away from the ferry landing, Cave-in-Rock arched fifty feet at its widest, looking out onto the river with a portentous mouth. Its 160-foot rooms and deep sanctuary had entered the chronicles of American travel lore before Thomas Jefferson became president.

Based at Cave-in-Rock, Mason was not so hospitable as his sign proclaimed. He either robbed his travelers blind or, in the case of the new cave landlords, the "Big" and "Little" Harpe brothers a few years later, carried out a reign of terror. The dark legends of southern Illinois's caves and woods and wild backwoods people quickly provided a staple of gore for travelogues and newspaper accounts, and untold numbers of songs and poems. One of the roads from the river through Eagle Creek to the Great Salt Spring became known as the "werewolf" trace; "Satan's ferrymen" commandeered the boats.

Even from his muddy riverside township to the east of Eagle Creek, James Hall lamented in 1828: "No place in the western country has been more vilified than Shawnee Town. Nor could the picture drawn of them have been much aggravated by adding the crimes of Sodom and the plagues of Egypt."

American folk hero Mike Fink, an infamous nineteenth-century keelboater and river brawler whose exploits turned into larger-than-life literary tales, battled the Cave-in-Rock pirates in a popular novel published in 1848.

In the 1870s, the Chicago newspapers followed a violent feud between a couple of families in southern Illinois—lacking violence in their own town, apparently—with such an obsession that readers could practically read daily dispatches from the war correspondents. "The feud is a disgrace," declared the *Chicago Tribune*, "to the whole state of Illinois."

Gary had his own obsession with outlaws. His biography on gangster Charlie Birger, *A Knight of Another Sort*, often overshadowed his decades of writing and editing at *Springhouse*, and his more literary poetry.

By the mid-1920s, in the midst of the Prohibition gangster wars, the *American Mercury* magazine appointed Birger, born into a Russian Jewish family and transplanted as a local bootlegger from the Harrisburg area, as the "baron of Egypt, America's Robin Hood." His murderous reign over rival bootleggers and politicians notwithstanding, Birger gained a measure of national fame for his acts of charity—those handfuls of coins thrown into a crowd of children on the Harrisburg square, those wagons of coal delivered to the poor in the bitter winter—and his defiant clashes with the Ku Klux Klan.

Birger's flashy looks also put a spell on American journalists. His marketing chutzpah kept Cicero's Al Capone from drifting into his territory. He commissioned his own gang's portrait in front of a jury-rigged armored-plated vehicle, replete with tommy guns and rifles unfurled for posterity. This didn't prevent a rival gang from dropping bombs from a single-engine airplane on Birger's Shady Rest hideout just west of Harrisburg.

Birger's violent ways finished in a violent end. He was hanged in 1928 for the murder of a small-town mayor. He declared on the gallows: "It's a beautiful world."

Possibly the bloodiest tale of backwoods slaughter, the ballad of Billy Potts, was lifted by famed writer Robert Penn Warren, who hauled the story across the river, replanted it in Kentucky, and immortalized the murder in his poem of the same name in 1944.

Ostensibly based on the Potts family inn on the eastern edge of Eagle Creek, the ballad recounts a gruesome epic of unwitting filicide as endemic of the backwoods lust for the blood of outsiders. The tavern owners accidentally killed their long-lost son, confusing him for a passing traveler.

Not that any of this had a lick of truth. But it did make for good copy.

Gary laughed. *Springhouse* had run numerous articles on Billy Potts, by Ron Nelson no less, debunking many of the theories and shreds of evidence, while always investigating the obsession of writers for Egyptian crimes.

Darcy O'Brien, a bestselling true-crime writer who grew up in Hollywood as the son of a cowboy actor, loved the association of the Billy Potts story with the Eagle Creekers in southern Illinois. In an article reprinted in *Springhouse*, he created his own colorful version of the events from his imagination:

> Billy Potts was as big and tough and rough a man as ever betrayed a friend, fleeced a guest, kicked a dog, beat a wife, or emptied a quart. . . . A curse and a fist in your face or worse was ever the way with Billy Potts.
>
> He had a foul-smelling little dark wife with a wart on her nose the size of a cockroach and a tongue in her mouth that would peal the paint off a church.
>
> And they had an ugly son, red-faced and snot-nosed, bigger than a prize hog by the time he could walk, flat-headed and bawling, filthy as a pig-sty at lunch time. And they loved him. . . .
>
> As soon as the travelers bent down over the spring to take their last drink on earth, Billy Potts would sneak up behind them and plunge his big sharp knife up to its hilt into their backs. And the spring ran red with their blood.
>
> Meanwhile upstairs at the inn, Mrs. Potts was . . . slicing up the women and children as they slept in their beds. . . . She could

carve up a man as quickly and skillfully with her stone-sharpened cutlery as she could a lamb or pig. Then she and Billy would bury the human pieces in the yard and count up the contents of the purses and change the bedding on the beds. . . .

In many respects, O'Brien chose to saddle the invented Potts story as a cautionary tale of the Egyptian code of violence—or, at least to someone who grew up in Hollywood, was educated as a Rhodes Scholar at Oxford, and whose last book had been about the Hillside Strangler in Los Angeles. It led to one of his top-selling books, *Murder in Little Egypt*. A real page-turner, the true-crime chronicle hit the *New York Times* bestseller list in the late 1980s, narrating another filicide case in Eldorado and the nearby Shawnee backwoods. In gripping detail that rivaled his re-creation of the Potts legend, O'Brien spun the tale of a popular doctor who maintained a diabolic double-life and was convicted for the murder of his son.

"This Egypt," he begins on the first page, "is a secretive sort of place, an outback and a throwback to earlier, murkier times." The Shawnee Forest was "idyllic if you care for isolation, but disrupted every few miles by enormous coal pits, strip mines scarring the land with their huge power shovels several stories high, tearing up the ground, leaving behind black heaps where not even weeds can grow."

The violent strip mining of the land, for O'Brien, served as a metaphor for the violent tendencies of the people. Of course, he failed to recognize that the largest strip-mining companies were from Chicago and other outside cities.

In another essay for *Springhouse*, "A Rose in Little Egypt," O'Brien cast the monstrous strip-mine shovels as menacing statues of doom. "Here and there black metal pipes shot blue-orange flames into the gloom of the late, overcast afternoon, sending a weird, orange light against the sky. The pit, the great heaps of black slag, that outsized shovel, the flares—to Marian it was a peculiar and forbidding vision. She remembered Dante from high school. This was how she had imagined the *Inferno*."

O'Brien claimed Saline County, where "violence had been an unbroken tradition for two centuries," ranked second only to the coalfields in "Bloody" Harlan County in Kentucky as the rural murder capital of the nation. That murder was essentially natural to the mores of the backwoods people.

Locals were outraged and offended by O'Brien's book and his portrait of backwoods savagery; some referred to it as "The Murder of Little Egypt," an uninformed assault on the region's true legacy and heritage for the sake of selling a true-crime potboiler.

In the end, O'Brien kept the violent criminal stereotypes intact, as the strip mines continued to spread across the region without a word of criticism.

◊   ◊   ◊

ON THE SAME FALL DAYS in 1933 that the intra-union war erupted between the Progressive Miners and the United Mine Workers, two other important announcements nudged their way into the busy newspaper headlines in Harrisburg: "Shawnee unit for forest" and "Prohibition virtually at end."

This was the axis of issues that defined the state of affairs for southern Illinois: In the depths of near starvation and economic depression, the locals could choose between the social and economic mayhem of coal, or the future of a "green" economy based around reforestation and ecotourism, and with the coming of legal liquor, the end of the one sustainable industry for the backwoods farmer.

Plotted out by various civil groups in Harrisburg for years, the creation of the Shawnee National Forest had resulted from an amazing grassroots effort to jump-start the ailing communities in southern Illinois. With an estimated 60 to 70 percent unemployment rate in the 1930s, the coal mines having collapsed and been abandoned for the most part, few men in the coal camps and towns could turn to the land for any relief. In many respects, the coal miners were trapped: Still on call for the illusive notice to go down into the pit—that tortuous hook of the boom-and-bust cycle of the coal industry—they couldn't find other work or risk leaving the area.

In the meantime, the *Chicago Tribune* asked, How did southern Illinois become such a wasteland? At one point around the turn of the twentieth century, the region hummed with over 250 working sawmills, churning out the railroad ties and mining ties that carted the coal out of the region. One other little detail was left out: Scores of abandoned mines and strip pits blotched the hills and open fields with pus-filled pockets of poisoned waters.

As Coles had predicted a century before, the encroaching pioneers had clear-cut much of the Shawnee forests and hillsides into oblivion, leading to massive erosion and fallow lands. And they had been joined by the coal companies. A government report in 1931 came to a startling conclusion: Reforestation was the only hope of redeeming the land and the heritage of the people. It noted:

"The general region has been farmed for 100 years and much of the farm soil is worn out. The cost of reclaiming it as farm soil by artificial methods is prohibitive. Many farms have been abandoned on account of worn out soil and erosion. A large percentage of these are on soil which should not have been cleared of timber. It was suitable only for tree crops. Practically the whole region has been logged from one to ten times."

The uniqueness of southern Illinois was its position as the craggy boot heel at the edge of the Wisconsin glacier. "By its antiquity and location with respect to other floristic centers," a botanist wrote in the 1960s, recognizing its hingelike position as a bridge between the two great rivers and the Ozark and Cumberland mountain ranges, it had become a "floristic melting pot" and included some of the most diverse forests and fauna found anywhere in the United States.

In a rare move of enlightenment that recognized the dwellers and their entwined fate with the land, the federal government launched a program of buying abandoned hillside farms and woodlands without invoking eminent domain or engaging in any mass removals. Most farmers sold off parts of their plots, not entire farms, and stayed in the region. Although out-migration to the factories in Chicago, St. Louis, and Indiana did occur, a sizeable majority of people stayed in southern Illinois. Despite the misery, most of those backwoods farmers didn't want to leave.

In the meantime, cobbled together from the purchase of nearly 200,000 acres stretching across the hills, the Shawnee National Forest was officially signed into existence in 1939 by President Franklin D. Roosevelt.

The Harrisburg newspaper raved about the forest projects with an enthusiasm to defy the depression of the period. "These will affect the molding of a great tourist trade into southern Illinois, especially Saline County," it declared. "This trade in the years to come may take the place of the prosperous mining and farming industries that prevailed a few years ago."

Through the Civilian Conservation Corps, a federal public relief program, locals were employed to assist in the reforestation and to build new roads—real roads—including a better access into the Eagle Creek valley. Over the next several years, nearly a fifth of the unproductive land was replanted with pines—not the original hardwoods. Nonetheless, the extraordinary rehabilitation of the forest and its depleted wildlife—one of the most successful campaigns in the country—progressed.

In the fall of 1933, the federal officials arranged a meeting for Eagle Creek residents at the Bethel Church on the edge of our family's land. The nearby Eagle Mountains and the eastern ridges eventually designated as the Garden of the Gods Wilderness, of course, were considered prime landmarks of the national forest. Over two hundred Eagle Creek farmers attended the meeting. They listened to the government's offer to buy their farms tucked into the hills and hollers for an estimated $1–$1.5 dollars an acre, roughly the same price paid by their ancestors in 1820.

Not one Eagle Creeker offered to sell a single acre. It would take a couple of years before the first acres were dislodged out of the grip of pioneer families.

When asked later about their resistance to sell out to the Forest Service representatives, some surmised that there must have been an ancient Baptist dissidence to government authority at play.

"Perhaps," said one farmer. Then again, he added, if he left Eagle Creek, where would he ever find such clean water to make moonshine?

There was no place like Eagle Creek and its clean waters.

◊ ◊ ◊

IN MANY RESPECTS, though, the resistance of the Eagle Creekers to work with the federal government ultimately had devastating impacts on their livelihoods.

The first strip mine had already torn at the Eagle Creek hillsides in the early 1930s. Over the next half century, a series of coal companies carved away at the valley with the ebb and flow of a tide that never ended. With each new mine, each round of blasts, and each dismantling of a valley or hill or poisoning of a watershed, Eagle Creek saw its farmland and farm population drain further.

The full-scale launch of strip mining—the process of clearcutting the forests and dynamiting or detonating explosives across the landscape and then using heavy machinery to remove anything overlaying the mineral seams—took a giant leap in 1910 when steam-powered shovels rolled from the railroad tracks and tore pits out of the land with increasing ease. Within a decade, electrical power equipment had been developed: shovels with 12-cubic-yard dippers mounted on the end of a 95-foot boom. They seemed like enormous monsters at the time. But they were tiny. By the 1950s, over a third of all coal in the region was being strip-mined by "walking draglines," stripping shovels that towered over 250 feet tall and sported buckets of 35 cubic yards. An estimated 67,000 acres had been stripped by 1952.

As Hovie Stunson pointed out, flipping through his three-ring notebook of photos one day, strip mining didn't find its real groove until the "Captain" arrived in the 1960s. At one point considered to be the largest dragline in the world, the "Captain" stood twenty-one stories tall, weighed over 28 million pounds, and could sweep up two seams of coal simultaneously in its 180-cubic-yard dipper.

The Captain was a monster. It dug out craters with the panache of a meteor, and once it had finished reaping all the coal out of the area, it walked itself like a surreal robot skyscraper down the road to the next mine.

It was the tallest building in the region, though a transient one.

The destruction from strip mining did not go unnoticed. On one hand, the progress of industry seemed like no match for nature. Clarence Bonnell, a science teacher and writer in Harrisburg, delivered a paper at the Illinois Academy of Science in 1916, comparing strip mining to the region's unique bluffs and undulating hills and valleys. Bonnell concluded: "The two thick veins of coal in the Saline and Gallatin counties, now worked from nearly two score mines, are scarcely disturbed as yet. Man can destroy in a few centuries but a small fraction of what nature has already destroyed of her own handiwork by the agencies of erosion, as is displayed in the hundreds of canon-like valleys of the counties."

These notions of the natural "badlands" as a parallel phenomenon to the strip mines gained a foothold among several observers. Writing in the *Scientific Monthly* in 1944, one author launched into a defense of strip mining as a way of making forests and prairies more interesting. It was just a question of semantics, he announced:

"It is indeed unfortunate that the term 'spoil bank' or 'strip mine dump' became associated with the strip mining industry. Both 'spoil' and 'dump' mean something undesirable, to say the least, to the average American; so upon hearing the words 'spoil bank' one visualizes an area of ground torn up by man and piled into unsightly dumps, yet the average person going to Yellowstone Park will spend additional money to see the Bad Lands, a rugged area of 25,000,000 acres developed by nature. We tend to see the good side of the Bad Lands, but the bad side of the strip mine hills."

In truth, the great machines were writing the region's destiny on the canyon's walls. Strip mining was not going away.

As early as 1922, critics called for restraint, or at least an element of preservation in the role of strip mining. At an Academy of Science conference in Rockford that year, one professor noted: "I have tried in this small way to discuss a slight portion of the most important resource which nature has left us. It is ours to use, not to abuse; to consume, not waste. Let us accept it as our treasure, use it as our friend and ally, and in turn pass it on to those who are to follow us with as little impairment as possible."

By 1940, Illinois became the national leader in strip-mining coal. It was not limited, of course, to the hilly ranges across southern Illinois. Throughout the midwestern states, over a million acres of prime farmland were lost to strip mining in the mid-twentieth century. The unbridled destruction of fertile farmland in central and western Illinois actually gave rise to a national movement to regulate surface mining. As early as 1940, Senator Everett Dirksen, a conservative Republican from Illinois, introduced federal legislation to require coal companies to reclaim the land to a certain degree of sustainable post-mining use.

This concern fell on deaf ears. Dirksen's bill didn't even manage to get out of a subcommittee, but it marked the beginnings of a new awareness about strip mining.

When the state of Illinois passed its own surface-mining regulations in 1962, however, the cautious legislation erred on the side of the coal companies. The state law did not mandate any firm post-mining reclamation policy but sought to "encourage the planting of forests, to advance the seeding of grasses and legumes for grazing purposes and crops for harvest, to aid in the protection of wildlife and aquatic resources, to establish recreational, home and industrial sites, to protect and perpetuate the taxable value of property and to protect and promote the health, safety and general welfare of the people of this state."

In the end, it was in the hands of the coal companies and the largely window-dressing state regulators who had no powers of enforcement.

To be sure, there were a number of efforts to minimize the extent of strip mining and preserve some of southern Illinois's most beautiful upland ranges and woods. This included Eagle Creek. In a 1953 study commissioned by Southern Illinois University, internationally renowned geographer Charles Colby proposed the creation of an Eagle Creek state park, as part of a chain of parks for ecotourism. The Eagle Creek area and its possibilities entranced Colby; his proposal called for establishing the state's largest and most varied park in the area. He called for creating a "scenic drive" around the ridge of Eagle Mountain, the Wildcat Hills, where with "numerous outlook points a visitor could get panoramic views of the lowlands" in the Eagle Creek valley.

"Tributaries of Eagle Creek drain the series of spectacular hollows cut deeply into the high southern flank of Eagle Creek Basin.

As has been stated, Pounds Hollow at the east already is a recreation area of the U.S. Forest Service. Taken together these eight hollows make up the most spectacular group of valleys in all Illinois. They have to be seen to be appreciated. Some of them might be kept as wilderness areas for folks who like to get off the beaten path; others could be treated as to emphasize their unique features. The floor of the Eagle Creek Basin could be left in private hands, but a fine golf course with cabin facilities would capture the interest of many."

Neither the golf course, nor the scenic drive and a state park ever emerged.

The strip mining plundered on through the east end of the valley, once known as Kedron—that hallowed namesake of the biblical Abraham, the father of the great religions.

With the narrow two-lane back roads weighed down by overburdened coal trucks, ecotourism failed to attract many outside visitors to the area. Only local hikers, horse riders, and hunters took full advantage of the Garden of the Gods and other Shawnee National Forest areas. A satirical postcard in the 1960s declared "Visit the Shawnee Hills Recreation Lands!" It showed a huge shovel like the Captain digging itself out of a wasteland.

Despite the growing alarm at strip mining, the timidity of any legislation underscored the power of the coal industry in determining the outcome of any regulations. Founded in the mid-1970s to assist farmers and rural people under assault from the coal industry, the Illinois South organization in Herrin, the infamous coal town that still nursed its wounds from the massacre in 1922 over a strike at a strip mine, showed in a study that "the 10 biggest Illinois coal companies were owned by Fortune 500 companies—corporations uninterested in preserving land for future generations."

Illinois South joined an extraordinary alliance of farm organizations, community groups, and coalfield delegations from the western states to the Midwest to Appalachia that had been campaigning for decades for the abolishment of strip mining. Hundreds of thousands—if not millions—of acres across the nation resembled, according to the coalfield residents, the "aftermath of Hiroshima."

It was not only a matter of the land, but also the economy. With 60 percent of our national coal production coming from strip-mining operations, everyone in the coalfields knew that the massive machinery and explosives would eventually wipe out the need for two out of every three coal-mining jobs. Ever since the 1922 massacre of the strikebreakers at the strip mine in Herrin—a conflict over the mechanization of jobs as much as the demands over wages—strip-mining operations had been pounding the final nails in the coffin of the large-scale shaft-mine employers in the region.

This was the cruel irony of strip mining, of course: It stripped the miners of their jobs. In fact, more jobs would be lost over the next decades to scaled-down heavy-machine-driven strip-mining operations than those impacted by any environmental legislation in the country.

In 1971, West Virginia congressman Ken Hechler had also spelled out the impending impact of strip mining on his region's broader economy:

"What about the jobs that will be lost if the strippers continue to ruin the tourist industry, wash away priceless topsoil, fill people's yards with the black muck, which runs off from a strip mine, rip open the bellies of the hills and spill their guts in spoil-banks? This brutal and hideous contempt for valuable land is a far more serious threat to the economy than a few thousand jobs which are easily transferable into the construction industry, or to fill the sharp demand for workers in underground mines."

Yet, there was a certain banality of evil in the strip-mining debate. The movement to abolish surface mining was effectively derailed by the Goliath-like resources of the coal companies, whose sway on Capitol Hill was no less powerful in the state and township corridors. In the end, federal legislators opted to "regulate" strip mining, instead of banning its undeniable wrath of destruction in the coal areas.

In 1977, in the afterglow of the OPEC energy crisis and a new scramble toward coal production, President Jimmy Carter signed the Surface Mining Control and Reclamation Act, an admittedly "watered down bill" that would enhance "the legitimate and much-needed production of coal." The president declared that it would also "assuage the fears that the beautiful areas where coal is produced were being destroyed."

Few residents in the coalfields agreed. In his classic *To Save the Land and People: A History of Opposition to Surface Coal Mining in Appalachia*, Chad Montrie described the sense of betrayal of the Appalachian coalition working with the midwestern heartland advocates, and those living in the ruins of the strip mines:

"The present bill was so weakened by compromise that it no longer promised effective control of the coal industry or adequate protection of citizens' rights. A press release listed the provisions (or absent provisions) the Coalition found particularly troublesome: an eighteen-month exemption of small operators; recognition of mountaintop removal as an approved mining technique (rather than a variance requiring special approval); language allowing for variance from restoration to approximate original contour; failure to impose slope limitations (or a partial ban on contour mining); and failure to fully protect surface owner rights with a comprehensive consent clause."

According to longtime anti-strip-mining activist Jane Johnson in Illinois, the act also allowed a flood of "grandfathering" of old mining contracts to circumvent the new requirements. Johnson wrote in the Illinois South newsletter in 1987, on the tenth anniversary of the surface-mining act:

"The State allowed thousands of acres of prime land to be mined without having to meet the requirements of PL 95–87. Also, farmland could be mined, but there were no criteria written for judging the success of land reclamation. Industry continued to defend its reclamation practices but citizens couldn't find the bountiful harvest of corn and soybeans alluded to in permit applications. People in the cornbelt felt betrayed."

So did the backwoodsmen in the Shawnee National Forest areas. So did virtually every resident in the affected coalfields in the heartland, Appalachia, and the western tribal areas. Over the next three decades, despite the new surface-mining laws, a land mass the size of some entire eastern states—including over five hundred mountains in Appalachia—would be strip-mined and eliminated from our American maps.

As part of the act, taxpayers would spend more than $3 billion over the next three decades to clean up the hazardous waste and spoils of thousands of abandoned mines.

The strip miners themselves were not even spared. In 2003, a truck driver hauling a load of coal from a nearby strip mine across the hills from Eagle Creek died when his truck overturned. Inspectors found that the coal company had falsified their records to hide their oversight in carrying out federally required training. The end result from this loss of life: MSHA proposed a $93,000 fine against the company for the violations.

In 1990, Congress passed the Illinois Wilderness Act, setting aside seven wilderness areas located in the Shawnee National Forest. Over 27,000 acres, including a virtual horseshoe around Eagle Creek, were ostensibly protected from logging, mining, any commercial tourist development, and motorized vehicles. In truth, an eight-year loophole remained for coal mining. The act drew a tremendous amount of negative reaction from the region for another reason: The Wilderness Act kept longtime horse riders from using their historic trails.

A section of the Garden of the Gods to the southern rim of Eagle Creek received a special protection status. The last remnants of Eagle Creekers, however, fell in that unprotected zone of private property or, as the Wilderness Act noted, an area of "resource attributes."

As the first historic community in the region, Eagle Creek remained an unprotected outpost of impending doom.

◊ ◊ ◊

IN 1912, a group of young students from the Eldorado high school did a hike along the hills of Eagle Creek and then camped at the summit of Eagle Mountain. According to a report in the *Saline County Republican* newspaper, "beautiful scenes" of Eagle Creek abounded on all sides. "Down below the side of the cliff was seen, rounded and rugged, the tops of oak trees showing the downward slope of the mountain, the green leaves looking as one vast meadow. Still farther away the farms in the Eagle Creek valley "looked very beautiful and the plowed ground shown up as smooth, even places." Log cabins dotted Eagle Creek like outposts of humanity.

More important, the students didn't need to carry water.

"As all were thirsty they satisfied that craving to their heart's content. The sun was very warm indeed and all the walkers were perspiring freely. Some cooled their faces by washing them in the brook, while some of the boys even dipped their heads in the clear, cold mineral water."

The last time Rick Abbey led a group of hikers from Eldorado or the River to River Trail club along the Eagle Mountains or Garden of the Gods Wilderness area, he instructed them to pack in their own water.

The springs were gone.

Strip mining had destroyed the aquatic life and waters of Eagle Creek and its tributaries; mining waste and slurry ponds had deposited heavy metals, sulfates, nitrogen, and high concentrations of dissolved solids. In essence, the creek was sterile. An intensive survey of the Saline River Basin, which included Eagle Creek, pinpointed the impact of strip mining and underground coal mining. There had been nearly five hundred mine sites in the Saline River area: twenty-three permitted sites had authorization for 109 "discharges" of waste from the mines. "Water quality standards violations were common at all sites for pH, TDS, sulfate, dissolved iron, manganese, and zinc."

Strip mining had killed the healing waters that had nursed Eagle Creekers through two centuries of cholera, malaria, scarlet and yellow fevers, and small pox. Those same waters had made David Owen, the first mining surveyor to declare Eagle Creek a wonderland of coal in the 1850s, also note that the same valley was a paradise of springs.

In 1928, University of Illinois scientists began to study the impact of strip mining on the fertile farm areas, as well as the forests in the southern part of the state. Given the erosion, they found that bindweeds and grasses were the most likely vegetation to gain a foothold on the stripped lands. Pines, those "coffin pines," did better than the native trees.

In truth, slipping through a loophole in the reclamation laws, the coal companies returned only a tiny percentage of the reclaimed land to its natural state.

Outside of a few heavily subsidized recreational areas, most strip-mined forests were turned into Birkbeck's beloved grassland prairies.

Nearly eight decades later, fellow scientists at Southern Illinois University came to the same conclusion in 2006, in a special study on sustainable strip-mine reclamation published in the *International Journal of Mining, Reclamation and Environment.* Despite all of

the laws and regulations on the books, and eighty years of reclamation efforts, the bottom line remained the same: The forests and
the fertile farmlands were not coming back. The report found:

"Mined land cropped for bond release commonly becomes unmanaged grasslands. Scant mineland is returned to trees, with
survival and growth poorer than on reclaimed minelands pre-
regulation. Problems include high soil strength, poor water relations and excessive ground cover. Sustainable plant communities
have not developed."

The most realistic fallback, the report concluded, "was to turn
the stripmined areas over to recreation purposes." This fallback plan
had always been held up by the coal boosters as an achievement of
the last resort, as if turning a strip-mined wasteland into a mas-
sively government-subsidized lake, with a fraction of the species
and flora, somehow made amends for the eradication of historic
communities and diverse forests and farmlands.

Reclamation programs suffered the most from amnesia; there
was almost an eerie giddiness about the announcement of their
recreation sites that acted as if they had been handed a clean slate
and transformed it into one of God's natural wilderness areas. The
precedent had already been in the works for a century, of course.
As with the removal of Native Americans, mining reclamation programs simply airbrushed the destruction of the past from the landscape and replanted an idyllic version of the future that had
deracinated any human connection or roots to the areas, other than
the coal company's sponsoring name.

One headline cheered: THE SAHARA WOODS NEAR HARRISBURG!
A 4,000-ACRE STRIP MINE TURNED INTO A FISH AND WILDLIFE AREA!
LAKES! DEER AND TURKEY HUNTING! FISHING! FAMILY COOKOUTS!

I wondered if any boater on those lakes ever looked down into
the water, felt a tug on the oars, and imagined the arbored prayer

meetings in the forest of the early pioneer preachers and their flocks
that had once taken place in the same area below, or the plots of
corn and sorghum that had allowed the backwoods farmers to raise
their families—the centuries of stories that had been cultivated into
the land and wiped out in an afternoon of stripping, and then covered up with a pool of water.

Did it matter that you couldn't gather at the river, as the old
gospel ballad went, to baptize your child in the contaminated black
waters?

Did a fisherman ever know that for every acre that had been
reclaimed into a recreational lake, untold miles of vibrant streams
and creeks and underground watersheds had been polluted and all
aquatic life destroyed with the toxic runoff of waste from abandoned mines and leaking slurry ponds?

Strangely enough, recreational cheerleaders bent over backward
to thank the coal companies for "donating" the razed land, as if
after decades of extracting tremendous profits from the region and
leaving behind a ravaged, abandoned landscape, it was a gift to hand
back the ruins of one of the most diverse forests in the Midwest and
require the taxpayers to subsidize its reclamation.

"Like putting on red lipstick to keep you from looking at a black
eye," one farmer in Eagle Creek once told me. "And thanking the
person who had walloped you in the first place."

In Appalachia, coalfield author Harry Caudill had referred to it
as "putting lipstick on a corpse."

Not one single recreation site from a strip mine ever noted who
or what had been lost in the plunder for the coal.

If the schoolchildren from Eldorado had made the same hike
along the Eagle Mountain ridges today, they would not see beauty
on all sides. They would not dip their heads into the clear, cold mineral waters. They would not see the splendid hillside farms below.
Instead, they would see a wasteland as hopelessly razed and eroded

and blackened as the 1930s ruts that forced the region's leaders to turn to reforestation as the last resort of survival.

But, back in their classrooms, the students would read the websites of the official state Illinois Coal Revival Program taught at all schools, which disingenuously trumpets to the young readers in the abandoned coal town: "Reclamation is returning the land to the way it was or better than before mining."

As specious as this kind of coal industry propaganda may be, the real tragedy was that not one single report on strip mining in the last century ever mentioned the removal and destruction of the inhabitants—those dreaded and criminalized woodsmen—from the area.

One day, Gary and I visited Harlan Booten, the octogenarian farmer on Eagle Creek. He showed us a plastic container he had fashioned as a sort of mini-greenhouse. He had planted some seeds from a catalpa tree, which was also known as a Shawnee or Indian bean tree. Harlan pushed his finger in the dirt at the tiny sprouts, he looked at us and smiled, and then told us how he loved the heart-shaped three-lobed leaves of the tree.

I knew that Harlan, unlike the coal companies, would plant these seedlings come spring, even though the older farmer knew he would not live long enough to see them bloom one day.

"There are no more moonshiners in Eagle Creek," Harlan told us.

Harlan's well had been destroyed years ago from blasting by the Peabody coal strippers; he had to truck in his water now. Like every avid fisherman in the area, in a land of fishermen and hunters, he had to get in his truck and drive out of Eagle Creek to find a place to fish along the Ohio River.

As we left his house, I looked across the Eagle Creek valley that now buckled like the bareback slopes of unmanaged grassland; the once dense forest looked like the anonymous prairies now. We could have been in Kansas; we certainly were not in the Shawnee National Forest anymore. Not a single house or puff of smoke from a chimney was in sight.

Eagle Creek looked like a wartime battlefield cemetery now. Looked like the naked burial mounds that dotted Egypt from a prehistoric period. Looked like the gob piles that had been overgrown and hidden under weeds and wild grasses in toxic monuments to coal waste.

In the end, Birkbeck got his way, yet his ghosts had to a pay a price; the woodsmen were eradicated from the forests, but the waterways and woodlands that should have bordered those tidy English prairie farms had been poisoned and destroyed in the process.

Coal collided with the timber. And coal mining turned the waters black.

As we quietly drove across the Gap, which the mining company had misspelled on the new street sign as "GAPE" HOLLOW ROAD in an eerie admission of their indifference to destruction, I imagined the famed Eagle Creek fiddlers and musicians gathering for one of their legendary hoedowns, only this time they played the old Jean Ritchie ballad on strip mining in eastern Kentucky, "Black Waters":

> In the coming of springtime we planted our corn
> In the ending of springtime we buried our son
> In the summer come a nice man saying everything's fine
> My employer just requires a way to his mine
> Then they tore down my mountain and covered my corn
> Now the grave on the hillside's a mile deeper down
> And the man stands a talking with his hat in his hand
> While the poison black waters rise over my land
> Well I ain't got no money, not much of a home
> I own my own land, but my land's not my own
> But, if I had ten million, somewheres thereabout
> Well, I'd buy Perry county and throw them all out

And just sit down on the banks with my bait and my can
And watch the clear waters run down through my land
Well, wouldn't that be just like the old promised land?
Black waters, black waters no more in my land
Black waters, black waters no more in my land.

One-handed miner. *(Doc Horrell photograph collection, Special Collections Research Center, Morris Library, Southern Illinois University Carbondale.)*

◊

Chapter Six

THE SHORT SWIFT TIME OF CLEAN COAL ON EARTH

Dirty Coal Has Left the Building

Doubtless the end of the coal, at least as an article of a mighty commerce, will arrive within a period brief in comparison with the ages of human existence. In the history of humanity, from first to last, the few centuries through which we are now passing will stand out prominently as the coal-burning period.

—SIR ROBERT BALL, *Chicago Tribune*, 1892

In the early hours of December 11, 1811, a rumbling noise swept across the southern Illinois region like a guttural moan of thunder. Then came the shocks and cracks. The shattering shakedown of forests. Log cabins collapsed like twigs. Crevasses opened. The worst recorded earthquake in the Americas broke from its epicenter in New Madrid, Missouri, just across the Mississippi River, causing it to reverse its course. The contours of streams and creeks shifted. Over 1,800 aftershocks followed over the next several months. Black gobs of sand and water spewed from fissures like coal blasts. Within hours of the first shock, a sulfurous vapor was cast into the atmosphere, darkening the skies in a portentous display of nature's power.

221

In 2007, when I first read Dr. James Hansen's testimony on climate-change science to Congress, I thought about the earthquakes of 1811–1812. As the head of NASA's Goddard Center, Hansen had served as the Paul Revere of the climate destabilization debate when he first testified about global warming in the 1980s. Now, as the foremost climatologist in the nation, Hansen had issued our marching orders for survival.

"My approach is to try to imagine how our forefathers would have viewed our present situation and how they may have dealt with the climate-change issue. A well-informed educated public was and is a premise of our democracy; it is easy for me to imagine Benjamin Franklin presenting an objective discussion of climate change that would be thoughtfully received. Another fundamental tenet of our democracy, separation of powers within our government, with checks and balances, is brought into focus by the climate crisis."

Hansen lamented the "downplaying of evidence about global warming" and its impact on the perception of climate change. He charged: "I believe that the gap between scientific understanding of climate change and public knowledge about the status of that understanding probably is due more to the impact of special interests on public discourse, especially fossil fuel special interests, rather than political interference with climate change science."

In the spring of 2008, Hansen and a group of scientists issued an even more dire warning in *Science* magazine: "If humanity wishes to preserve a planet similar to that on which civilization developed and to which life on earth is adapted, paleoclimate evidence and ongoing climate change suggest that CO_2 will need to be reduced from its current 385 ppm to at most 350 ppm."

For author Bill McKibben, whose own book, *The End of Nature*, served as a clarion call on global warming two decades ago, the numbers provided a road map of sorts for engagement:

"Since the pre-Industrial Revolution concentration of carbon in the atmosphere was roughly 275 parts per million, scientists and policymakers focused on what would happen if that number doubled—550 was a crude and mythical red line, but politicians and economists set about trying to see if we could stop short of that point. The answer was: not easily, but it could be done.

"In the past five years, though, scientists began to worry that the planet was reacting more quickly than they had expected to the relatively small temperature increases we've already seen. The rapid melt of most glacial systems, for instance, convinced many that 450 parts per million was a more prudent target. That's what the European Union and many of the big environmental groups have been proposing in recent years, and the economic modeling makes clear that achieving it is still possible, though the chances diminish with every new coal-fired power plant.

"But the data just keep getting worse. The news this fall that Arctic sea ice was melting at an off-the-charts pace and data from Greenland suggesting that its giant ice sheet was starting to slide into the ocean make even 450 look too high. Consider: We're already at 383 parts per million, and it's knocking the planet off kilter in substantial ways."

Coal was at the top of Hansen's list for a complete change in policy. He called for a "moratorium on new coal-fired power plants until the technology for CO_2 capture and sequestration is available. The reason for this is that about a quarter of CO_2 emissions will remain in the air 'forever,' i.e., more than 500 years. As a result, I expect that it will be realized within the next decade or so, that all power plants without sequestration must be 'bull-dozed' before mid-century."

In the spring of 2009, providing testimony at a utility board meeting in Iowa that was considering the construction of a new coal-fired plant, Hansen shifted his scientific equation into a stark image:

"If we cannot stop the building of more coal-fired power plants, those coal trains will be death trains—no less gruesome than if they were boxcars headed to crematoria, loaded with irreplaceable species."

◊ ◊ ◊

EVERY TIME I heard someone talk about "clean coal," I thought about Burl Collins. I ended up spending a good part of the summer on his front porch in 1983, during my first visit to Appalachia as a young man. One day Burl rolled up his pants and showed me the leg that had been mangled in a mining accident. The scars snaked down to his ankles.

I told him about my grandfather's accident in the mine. "He had these blue marks and bits of coal buried in his face."

"Coal tattoo." Burl wheezed. "Don't let anyone ever tell you that coal is clean."

"Clean Coal." Never was there an oxymoron more insidious or more dangerous to our public health. Invoked as often by the Democrats as by the Republicans and by liberals and conservatives alike, this slogan blindsided any meaningful progress toward a sustainable energy policy.

In one of the creepiest displays of propaganda in years, the coal industry's front group—American Coalition for Clean Coal, formerly organized as Americans for Balanced Energy Choices in 2000—had spent over $55 million on public relations stunts during the election year of 2008. That year they had saturated the Democratic Party presidential convention in ads, billboards, T-shirts, and even hand-held fans for Obama's outdoor acceptance speech. They celebrated the winter holiday season with Christmas "coal" carols, rewriting religious songs with blasphemous lyrics; the venerable "Silent Night" turned into a hair-raising "Clean Coal Night" rendition.

An internal memo released by the public relations firm in charge of the "Clean Coal" campaign declared around the New Year of 2009: "Even in a communication-saturated environment we achieved, even exceeded, our wildest expectations (and we believe those of our client!)."

And perhaps they were right: The use of the "clean coal" jargon had seeped into everyday language and headlines, as if it actually meant something. Even President Obama used the two words together as if they existed as a single entity.

"Big coal is on a roll in the nation's capital," began a *Wall Street Journal* article at the time of President Obama's inauguration in 2009.

In truth, this "clean coal" charade had more to do with another campaign, back in the cold winter of 1992. The National Coal Council held a conference to come to grips with a disturbing marketing reality: "Coal has a dismal image." Coal was "maligned and misunderstood." According to the Coal Council report, "Its detractors feel contempt for coal's reputation for dirt, pollution, and human tragedy." Worse yet, "Most Americans do not think about coal at all."

The convention of coal companies grappled with these popular images: air pollution and visibility, mine safety and labor regulations, unregulated strip mining, local apprehension, global warming, acid rain, soot and particulates, acid mine drainage and abandoned mines and more subsidence, the dreaded images of coal-draped Eastern Europe, and an unfair media. Coal was destined to play the villain unless "effective actions are taken to alter the public's perception of coal."

What to do?

By 1895, newspapers ran ads for smoke-free "clean coal" in Chicago and around southern Illinois, as the boom in coal-fired plant electricity was about to launch a new era.

During the war years in the 1940s, coal boosters raved about the new process to wash, dedust, and screen coal, which when plated with oil removed various impurities. The end result was a refined "clean coal."

In 1950, schoolchildren across the Midwest put on coal industry–funded plays such as "Old King Coal Reigns Here," which taught people how to fire their furnaces correctly to have "clean coal."

In the 1960s and 1970s, "clean coal" institutes and agencies and commissions and programs popped up like industrial car-wash fronts on every corner to deal with the sulfur dioxide emissions behind acid rain.

Former Illinois governor Dan Walker, who had once proposed creating a department of coal, touted illusory "clean coal" fuel for cars ideas during the OPEC crisis in the 1970s. Walker hosted a "Clean Coal/The Energy Alternative" conference, according to his own press release, to "escalate the commitment to tap Illinois' vast coal reserves" and unveil the "first coal-powered automobile." As the nation panicked, the coal industry and its political allies announced a massive "clean coal" plan for coal-to-liquid gas conversion that would free the nation from foreign-oil dependence. Alas, the coal conversion program turned into a prohibitive boondoggle, and the grand plans disappeared into the dirty air once the OPEC crisis subsided.

As the debate has shifted in recent years to the reality of climate change and coal's indubitable role as a leading contributor of carbon dioxide emissions, the new "Clean Coal" campaign has been brought out of the closet and refashioned as a miracle cure to capture and store carbon emissions. Not that any scientist concurred that a feasible and safe implementation for a carbon capture-and-storage plan for coal-fired plants on a nationwide utility scale had any chance of happening within the next generation. A Government Accountability Office report in 2008 concluded that federal agencies had not begun to address the "full range of issues that would require resolution for commercial-scale CCS [carbon capture and storage] deployment."

In essence, over the past century "clean coal" came to represent the coal industry's response to any dirty mess it had created.

Within minutes of President Obama taking his seat in the Oval Office, the coal lobby was running TV ads featuring the president's own campaign speeches on the future of "clean coal."

Although Federal Trade Commission and Federal Communications Commission standards called for advertising claims that must be truthful and substantiated, the "clean coal" ads willfully engaged in "deception by omission" and supplanted truth with trickery. Using footage from a campaign appearance by President Obama in Virginia in September 2008, the ad replayed a line from Obama's speech that "clean coal technology is something that can make America energy independent." The ad then ran the text "Clean Coal—Creating Jobs" as it spliced another clip from the president: "And by the way, we can create five million new jobs, in clean energy technologies."

The inference: "Clean coal" will create five million new jobs.

Was that what our president said? Of course not. If anything, the tricky ad just made coal seem dirtier. Not that the Obama administration objected to the ads.

"Clean coal" was really another way of saying dirty coal needed to clean up its act.

◊ ◊ ◊

THE PROPONENTS of clean coal tended to forget about the dirty realities of extracting coal from the earth. Long before the black rock reached a coal-fired plant, it still had to be mined, cleaned and processed, trucked and transported, and then burned with coal ash. Yet, pummeled by warnings that global warming was triggering the apocalypse, many politicians and even environmentalists increasingly fell for the ruse of futuristic science that was "clean coal"—this chimera of capturing and storing carbon dioxide emissions, as if once that problem was solved, we could continue to mine coal without any worries.

Here was the hog-killing reality that a coal miner like Burl or my grandfather knew firsthand: No matter how cap-and-trade and carbon cap-and-storage schemes panned out in the distant future for coal-fired plants, strip mining and underground coal mining remained the dirtiest and most destructive ways of making energy.

Coal wasn't just dirty. Coal was still deadly and costly.

More than 104,000 miners in America died in coal mines since 1900. Every day, three coal miners die from black lung disease; over 250,000 Americans suffered and perished from black lung–related diseases in the last century; 10,000 miners, according to the National Institute for Occupational Safety and Health, died in the last decade. In the meantime, the external economic costs of the Black Lung Program tallied in tens of billions.

The injuries and deaths caused by overburdened coal trucks were innumerable.

Miners were not the only Americans to suffer from the dangerous pollutants, including mercury, that filtered into our air and water from the mines. According to the American Lung Association, 24,000 Americans die prematurely from coal-fired plant pollution each year. Another 550,000 asthma attacks, 38,000 heart attacks, and 12,000 hospital admissions are also attributed to coal-fired plants. An Environmental Protection Agency study found that long-term exposure to "particulate matter of 2.5 microns and smaller (Pm2.5)," which coal-fired plants contributed, "shortens the average lifespan by 14 years."

The external health care costs, as well, were enormous. According to a study by Princeton University, "the mean cost premium per kilowatt due to pollution from the average US coal plant is an additional 13.5 cents." Using those measurements, a follow-up study by the Environmental Affairs Board at the University of California in Santa Barbara concluded that these overlooked health care costs amounted to $268 billion for the public each year.

This was from burning coal; storing the ash had become another crisis. When 1.1 billion gallons of toxic coal-ash sludge broke past an earthen pond at a Tennessee Valley Authority (TVA) coal-fired plant a few days before Christmas in 2008, the nation was reminded that our network of Jurassic-era coal-fired plants and fly-ash ponds had become a national problem. Over 1,300 other coal-ash piles around the country slumped during those winter and spring months of freezing and flooding like calamities waiting to happen. Contrary to the image of their remote locations, hundreds of coal-fired plants and coal mounds resided within thirty minutes of half the American population.

According to Eric Schaeffer, director of the Environmental Integrity Project and a former Environmental Protection Agency official, "The industry's indiscriminate attempts to market 'clean coal' are starting to look like the tobacco industry's efforts to sell 'safe cigarettes.'" In the face of the TVA disaster, he added, "No public relations strategy can hide the dozens of plants the industry is still trying to build, using old technologies that would add more than 150 million tons of carbon dioxide to the atmosphere—the amount of global warming pollution created by more than 20 million Hummers. And it certainly can't hide the back-to-back spills of toxic coal ash at TVA's plants only weeks after the election."

An Environmental Integrity Project report found:

Between 2000 and 2006, the power industry reported depositing coal ash containing more than 124 million pounds of the following six toxic pollutants into surface impoundments: arsenic, chromium, lead, nickel, selenium, and thallium. These pollutants are present in coal ash, prone to leaching from ash into the environment and highly toxic at minute levels (parts per million or billion) to either humans or aquatic life, or both.

In May 2009, the Obama administration released a 2002 study carried out by the Environmental Protection Agency on the dangers of toxic coal-ash ponds. Held in secret during the Bush administration, the report concluded that coal ash contamination could last a hundred years. *Charleston Gazette* reporter Ken Ward noted: "The EPA estimates that 1 in 50 nearby residents could get cancer from exposure to arsenic leaking into drinking water wells from unlined waste ponds that mix ash with coal refuse. Threats are also posed by high levels of other metals, including boron, selenium and lead."

Meanwhile, millions of acres across more than twenty-five states had been subjected to explosives, torn and churned into bits by strip mining in the last 150 years. More than 60 percent of all coal mined in the United States today, in fact, came from strip mines.

As the poster child for strip mining's worst depravations, mountaintop removal in Appalachia—the radical process of literally blowing up the top of a mountain and dumping it into the valley and waterways—had erased an estimated 1.5 million acres of hardwood forests, a thousand miles of streams, and more than five hundred mountains and their surrounding historic communities—an area the size of Delaware—from the southeastern mountain range in the last two decades. Millions of pounds of explosives—the equivalent of several Hiroshima atomic bombs—were set off in Appalachian communities every week.

According to a West Virginia University study released in June 2009, "Mortality in Appalachian Coal Mining Regions: The Value of Statistical Life Lost," the negative impact of coal mining on Appalachia alone totaled $42 billion annually and resulted in thousands of premature deaths. The study concluded: "The heaviest coal mining areas of Appalachia had the poorest socioeconomic conditions. Before adjusting for covariates, the number of excess annual age-adjusted deaths in coal mining areas ranged from 3,975 to 10,923, depending on years studied and comparison group. Corresponding VSL [value of statistical life lost] estimates ranged from $18.563 billion to $84.544 billion, with a point estimate of $50.010 billion, greater than the $8.088 billion economic contribution of coal mining. After adjusting for covariates, the number of excess annual deaths in mining areas ranged from 1,736 to 2,889, and VSL costs continued to exceed the benefits of mining. Discounting VSL costs into the future resulted in excess costs relative to benefits in seven of eight conditions, with a point estimate of $41.846 billion."

Finally, nearly 15 percent of our coal production came from longwall mining, the supermechanized process of shearing the walls of an underground mine without any pillars and allowing for the mine to ultimately cave in, or, as the industry defined it, "planned subsidence." Such longwall mining under residences and farms had destroyed underground aquifers, shattered the foundations of homes, and rippled across thousands of acres of farmland in central and southern Illinois, the Midwest, and northern Appalachia like an earthquake.

Standing in front of a wonderful bulwark of old-growth forest across the Williamson County line, retired coal miner George Strunk showed me a layer of coal dust that coated the side of his house as a result of a nearby mining operation during the summer of 2008. Dust, though, had become the least of his concerns. After five agonizing years of legal battles and regulatory entanglements, Strunk's plea for statewide enforcement of mining laws had fallen wayside to the encroachment of a longwall mining operation, which was plowing under his century-old family farm and George's recently built house with irreversible damage to their foundations. The house would inevitably collapse and the Strunks would be forced to move.

"The whole county is going to sink," Strunk said, "and our dreams are going down with it."

How much more death and destruction would it take to strip coal of this bright, shining "clean" lie?

◊ ◊ ◊

DENIAL WAS ESSENTIALLY another form of abuse.

Although black lung was first diagnosed in 1831, it took until 1969 to pass federal legislation to deal with its ravages.

Although scientists recognized the deleterious impact of sulfur dioxide emissions as early as the 1860s, it took an aggressive grassroots movement to pass the Clean Air Act of 1990 to overcome the denial of acid rain, which had scorched the forests from the Appalachians to Canada.

According to a Gallup poll in 2008, the majority of Republicans did not believe global warming had begun, or that coal-fired plants generated over 40 percent of our carbon dioxide emissions. A quarter of the Democrats were on the same side of denial.

In the meantime, despite a protracted legal battle by local and environmental groups like the Sierra Club, a new 1,600-megawatt pulverized-coal plant was being built by Peabody Energy in Lively Grove, southern Illinois—the biggest in the nation. It not only stood to emit 12 million tons of greenhouse gases annually, but also sat on the edge of the New Madrid earthquake fault line.

Peabody, though, had learned its lesson. With twenty of the largest cranes in the country at work on the construction site, and a seven-hundred-foot chimney towering over the unfinished compound like a haunting battleground outpost, the world's largest coal provider had decided to refer to the nearly $4 billion coal-fired plant as the "Prairie State Energy Campus." The unveiling of the "campus" was scheduled for 2011.

The "campus" overlooked a teaching moment: The past is prologue. First, it was placed between the Wabash seismic and New Madrid fault lines, whose activity had caused what local histories in Lively Grove had referred to as the "Big Shake" in 1811. Geologists believe these active faults led to sinkholes and "flats" and altered the very waterways that would feed into the Peabody mine-mouth operation. According to a scientific report published in *Nature* magazine in 2005, conferring with a U.S. Geological Survey, there was a 90 percent chance that a magnitude 6 or 7 earthquake would occur in the New Madrid seismic area within the next fifty years.

Moreover, this coal-fired plant was also being built in the scattered ruins of a prehistoric Cahokia mounds civilization, right off Mud Creek.

The Cahokia empire ultimately collapsed in the thirteenth century as an environmental disaster, unable to sustain its urban demands and resources.

◊ ◊ ◊

IN THE FACE OF a new clean energy movement and the recognition of coal's proven role in carbon dioxide emissions and climate destabilization, Illinois clung to its past and in the last decade proposed the construction of more coal-fired plants than any other state in the union. The state's Coal Revival Program invested hundreds of millions of taxpayer dollars into "advanced technology" coal-fuel projects, including a synthetic-gas-from-coal plant. Carbondale—its name notwithstanding—the home of Southern Illinois University, had become one of the prime think tanks for "clean" coal research.

Mount Carbon stood nearby with its moniker of doom.

That was just for starters. Illinois prided itself as the rightful home of the nation's first proposal in 2007 for an experimental plant in carbon capture-and-storage technology, otherwise known as FutureGen. In many respects, FutureGen was a new form of mining, seeking to bury the captured carbon emissions from burning coal into holes sunk into underground chambers. The plan was as unreal as it sounded.

As the site manager for the virtual FutureGen plant once declared: "To fully remove the shackles from the Illinois coal industry is going to require some advances in technology to deal with greenhouse gases and global warming. We, meaning anybody who is involved in coal in this administration in Illinois, has believed that for some time. It's a question of how and when, and not if."

Abandoned in 2008 by the George W. Bush administration as a spiraling boondoggle in the billions of dollars, FutureGen had no hope of becoming a zero-emissions reality for more than a decade, if not two decades. As the Center for American Progress climate expert Joseph Romm declared in its wake, FutureGen was "either doubly pointless or doubly cynical," given that "the climate will have been destroyed irrevocably before FutureGen could have accomplished anything useful in the marketplace."

"What we do in the next two to three years will determine our future," Rajendra Pachauri, chairman of the UN's Intergovernmental Panel on Climate Change, had earlier declared in 2007. "This is the defining moment."

A report by the House Subcommittee on Investigations and Oversight of the Committee on Science and Technology in the winter of 2009 was even less generous. It likened FutureGen's relevant future to a "Humpty Dumpty that couldn't be put back together with all of the Department of Energy, press releases and Power-Point presentations." The report declared:

"In retrospect, FutureGen appears to have been nothing more than a public relations ploy for Bush Administration officials to make it appear to the public and the world that the United States was doing something to address global warming despite its refusal to ratify the Kyoto Protocol."

In truth, FutureGen was a colossal albatross devised by a funding partnership among the Department of Energy and the world's biggest extraction and utility corporations, such as Peabody Energy. Debunked by energy experts as infeasible and prohibitively expensive, it ultimately put the down payment of our coal-fired future on the taxpayers and burdened the government with potential accidents, leaks, disposal problems, and the enduring issue of mercury and carbon dioxide emissions.

In effect, the dillydallying of FutureGen politics simply allowed the coal industry to continue to mine coal at record profits, carry out the unremitting devastation of our environment and communities, and keep open the floodgates for greenhouse gases to continue their irreversible assault on our future.

Not that the Bush administration's decision in 2008 to jettison the FutureGen project had ever stopped Illinois lawmakers, such as Senator Dick Durbin, a liberal Democrat, from continuing their lobbying efforts with their former Illinois colleague President Obama. Durbin proclaimed: "We are going to work hard to make sure that the new Secretary of Energy and the new Administration make an early commitment to FutureGen so we can move forward." Durbin had called FutureGen "my longest, most difficult battle in Congress."

In truth, Illinois emerged in 2009 as the symbolic litmus test for the Obama administration's commitment to break our nation from its dependence on fossil fuels, or remain beholden to the centuries-old whims of King Coal.

Peabody Energy celebrated an eightfold increase in profits in the last quarter of 2008, in large part due to expanding international operations, and announced its intention to reopen the controversial strip mine on tribal lands on Black Mesa in Arizona. At the same time, Senator Durbin was arm-twisting Department of Energy Secretary Steven Chu and President Barack Obama into subsidizing Peabody's—and a host of the world's largest extraction companies'—FutureGen billion-dollar boondoggle.

No constituent, especially in an economically depressed area, begrudged a senator who wanted to bring home the bacon in the form of a massive jobs program. Because, when the cards were put on the table, everyone in Illinois knew that the $1.8–$2.2 billion price tag for the no-longer "zero emissions" but now "near zero-emissions" FutureGen experimental plant had nothing to do with the delusion of carbon capture and storage of carbon dioxide emissions from coal-fired plants.

It was all about 1,500 construction jobs, 150 permanent jobs, and revamping the state's collapsed coal industry.

As the *Southern Illinoisan* newspaper's editorial board wrote in the summer 2008, FutureGen "was seen as a first step in developing a market for our region's ample stores of bituminous coal."

In that same month, former vice president Al Gore unveiled his plan for "A Generational Challenge to Repower America," which called for an energy policy based on 100 percent renewable sources within a decade. Gore challenged the country to look beyond coal and other fossil fuels:

"What if we could use fuels that are not expensive, don't cause pollution and are abundantly available right here at home?

"We have such fuels. Scientists have confirmed that enough solar energy falls on the surface of the earth every 40 minutes to meet 100 percent of the entire world's energy needs for a full year. Tapping just a small portion of this solar energy could provide all of the electricity America uses.

"And enough wind power blows through the Midwest corridor every day to also meet 100 percent of US electricity demand. Geothermal energy, similarly, is capable of providing enormous supplies of electricity for America.

"The quickest, cheapest and best way to start using all this renewable energy is in the production of electricity. In fact, we can start right now using solar power, wind power and geothermal power to make electricity for our homes and businesses. . . . "

Appearing on *Meet the Press* on July 20, 2008, Gore provided a reality check to the FutureGen campaign: "We're building up CO_2 so rapidly that we're seeing the consequences scientists have long predicted. And the only way to take responsible action is to get at the heart of the problem, which is the burning of fossil fuels." Gore concluded: "The phrase clean coal is a contradiction in terms. There's no such thing as clean coal now."

Whether they recognized Gore's challenge or accepted the urgency—the reality—of climate change, the eyes of the powerful Illinois politicians were focused on the prize of "38 billion tons of coal" that sat under our feet in the Illinois coal basin. In the meantime, they were missing the green revolution of renewable energy that was sweeping the rest of the nation. The clean coal dogs barked, ultimately, as the green energy caravan moved on to other states.

Nonetheless, the powerful coal lobby and Illinois politicians behind FutureGen got their spoils; or, as one headline read, a new bridge to nowhere. On June 12, 2009, on the heels of a major *Wall Street Journal* report that we were reaching "peak coal," and revelations that the Bush administration had buried a 2002 report on the cancer risks associated with coal ash, Secretary of Energy Steven Chu made a $1.073 billion down payment on the still-illusory construction of FutureGen, "the first commercial scale, fully integrated, carbon capture and sequestration project in the country in Mattoon, Illinois."

Chu's buy-in of "clean coal," a phrase that young liberal Democrat Francis Peabody first used back in the 1890s to peddle his brand of "smoke-free" clean coal in Chicago, placed him in the company of FutureGen Industrial Alliance promoters like Peabody Energy, whose 2009 first-quarter profits "only tripled" that spring.

Given that Chu still did not know whether FutureGen's attempt to capture CO_2 emissions and bury them in the earth would be economically feasible, safe (in terms of leaks or accidents or earthquakes), or even possible within the next decade, his extraordinary commitment of $1.073 billion tax dollars essentially functioned as a down payment on a risky, if not chimerical, scheme. Chu announced: "Following the completion of the detailed cost estimate and fundraising activities, the Department of Energy and the FutureGen Alliance will make a decision either to move forward or to discontinue the project early in 2010."

In the meantime, one truth remained: FutureGen meant we would be extracting even more coal. Even in the best scenarios, according to most estimates FutureGen-type CCS plants required increased fuel needs by 25 to 40 percent.

In the "Saudi Arabia of coal," as the *Wall Street Journal* reported on June 9, 2009, the estimates for our American coal reserves—such as those 38 billions tons of coal wedged into the seams underneath Illinois—were "wildly overconfident." According to a new survey by the federal Energy Information Administration, the agency in charge of tabulating our coal reserves: "While there is almost certainly as much coal in the ground as Mr.

Warholic's Energy Information Administration believes, relatively little of it can be profitably extracted."

Unlike previous coal reserve studies, the *Wall Street Journal* noted, the study broke ground by incorporating an economic feasibility factor. "Jim Luppens, an industry veteran who is now chief of the coal-assessment project for USGS, says policy makers often confuse the total coal resource—which he describes as the 'blood, guts and feathers' number—with coal reserves, which he likens to the edible meat. 'They mix up the R-words,' he says."

"'We really can't say we're the Saudi Arabia of coal anymore,' says Brenda Pierce, head of the United States Geological Survey team that conducted the study," reported the *Wall Street Journal*.

◊ ◊ ◊

ON THE EVENING OF February 24, 2009, in his first major address to the nation, President Barack Obama spoke before a joint session of Congress in Washington, DC, and introduced the American Recovery and Reinvestment Act. Calling on the nation to "confront boldly the challenges we face, and take responsibility for our future," the president also presented a plan for a new era of clean energy in our nation.

"We are a nation that has seen promise amid peril, and claimed opportunity from ordeal. Now we must be that nation again. That is why, even as it cuts back on the programs we don't need, the budget I submit will invest in the three areas that are absolutely critical to our economic future: energy, health care, and education."

According to the president, the new vision "begins with energy."

"We know the country that harnesses the power of clean, renewable energy will lead the 21st century. And yet, it is China that has launched the largest effort in history to make their economy

energy efficient. We invented solar technology, but we've fallen behind countries like Germany and Japan in producing it. New plug-
in hybrids roll off our assembly lines, but they will run on batteries
made in Korea.

"Well, I do not accept a future where the jobs and industries of
tomorrow take root beyond our borders—and I know you don't either. It is time for America to lead again."

The Obama administration called on Congress to pass legislation to double our nation's renewable energy production in three
years, planned to invest $15 billion a year, and provided for billions
of dollars in tax incentives and investment loans for clean energy
production, and called for cap-and-trade legislation to limit carbon
emissions.

With this new era of clean energy prowess entering Washington, DC, thousands of climate-change and coalfield activists converged on the snow-swept streets of Washington, DC, a week after
Obama's breakthrough speech, to remind Capitol Hill that a growing and incredibly organized movement was ready to make this new
clean energy era a reality.

Rallied by a clarion call from the beloved farmer–poet laureate
Wendell Berry and pioneering climate-change author Bill McK-
ibben, a historic protest was staged at the symbolic meeting point of
Capitol Power Plant in Washington, DC, on March 2, 2009. The
protesters declared:

"The industry claim that there is something called 'clean coal'
is, put simply, a lie. But it's a lie told with tens of millions of dollars, which we do not have. We have our bodies, and we are willing
to use them to make our point. *We don't come to such a step lightly.*
We have written and testified and organized politically to make this
point for many years, and while in recent months there has been real
progress against new coal-fired power plants, the daily business of

providing half our electricity from coal continues unabated. It's time to make clear that we can't safely run this planet on coal at all."

As a hundred-year-old relic, the Capitol Power Plant spewed over 60,000 tons of carbon dioxide emissions annually to keep government buildings warm. Not far away, the Potomac River Plant operated on coal hauled from mountaintop-removal strip mines that had left parts of Appalachia in ruin.

And then something historic happened.

In anticipation of this first mass act of civil disobedience regarding climate change in our nation's history, on March 2, 2009, Speaker of the House Nancy Pelosi and Senate Majority Leader Harry Reid wrote to the acting architect of the Capitol asking for the end of coal use at the Capitol Power Plant as "an important demonstration of Congress' willingness to deal with the enormous challenges of global warming, energy independence and our inefficient use of finite fossil fuels."

That was one small step for Congress—the coal-fired plant would eventually convert to natural gas, another fossil fuel. But it was one giant leap for the nation, if it had truly set in motion the march to retire the oldest and dirtiest coal-fired plants at a similar pace.

In essence, the congressional leaders recognized that it was time for dirty coal to leave the building.

In the meantime, at the other 635 coal-fired plants around the country, nearly 40 percent of our nation's carbon dioxide emissions continued to flow from electricity plant silos like a silent tsunami of death.

Thanks to a growing citizens' movement, however, there were glimpses of local, state, and national resistance to more coal-fired plants. Bruce Nilles, director of the Sierra Club's "Beyond Coal" campaign, announced in the summer of 2009 that "100 coal plants have been defeated or abandoned since the beginning of the coal rush" in 2001. Nilles added: "This also comes just a week after Los Angeles Mayor Antonio Villaraigosa announced the city would end coal use by 2020, and it was announced the same day as a decision by Basin Electric Power in South Dakota to pull plans for a new coal-fired power plant."

The incoming Obama administration was not far behind the congressional leadership. In one of her first acts as head of the Environmental Protection Agency (EPA), in the spring of 2009 administrator Lisa Jackson made a significant stride toward curbing CO_2 emissions. The EPA had first put a hold on the approval of a coal-fired plant in South Dakota on January 22; in mid-February, the EPA announced its intention of more closely regulating carbon dioxide emissions from coal-fired plants. After reviewing a scientific analysis of carbon dioxide, methane, nitrous oxide, hydrofluorocarbons, perfluorocarbons, and sulfur hexafluoride, on April 17, 2009, the EPA made the extraordinary decision to propose a ruling to recognize greenhouse gases as a cause of climate change and an accountable threat to public welfare.

"This finding confirms that greenhouse gas pollution is a serious problem now and for future generations," EPA head Lisa Jackson said in a statement. "Fortunately, it follows President Obama's call for a low carbon economy and strong leadership in Congress on clean energy and climate legislation. This pollution problem has a solution—one that will create millions of green jobs and end our country's dependence on foreign oil."

"The current global atmospheric concentrations of the six greenhouse gases are now at unprecedented and record high levels compared to both the recent and distant past," the ruling says. "It is also unambiguous that the current elevated greenhouse gas concentrations are the primary result of human activities."

Responding to the president's call for a cap-and-trade bill to limit greenhouse gases, a movement took foot in Congress that spring to pass a bill that would put a cap on CO_2 emissions. The American Clean Energy and Security Act—or Waxman-Markey bill, named after the bill's authors, Democratic congressmen Henry Waxman and Edward Markey—emerged from a vigorous debate as a historic endeavor by Congress to tackle the issue of climate change on a national level. In the end, the bill called for a reduction of U.S. carbon emissions by 17 percent below 2005 levels by 2020 and 83 percent below by 2050. This was a significant step toward reversing climate change, though one which fell far short of the call by the world's scientific community to reduce greenhouse gas emissions by 25 to 40 percent from 1990 levels by 2020.

"The bill includes a raft of energy-efficiency provisions and a renewable-energy standard that will require 20% of all U.S. electricity to come from alternative sources by 2020," Bryan Walsh reported in *Time* magazine. "Chiefly, though, Waxman-Markey puts a cap on almost all of the greenhouse-gas emissions produced by the U.S. economy—everything from utilities to industry to transportation—setting a limit on how much carbon the country can produce. Industries are issued allowances each year that give them the right to emit a certain amount of carbon; they have to reduce their emissions to meet the cap, or buy allowances from other companies if they exceed the cap. (Companies will also have the option to buy carbon offsets, which involve investing in projects that reduce carbon, like tree-planting.) The idea is that cap and trade gives you more bang for your climate buck."

"We are at an extraordinary moment, with a historic opportunity to confront one of the world's most serious challenges," former vice president Al Gore announced after the bill passed in the House by a vote of 219–212 on June 25, 2009. "Our actions now will be remembered by this generation and all those to follow."

Later that day, President Obama made his own remarks on the passing of this "historic" legislation:

"The energy bill before the House will finally create a set of incentives that will spark a clean energy transformation of our economy.
It will spur the development of low-carbon sources of energy—
everything from wind, solar, and geothermal power to safe nuclear
energy and cleaner coal."

Cleaner coal.

Although virtually every environmental organization and advocate, including Gore, praised the legislation as a step in the
right direction, many critics pointed at the "watered-down" com-
promises to appease the coal lobby. "Coal-fired power plants are
the largest source of heat-trapping gases that cause global warming," Jim Tankersley reported in the *Los Angeles Times*, "but
President Obama's plan to fight climate change would result in
the nation burning more coal a decade from now than it does
today." Tankersley continued: "But to attract vital support from
congressional Democrats representing heavily coal-dependent
areas, authors of the legislation, including Rep. Henry A. Waxman (D-Beverly Hills), have made a series of concessions that
substantially soften its effect on coal—at least over the next
decade or so.

"As a result, the Environmental Protection Agency projects that
even if the emissions limits go into effect, the U.S. would use more
carbon-dioxide-heavy coal in 2020 than it did in 2005.

"That's because the bill gives utilities a financial incentive to
keep burning coal by joining the cap-and-trade system—a kind of
marketplace where polluters could reduce their emissions on paper
by buying pollution reductions created by others. These so-called
offsets, for example, could be created and sold by farmers who
planted trees, which filter carbon dioxide from the atmosphere.

"Environmental groups also say the bill could set off a boom in
the construction of new coal plants because of provisions that would
restrict legal efforts to block such projects.

"Leading Democrats—and some major conservation groups, such as the Natural Resources Defense Council—say the moves have helped attract coal-district Democrats to support the bill without undermining the plan's environmental goals.

"'We've ensured a role for coal' in the nation's energy future, said Rep. Rick Boucher (D-Va.), one of the leading coal champions in the House."

In an editorial on the day of the historic vote in the House, the *Washington Post* concurred: "But, among many, many other things, the 1,200-page bill would also devote $60 billion to making sure clean coal isn't a loser. . . . The bill essentially guarantees that carbon capture and sequestration will play a large role in America's energy mix, at first by offering coal plants that capture and sequester most of their emissions 10 years of compensation that is many times the market value of the carbon emissions they avoid—on top of the savings they would accrue by not polluting under the cap-and-trade regime. After phase one, the Environmental Protection Agency would take more control. At that point, a complicated regulatory framework would aim to reduce the subsidy for new facilities so that it covered only capital and operating costs of carbon capture and storage for 10 years.

"Uncertainties abound: What if the costs of clean coal don't come down enough to make it economical relative to other measures? If clean coal turns out to be less than its advocates envision, can Congress ever work up the political will to kill the subsidy program? Subsidies are set to phase out after 10 years of paying for operating costs, but won't powerful coal-state lawmakers fight to keep them going? And even if it does work, won't members of Congress insist that big carbon repositories not be located in their districts?

"As with the whole of Waxman-Markey, these coal provisions have real attraction in their billed potential to cut greenhouse emissions. But they also bring with them the huge risk that federal regulation will not achieve the reforms most needed to efficiently fight global warming."

As the legislative climate battle then shifted to the Senate in the fall of 2009, Sierra Club's "Beyond Coal" campaign director Bruce Nilles delivered an impassioned call to end Big Coal's free pass. Nilles wrote:

> There is some modestly good news for new plants that don't yet have their construction permit: no later than 2025, they will have to cut their carbon emissions in half. But the bad news is that the bill exempts a slug of plants permitted but not yet built, plus the huge fleet of America's oldest and dirtiest coal plants, from any requirement to clean up and cut their CO2 emissions.
>
> This is a disaster in the making, because it threatens to block the way for the U.S. to transition rapidly to a clean energy economy. These old dirty coal plants need to clean up or be retired. But the way the bill works right now, instead of encouraging investment in new industries and new plants that are subject to stringent standards, it leaves the door open to expand the old plants with no added safeguards.
>
> By "grandfathering" existing coal-fired capacity, which accounts for 44 percent of U.S. electricity generation, the bill repeats the mistakes of the 1977 Clean Air Act—mistakes that we have been paying for in the form of deadly air pollution ever since.
>
> Three decades ago, Congress exempted older plants from soot and smog limits that applied to new units, on the assumption (and promise by the industry) that they would soon be retired. Instead, the industry took full advantage of this loophole to refurbish old plants and, in some cases, to expand their capacity and emit even more of the air pollution that causes tens of thousands of asthma attacks, hospitalizations, heart attacks, and premature deaths every year. We can't repeat that mistake.

While ACES does make some good strides in reducing global warming pollution, Big Coal cannot be allowed to vent billions of tons of pollution without consequence.

To close this huge loophole and level the playing field between coal and clean energy, the Senate must insist that the oldest, dirtiest plants will retire by a date certain or meet the same pollution standards as new plants. And, until they retire or clean up, existing plants must be prohibited from expanding their capacity and increasing carbon pollution. These measures would create an incentive for industry to use cleaner technologies instead of continuing to lean on the dirty dinosaurs that generate too much of our electricity today. Finally, if Congress cannot muster the backbone to clean up the nation's oldest and most dangerous coal plants, it ought to restore the Environmental Protection Agency's authority to do so.

The stakes could not be greater. We cannot let Big Coal get away with another massive loophole to continue polluting at the same level as today for 1–2 more decades. Congress must close the coal loophole and make the coal industry slash its pollution. Our future depends on it.

◊   ◊   ◊

AS THE PROTEST at the Capitol plant in Washington, DC pointed out, the urgency of this new climate-change movement emerged from the daily burdens of those in the coalfields of the heartland, Appalachia, and the West. The scientific reality of climate change mean we all live in the coalfields now, and that we must choose clean energy options to ensure a sustainable future.

For me, that urgency forced me to return to the very place that had first awakened me to the horrific realities of strip mining: Appalachia. At Coal River Mountain in West Virginia, a new movement to transform the coalfields had reverberated across the country in 2008, with a unique proposal to break the stranglehold of Big Coal on the region.

For the first time ever, an alternative energy source to coal was being proposed, in the coalfields.

On January 16, as Barack Obama visited a wind-turbine factory in Ohio, Coal River Mountain Watch activist Rory McIlmoil snaked along a muddy mountain road in West Virginia on a similar mission. He was headed up Coal River Mountain, the last peak left untouched in a historic range ravaged by strip mining.

On a ridge, the twenty-eight-year-old activist brought his four-wheeler to a skid. He couldn't believe what he saw. Bulldozers had begun clearing the site for the first phase of a mountaintop-removal operation, a radical strip-mining process that would clear-cut 6,600 acres of hardwood trees, detonate thousands of tons of explosives, and topple the mountain range into the valley. A hundred-foot swath of forest just below the ridge lay like an open wound.

For McIlmoil, this should have been ground zero in Obama's green recovery plan. Not a future wasteland.

Less than a year earlier, McIlmoil had climbed the same ridge, looked out over a breathtaking quilt of lush forests and envisioned an industrial wind farm. With boundless enthusiasm for alternative energy, he soon began to draft a proposal. As the year wore on, he showed—even in the deep heart of coal country—that a row of whirling wind turbines could produce enough megawatts to serve the entire region, provide hundreds of clean energy jobs, and generate significantly more tax revenues than the mountaintop-removal operation.

With his ruddy good looks and the deep cracker-barrel voice of a young Johnny Cash, McIlmoil emerged as a champion of clean energy and green jobs in West Virginia, and around the country. Joining forces with the Coal River Mountain Watch, a tenacious group of coal-mining families and environmentalists, he helped launch the Coal River Wind Project as a breakthrough initiative to transcend the century-old stranglehold by the state's politically powerful coal industry.

"The benefits of economic diversification, new safe jobs, and reducing CO_2 emissions are important," McIlmoil told me. "But for most residents, if a wind farm is what it takes to save their mountain, then they're all for it.

"When I first came here," he added, "I was all about just beating Massey and driving a wind turbine into the heart of their territory. But now there are hands and hearts, lives and histories, all holding on to that turbine, and I dream of a day when one of the community folks gets to hit the 'On' switch that turns on the first turbine."

Mountaintop removal had literally brought central Appalachia to its knees; it had decimated over five hundred mountains and adjacent communities, wiped out 1,200 miles of streams, and prevented any diversified economy from emerging from the ruins. The areas of mountaintop removal, like the strip-mined lands in southern Illinois, had the highest rates of poverty in the region.

As a final wake-up call, in December 2008, West Virginians saw what happened at the Tennessee Valley power plant. A restraining wall burst and a billion gallons of coal ash poured out of a pond and deluged four hundred acres of land in six feet of sludge. The proposed mountaintop-removal site on Coal River Mountain rested beside a 6-billion-gallon toxic coal-waste sludge dam above underground mines. If the proposed blasting took place, a fracture along the sludge lake could be catastrophic for the communities downstream.

The residents asked, Why should Coal River Mountain be the last mountain to die for a mistake?

In West Virginia, turning around the two-hundred-year-old colossus King Coal is tantamount to blasphemy for many. Second only to the state of Wyoming, West Virginia produced 158 million tons of coal in 2007 and generated $338 million in severance taxes. In a nation that still depends on coal for roughly 44 percent of our electricity, West Virginia plays a key role in keeping on the lights. The Marfork Coal Company, a subsidiary of the Virginia-based Massey Energy, the largest coal company in West Virginia and fourth largest in the nation, remains a major force in the state's economy and politics.

"When you look into the climate implications of coal, you realize that Rory and the Coal River group are at the forefront of an important struggle," said filmmaker Adams Wood, who has been following the events at Coal River Mountain for a documentary, *On Coal River*. "He is taking on an enormously powerful industry and doing it with extremely limited resources and mostly on-the-job training."

McIlmoil's scrawny frame begged a David comparison to the coal companies' Goliath. He grew up in suburban Atlanta and Charlotte, North Carolina, raised by a single mother, with the dream of playing professional baseball. During his freshman year in college, an eye-opening trip to Mount St. Helens shifted his studies to earth and environmental science. After a post-college stint in Ecuador, studying environmental issues in indigenous mountain communities, McIlmoil moved to Washington, DC, to study at American University. One day, after hearing a bluegrass jam about the effects of mountaintop removal in Appalachia, he was done for. He never looked back, throwing himself into the nitty-gritty of coal-mining analysis.

"The more I learn about the state and coal economy, and the people living in the communities around the mountain, the harder I work," McIlmoil told me. "Without a strong legal and political push to upset the status quo, the whole area is doomed to destruction and contamination."

While writing his master's thesis on the impacts of mountain-top removal, McIlmoil jumped at the opportunity for an internship at the North Carolina–based Appalachian Voices, an environmental organization that dealt with mountaintop removal. Soon he began imagining how wind energy could replace coalfields. According to J. W. Randolph, the Washington legislative aide for Appalachian Voices, McIlmoil's timing was impeccable, as the anti-mountain-top-removal movement was growing.

"What the movement needed was someone who could speak to the future beyond the coal status quo," Randolph wrote in an email. "Legislators, investors and those who work on strip-mines wanted to know what's next. Rory provided that much needed voice that can explain, in excruciating detail, how much benefit we could bring to our region from wind power and alternative energy. He can show people our new Appalachian future and back it up with data three miles long."

Within months of landing at the Coal River Mountain Watch office in Whitesville, West Virginia, whose mission is to "stop the destruction of our communities and environment by mountaintop removal mining," McIlmoil's sleep-deprived passion for wind energy became famous. Hunched over permit maps and satellite imagery for hours, he meticulously traced the outlines of old strip and mountaintop removal mines on the computer and analyzed wind farm models. He slept a few nights out of each week on the couch at the office.

"His technical knowledge fits like hands folded in prayer with our local knowledge of the mountains and strip mining," declared Julia Bonds, codirector of Coal River Mountain Watch, whose long-time advocacy for social justice in the coalfields was recognized with a Goldman Environmental Prize in 2003.

McIlmoil quickly found a partner and codirector of the wind project in Lorelei Scarbro, a coal miner's widow and grandmother whose back fence literally demarcated the front lines of the impending mountaintop-removal site. Hired as a community organizer for Coal River Mountain Watch in the fall of 2007, Scarbro had seen hundreds of well-meaning young activists trundle through the area. In her eyes, what McIlmoil lacked in the department of mountain heritage, he made up for in his willingness to listen to and understand the local residents in rural Appalachia.

"What we need most are people to stand beside us, not in front of us or behind us," Scarbro said. "My husband, who spent thirty-five years as an underground union coal miner and died of black lung in 1999, is buried in the family cemetery next door. There is no price you can put on the memories we have here. We have a sense of place here that many people don't know and can't begin to understand. There are many Appalachians who know this sense of place."

By working with other energy analysts and mining experts, Scarbro and McIlmoil drew up a virtual plan for a wind farm on Coal River Mountain. As McIlmoil envisioned it, the wind potential on Coal River Mountain blew away the short-lived economic benefits of the proposed mountaintop-removal sites. In fact, coal mining provided only 11 to 13 percent of the economic activity in West Virginia. And the state could use all the economy activity it could get. In 2008, Forbes ranked West Virginia fiftieth among the best states to do business.

On less than one hundred cleared acres across the same mountain range, McIlmoil concluded that the wind farm would create two hundred local jobs during construction, and fifty permanent jobs during the life of the wind farm. In the process, it would provide 440 megawatts of electricity, or enough energy for 150,000 homes, and allow for sustainable forestry and mountain tourism projects. The plan also called for a limited amount of underground coal mining.

After the launch of the Coal River Wind website and its virtual plan for the valley in April 2008, McIlmoil and Scarbro, along with other members of the Coal River Mountain Watch, spent the next six months going to battle in the community for their plan.

At the wind partners' first local presentation in the Marsh Fork area, only five people showed up. Undaunted, the two held meetings there for several weeks and began to note that crowds kept getting bigger and more welcoming. At the third meeting, McIlmoil realized the wind plan had taken root in the community when a Massey coal miner listened quietly to the presentation, left the meeting, and then halfway from home, turned back and asked for materials to pass around.

For filmmaker Catherine Pancake, at work on a study chronicling the rise of clean energy, the Coal River Wind Project emerged as a bellwether for renewable energy. "They are showing what happens when citizens with a viable green energy plan come into brutal contact with a multibillion-dollar industry," she told me. "Rory and Lorelei are effectively killing the popular and bogus 'jobs vs. the environment' argument used ad infinitum in local and state politics."

Despite the positive receptions by several county and state agencies and public officials, McIlmoil soon learned that the vicelike grip of the coal industry locked down any governmental or legislative support for the wind farm. Marfork Coal Company simply had no intention of halting its demolition plans on Cold River Mountain. With nineteen Appalachian mining operations valued at $2.6 billion in 2008, parent company Massey had demonstrated a merciless coveting for coal at any expense.

In a haunting parallel to the Tennessee coal ash disaster, a Massey subsidiary in eastern Kentucky had been responsible for the largest coal slurry spill in 2000, leaking over 300 million gallons of toxic sludge into the area's waterways and aquifers. Massey's political connections in the Bush administration, however, resulted in a slap-on-the-wrist fine and the firing of one of the industry's veteran whistle-blowers.

Not that Massey altered its policies. By 2008, it had been forced to pay $20 million in penalties for dumping toxic mine waste into the region's waterways; before the year was out, Massey shelled out a record $4.2 million for civil and criminal fines in the deaths of two coal miners in West Virginia.

In the dog days of summer, McIlmoil and Scarbro kept the pressure on. After receiving a grant from the Sierra Club for an in-depth economic study of the wind proposal, McIlmoil and Scarbro made their first presentation to representatives of Governor Joe Manchin's office. The polite indifference from the pro-coal governor's office didn't surprise them, so they launched a national campaign.

Overwhelmed with supportive calls, national media attention, and an online petition calling for the halt of the proposed strip mine and the creation of the wind farm, which topped 10,000 signatures, the Coal River wind advocates received a special award from Co-op America (now Green America), a nonprofit group devoted to sustainability.

There was no celebration. Days earlier, McIlmoil and Scarbro had read in the local Beckley *Register-Herald* of Massey's intention to begin blasting on the first area of the strip mine. The company had taken out a classified ad in the newspaper to alert the community. The activists' concern with the bold move by Massey turned to outrage when they discovered the coal company lacked certain blasting permits and state-agency approval of the mining plan revision.

Drawing from their growing support across the country, McIlmoil and Scarbro managed to flood Governor Manchin's and state agency offices with thousands of emails and phone calls, resulting in a suspension of any blasting. All eyes were now on the governor to reconsider the economic ramifications of mountaintop removal, and form a commission for renewable energy sources, such as the Coal River wind proposal. It didn't happen. "It would be inappropriate for the governor to interfere in the regulatory process," Manchin's communications director, Lara Ramsburg, said in an email statement to the *Charleston Gazette.*

On November 20, at the same time President Obama announced a forthcoming economic recovery package and clean-energy job programs, the West Virginia Department of Environmental Protection, with the approval of Manchin, granted Massey the surface-mining permit revision for the initial part of their proposed mountaintop removal of Coal River Mountain.

"Once the demolition begins," Scarbro declared at a local hearing, "it will be very difficult to stop it, and once the mountain is removed, it won't grow back. The potential for wind energy and good jobs will be gone forever, along with our renewable water and forest resources."

Disheartened but not stymied by the news, the Coal River wind advocates released the results of a four-month economic study by West Virginia–based Downstream Strategies. According to the report, the first of its kind in coal country, the proposed wind farm on Coal River Mountain, consisting of 164 wind turbines and generating 328 megawatts of electricity, would provide over $1.74 million in annual property taxes to Raleigh County. By comparison, the coal severance taxes related to the mountaintop-removal mining would provide the county with only $36,000 per year. More so, it noted that the coal reserves in the area would only last seventeen years at best, compared to the eternal supply of wind.

As a reminder of the disastrous loopholes of the Surface Mining Control and Reclamation Act (SMCRA) of 1977, a Fourth U.S. Circuit Court overturned a lower federal court decision in January 2009, limiting greater environmental review of mountaintop-removal actions by coal companies. The circuit court's ruling effectively ushered in scores of mining permits through the gates of the U.S. Army Corps of Engineers—mountaintop removal now had no barriers. A surface mining board turned down the last appeals by Rory and his organization to stop the blasting on Coal River Mountain.

The fate of Coal River Mountain now rested in the hands of the Obama administration, or the passing of federal legislation for a clean water protection act to prohibit the dumping of mining waste—a key component of mountaintop removal—into waterways.

But it was not just the fate of Coal River Mountain at play—this was truly ground zero, like Eagle Creek had been in the past, of the coal industry's two-hundred-year grip on our nation that allowed it to plunder the coal at any cost. Even our future.

How seriously the nation appreciated the vanguard role of clean-energy advocates like McIlmoil would ultimately decide whether Coal River Mountain was to be the first mountain to resist mountaintop removal in Appalachia.

Or the 501st mountain to be eliminated from American maps.

With the incoming Obama administration in the spring of 2009, hopes were raised in the coalfields when the Environmental Protection Agency announced its intent in February to conduct greater scrutiny of mountaintop-removal permits. The reaction from the Big Coal lobby in Washington, DC, and from the various union and state officials from the coalfields, however, rattled the corridors in the new administration. Within a month, the EPA responded to the repeated questioning of Congressman Nick Rahall, a Democrat from West Virginia, on the status of the mountaintop-removal permits. In a stunning blow to coalfield residents and environmentalists, the EPA announced through a curious letter to Rahall in April that it had cleared forty-two out of forty-eight mining permits.

Acting Assistant Administrator Michael H. Shapiro wrote: "I understand the importance of coal mining in Appalachia for jobs, the economy and meeting the nation's energy needs. I also want to emphasize the need to ensure that coal mining is conducted in a manner that is fully consistent with the requirements of the [Clean Water Act], the Surface Mining Control and Reclamation Act, the National Environmental Policy Act and other applicable federal laws."

A few years earlier, at an oversight hearing of the U.S. House Committee on Natural Resource (on the thirtieth anniversary of the SMCRA), Joe Lovett, executive director of the Appalachian Center for the Economy and the Environment, had testified: "When Congress passed the Surface Mining Control and Reclamation Act in 1977, it thought that it was enacting a law to protect the environment and citizens of the region. OSM has used, and has allowed the states to use, the Act as a perverse tool to justify the very harm that Congress sought to prevent. The Members of Congress who voted to pass the Act in 1977 could not have imagined the cumulative destruction that would be visited on our region by the complete failure of the regulators to enforce the Act."

On June 11, 2009, the Obama administration announced its plan to take "unprecedented steps to reduce environmental impacts of mountaintop coal mining" and "to strengthen oversight and regulation, minimize adverse environmental consequences of mountaintop coal mining."

In truth, only two days after the U.S. Supreme Court reprimanded the West Virginia Supreme Court's Big Coal–financed justices for making conflict-of-interest decisions—and one day after the West Virginia Supreme Court upheld a decision to build an additional toxic coal silo on an elementary school playground in Coal River Valley, which sat under a 2.8-billion-gallon toxic coal-sludge pond jeopardized by mountaintop-removal blasting—the Obama administration had decided to "regulate" the crime of mountaintop removal, not abolish it as coalfield residents had requested.

A *Washington Post* editorial cut to the chase of the regulatory banter with its headline OBAMA IS RIGHT TO ALLOW MOUNTAINTOP REMOVAL MINING.

All well-meaning intentions aside, if the Obama administration truly wanted to "enforce" mountaintop removal regulations and protect American watersheds, drinking water, and communities from catastrophic flooding and toxic blasting, it would have simply worked to reverse a 2002 Bush administration manipulation of the Clean Water Act and restore the original definition of "fill" material to no longer include mining waste.

Instead, in an extraordinary move, the Obama administration disregarded a thirty-eight-year rap sheet of crimes of pollution, harassment, and forced removal of some of our nation's oldest and most historic communities—including the destruction of over hundreds of mountains and deciduous hardwood forests in Appalachia's carbon sink. Its intent to "minimize the adverse environmental consequences" of mountaintop removal reminded coalfield residents of the disastrous 1977 betrayal that granted federal sanctioning of mountaintop removal in the first place.

Back in the spring of 1977, President Carter had addressed the American people in a televised speech on his proposed energy policy. Carter pulled no punches. He declared: "We must look back in history to understand our energy problem."

On August 3, 1977, surrounded in the White House Rose Garden by beleaguered coalfield residents and environmentalists who had waged a ten-year campaign to abolish strip mining, President Carter signed the Surface Mining Control and Reclamation Act with great fanfare. President Carter may have attempted to put on a good face, but, according to the *New York Times*, he admitted to the three hundred guests: "In many ways, this has been a disappointing effort." Calling it a "watered down" bill, Carter added,

"I'm not completely satisfied with the legislation. I would prefer to have a stricter strip mining bill."

"The President's other main objection to the bill," wrote the *New York Times*, "is that it allows the mining companies to cut off the tops of Appalachian mountains to reach entire seams of coal."

Three decades later, President Carter's worst fears had been realized.

"I am not here as a public official, but as a citizen of a troubled world who finds hope in a growing consensus that the generally accepted goals of society are peace, freedom, human rights, environmental quality, the alleviation of suffering, and the rule of law," Carter said in his 2002 Nobel Peace Prize lecture.

In the name of peace, human rights, environmental quality, the alleviation of suffering, and the rule of law, coalfield residents were left wondering when this crime of mountaintop removal would end.

◊ ◊ ◊

"HOW LONG CAN the earth sustain life," wondered an editorial in the *Chicago Daily Tribune* in 1892, if we depend on the "wonderful power of coal?" The editorial lambasted Americans for our lack of vision and sense of energy conservation, and our need to "invent appliances to exhaust with ever greater rapidity the hoard of coal."

A century later, this ultimate reckoning had come: From the coal-fired plants fed by our insatiable demand for coal, the silent volcanoes of climate destabilization would continue to erupt until our nation decided to make another choice and bring an end to the coal-burning period.

Garden of the Gods. *(Photo by Charles F. Hammond.)*

◊

Epilogue

THE LAST EAGLE CREEKERS

These hills impound
Archaic silence
Much as misers with their gold
They do not waste it on the world

—GARY DENEAL,
Blue Hills, Blue Shadows

Tenney Tarlton was bare chested the first time I met him, sitting at the counter of his kitchen, checking his Peabody Energy stock on a laptop. Square jawed, his hair thinning, Tenney was somewhere in his early sixties, but he always hustled his short muscular frame in a way that made him seem younger, like an ambitious young man still intent on working overtime to move himself up the ladder.

As a young boy growing up on a hardscrabble farm in Eagle Creek, Tenney had promised himself to become a millionaire by the age of thirty-seven. He had not inherited that drive from his father, "Doc" Tarlton, who earned his nickname as a brilliant mechanic who could fix any machine, but from his grandmother, Elma Brinkley, a no-nonsense backwoods matriarch who woke up everyone at dawn and had the extended family doing chores on the farm before breakfast. Watching as she labored in the fields into her later years,

Tenney learned quickly that, with a fierce resilience, the women coaxed wonders from the beleaguered soils of Eagle Creek.

Another coal miner once described Tenney as "always running on high tram" during their shifts in an underground mine near McLeansboro, where Tenney had worked as a contractor, bricklayer, and carpenter. In the minds of his coworkers, he shattered the hillbilly stereotype of Eagle Creek, where the country boys were thought to be too lazy to scratch, too indolent to keep a job.

"Tenney acted like he owned the mine," another coal miner told me. "He worked harder than anyone else."

Tenney's drive raised eyebrows, and then they watched him walk off his shift in the coal mines, change his clothes, and work another shift as an independent contractor and carpenter in Eldorado, where he had moved and was married in the 1960s. At one point, Tenney had so many customers lined up that he had to sneak into his beautiful house on Main Street through a back door to avoid getting pigeonholed for a new job. In effect, Tenney lived a double life, working around the clock to achieve his millionaire dream.

In the late 1970s, Tenney purchased five acres of land near his parents in Eagle Creek, just across the ridge from our old homeplace near Colbert Hill.

The millionaire plan, however, hit a brick wall. Tenney's marriage crashed. His wife twisted the child custody suit into increasingly higher payments; he suddenly found himself working overtime to pay off bills and expenses he had never known about.

One day in the darkness of a room in a coal mine, sleep deprived and exhausted to the point of collapse, Tenney broke down and dropped into the coal dust. He couldn't take it anymore. He let go of the millionaire dream. He handed over his life to the Lord. And then he walked out of the mine, drove out to his shack on his five acres in the woods of Eagle Creek, and took refuge on his hill for the next three years.

"I realized when I was on the hill, out in the country, I was finally free," Tenney told me, putting on his shirt. "I became a new person, a complete person again."

It was a hot summer day, when the humidity clung like chiggers, but that had not kept Tenney's second wife, Sharon, from crossing the road to our family cemetery, mounting her power mower, and shaving the grass between the lanes of slumped tombstones under a canopy of towering oaks and hickories and dogwoods. With short-cropped hair, Sharon smiled behind her glasses. In her fifties, she looked as fit and youthful as Tenney. She seemed delighted to be outside. She walked as if untroubled by the heat, or the back-breaking work of trimming the weeds along the edges of the sloping cemetery fence.

With her own marriage on the rocks, she met Tenney one day in Eldorado, where she had found herself in a similar bind of treadmill exhaustion, running one of the town's most successful hair salons. When they started dating, Tenney would whisk her out to Eagle Creek under the cover of darkness, as if to keep his peaceful refuge in the hills a secret.

That secret didn't last long. Sharon fell in love, not only with Tenney, but also with the freedom of the Eagle Creek hills, and soon the two decided to start the second act of their lives in the hollow. They shed their dependency on the amenities of town life and plunged themselves into a lifestyle of self-reliance, maintaining a huge garden, canning their own food, attempting to live as simply as possible in the freedom of the countryside. As part of the plan, though, Tenney occasionally commuted to carpentry or brickwork jobs in the mines.

If we looked deep enough into the woodpile of our families, of course, I was related somehow to Tenney: some distantly related cousin. The Tarltons had been part of the area for nearly two hundred years. Our families had intermarried at various points, my grandfather's sister being the last Tarlton in our immediate family. Another Tarlton family actually ran one of the first taverns in Shawneetown in 1819.

Like my mom and Uncle Richard, Tenney recalled one of our forefathers' traditions: making sorghum molasses from sugar cane at a horse-drawn mill.

Without electricity or running water, our families had scraped a way of life from the hills: self-sufficient, but also aware of the limitations of the Eagle Creek soils and woods. They canned food from the garden, lived off the farm, made their clothes, quilts, toys, and soap.

Tenney and Sharon's house, though, situated across from the Colbert cemetery, was a temporary place Tenney had built a few years ago. He had also rebuilt the historic Bethel Church next to this new home, which had been torn down for the nearby strip mine.

Within a few years of moving down to Eagle Creek, Sharon and Tenney had to confront the increasing traffic of coal trucks. As a miner himself, Tenney recognized the violations of blasting, dusting, and maintenance and attempted to appeal to the coal companies on a friendly basis. It had no impact.

By the time our old homeplace had been blasted into a 200-foot canyon, and the seams of coal removed, Tenney and Sharon found themselves living in a virtual war zone. Coal dust covered their house like an extra coat of paint. Their chandeliers shook like chimes every time a 1,600- to 2,000-pound round of ammonium nitrate–fuel oil (ANFO) explosive detonated within a football field's distance from their house.

They watched as, one by one, their neighbors surrendered to the encroaching plans of the various coal companies, which had divvied up the entire Eagle Creek valley like a chessboard. Tenney and Sharon, and his family, were the last holdouts. When a rock the

size of a bowling ball smashed through the ceiling of Tenney's sister's trailer next door, Tenney marched out of the house and confronted the coal companies.

Problem was, this was all legal. The blast designs had received
stamped approval from the state's Office of Mines and Minerals. A
2,500-pound ANFO blast less than a thousand feet from a residence
was written up as an "insignificant" revision to a permit; the mine
blaster was granted the right to use his own judgment to determine
if residents were at risk or needed to be removed. All the preblast-
ing surveys had taken place; all the papers were in order.

So, Tenney explained his compromise. He went to the same coal
company that had badgered his parents until their deaths and cut a
deal. Tenney agreed to sell off part of his family's land and his own
acreage in exchange for a ridge top lot, where he knew the contours
of a fault line would prevent any mining from ever taking place.
As part of the deal, Tenney and Sharon temporarily relocated across
from Colbert cemetery, where they simply planned to wait out the
strip-mining and reclamation operations.

They put their lives and dreams on hold for six years, at least.

In 2003, they received a slight reprieve. The strip mining
stopped not because of any environmental regulations but, according to the coal company's report, "due to coal market conditions and
lack of adequate sales." This was a reminder that the miners' lost
jobs took a backseat to coal company stock prices.

"This has nothing to do with coal," Tenney lectured me one
day. "This is about greed. The same thing would have happened if
there was silver or lead or just timber in the area. It's not about coal
mining, but how far a company is willing to go to get it."

One day, Tenney had me hop into his truck, and we wound up
the back road to his hillside property. A gorgeous stand of the
Shawnee forest jutted off the ridge like a single column of
marchers. He had already planted a dozen or so fruit trees and had

set up several boxes of honeybees. As one of the best contractors and carpenters in the region, Tenney was slowly building his own dream home on the edge of a hill that overlooked a pristine pond. He had been exploring various possibilities to live off the grid; he had set up a modern woodstove to heat the house.

The rest of Eagle Creek terrain rolled like high chaparral grasslands until it climbed the foothills of the Eagle Mountains. On the edge of Colbert Hill, the Shawnee forests may have been destroyed for the most part, but the blue hills in the distance rolled like a fortress that forever kept Eagle Creek enclosed within its own kingdom.

Tenney smiled. He just watched.

For me, Tenney and Sharon represented the last generation of the frontier people on Eagle Creek—truly, the last Eagle Creekers. Their decision to return to the hills reminded me of my uncle Richard's letter, written to my mother at the time of the strip-mining of our homeplace: "A part of our lives now exists only in our minds and will be completely erased when we die; as if it never existed."

Now I knew that part of their lives hadn't died; it had refused to be erased.

Far from any sense of nostalgia, Tenney and Sharon were intent on keeping the Eagle Creek heritage alive, as fractured and decimated and depopulated as it was, precisely because they found the hills and hollows to be the only sustainable place to live. They seemed truly in love, and truly happy.

"One day there won't be any more coal," Tenney said. "But we'll still be here."

And so would Eagle Creek. Forever changed of course, but forever waiting to be discovered again.

COALFIELD AND CLIMATE CHANGE
RESOURCES AND ORGANIZATIONS

Organizations

Alliance for Appalachia: www.theallianceforappalachia.org
Appalachian Voices: www.appvoices.org
Black Mesa Water Coalition: www.blackmesawatercoalition.org
Citizens Coal Council: www.citizenscoalcouncil.org
Coal River Mountain Watch: www.crmw.net
Energy Action Coalition: www.energyactioncoalition.org
Greenpeace: www.greenpeace.org
Heartwood Council: www.heartwood.org
Illinois Sierra Club: www.illinois.sierraclub.org
Kentuckians for the Commonwealth: www.kftc.org
Mountain Justice: www.mountainjustice.org
Natural Resource Defense Council: www.nrdc.org
Ohio Citizens: www.ohiocitizens.org
Ohio Valley Environmental Coalition: www.ohvec.org
1Sky: www.1sky.org
Orion Grassroots Network: www.oriongrassroots.org
Rainforest Action Network: www.ran.org
Sierra Club Beyond Coal Campaign: www.sierraclub.org/coal/
Shawnee Sierra Club: www.illinois.sierraclub.org/shawnee/
350: www.350.org
United Mine Workers of America: www.umwa.org

Additional Websites and Blogs

Burning the Future: www.burningthefuture.org/
Climate Ground Zero: www.climategroundzero.org

Climate Progress: www.climateprogress.org
Coal Tattoo: http://blogs.wvgazette.com/coaltattoo/
Coal Is Dirty: www.coal-is-dirty.com
Coal Country: http://www.sierraclub.org/scp/coalcountry.aspx
Daily Yonder: www.dailyyonder.com
Grist Environmental News: www.grist.org
Illinois Mine Wars: www.minewars.org
NY Times Dot Earth: http://dotearth.blogs.nytimes.com/
OHVEC Daily News: www.ohvec.org
On Coal River: www.oncoalriver.org

BIBLIOGRAPHY

My work owes a tremendous debt to *Springhouse* magazine and its stable of writers and chroniclers of southern Illinois's history and ways over the past twenty-five years.

I also drew on news reports and stories from various regional newspapers, magazines, and historical and genealogical society newsletters, including:

Chicago Daily Tribune, 1872–1963
Daily Register, 1917–present
Egyptian Key
Gallatin Democrat (Shawneetown)
Illinois Republican (Shawneetown)
Illinois South, 1979–1990
Journal of the Illinois State Historical Society
St. Louis Post-Dispatch
Saga of Southern Illinois
Saline County Register, 1898–1905
Southern Illinois (Shawneetown)

Prologue

Abbey, Edward. "Shadows from the Big Woods." *The Journey Home*. New York: Plume, 1991.
Biggers, Jeff. "Down in Eagle Creek." Public Radio International's *Savvy Traveler*, March 1, 2001.
Dickens, Charles. *Martin Chuzzlewit*. New York: Penguin, 2000.

Introduction

News reports on President Barack Obama and his statements on the "Saudi Arabia of coal" and "clean coal" abound. I drew primarily from news reports made during the 2008 presidential campaign and Obama's nascent administration in 2009.

Angle, Paul. *Bloody Williamson: A Chapter in American Lawlessness.* New York: Knopf, 1952.

Bauerlein, Monika. "Every Breath You Take." *Sierra Magazine*, July 2006.

"Feds Blame Mine Operator for Fatal Collapse." CNN, July 24, 2008.

Illinois Coal Fact Sheet. Illinois Department of Commerce and Economic Opportunity—Coal, http://www.commerce.state.il.us/NR/rdonlyres/ED8AD879–93FE-47E4–8EE9-E30069A721FA/0/Illinoiscoalfacts Dec2006.pdf.

Illinois Coal Industry. Report of the Office of Coal Development, June 2006, http://www.commerce.state.il.us/NR/rdonlyres/1C724CC6-E056 -41A4-836C-1CC8A74BF710/0/TheIllinoisCoalIndustryJune2006.pdf.

Kalisch, Philip. "Death Down Below: Coal Mine Disasters in Three Illinois Counties, 1904–1962." *Journal of the Illinois State Historical Society* 65, no. 1 (Spring 1972).

MacGillis, Alec, and Steven Mufson. "Coal Fuels a Debate Over Obama." *Washington Post*, Sunday, June 24, 2007.

Monforton, Celeste. "Illinois's Subsidy to Coal's Bob Murray, Wilbur Ross and Exxon." October 18, 2007, www.pumphandle.wordpress/2007/10/18/illinoiss-subsidy-to-coals-bob-murray-wilbur-ross-and-exxon/.

Obama, Barack. *Audacity of Hope.* New York: Crown, 2006.

O'Brien, Darcy. *Murder in Little Egypt.* Philadelphia: Running Press, 2002.

Testa, Dan. "Obama, Clinton Make Closing Arguments as Montana Primary Looms." *Flathead Beacon*, May 28, 2008.

"U.S. Will Respect Trade Pacts 'as We Always Have': Obama." CBC News, February 17, 2009.

Chapter One

Caudill, Harry. *Night Comes to the Cumberlands.* Ashland: Jesse Stuart Foundation, 2001.

"Deforestation Causes Global Warming." Food and Agricultural Organization, http://www.fao.org/newsroom/en/news/2006/1000385/index.html.

DeNeal, Gary. *A Knight of Another Sort: Prohibition Days and Charlie Birger.* Carbondale: Southern Illinois University Press, 1998.

Goodell, Jeff. *Big Coal: The Dirty Secret Behind America's Energy Future.* Boston: Houghton Mifflin, 2006.

Roth, Philip. "The Most Original Book of the Season." *New York Times*, November 30, 1980.

Still, James. "Let This Hill Rest." *From the Mountain, From the Valley.* University of Kentucky Press, 2005.

West, Don, Jeff Biggers, and George Brosi. *No Lonesome Road: Selected Prose and Poems of Don West*. Urbana: University of Illinois Press, 2005.

Wilder, Thornton. *The Eighth Day*. New York: HarperCollins, 2007.

Chapter Two

Allen, John. *It Happened in Southern Illinois*. Johnson City, AERP Publisher, 1968.

———. *Legends and Lore of Southern Illinois*. Carbondale: Southern Illinois University Press, 1963.

Blackman, W. S. *The Boy of Battle Ford and the Man*. (city of pub. unknown) McDowell Publications, 1978.

Boggess, Arthur. *The Settlement of Illinois, 1778–1830*. Chicago Historical Society, 1908.

Bush, Barney. *Inherit the Blood*. New York: Thunder's Mouth Press, 1985.

———. *My Horse and a Jukebox*. Los Angeles: American Indian Studies Center, University of California, 1979.

———. *Petrogylphs*. Greenfield Center, NY: Greenfield Review Press, 1982.

———. *Remake of the American Dream*. Nato CD, 1992.

Calloway, Colin. *Shawnees and the War for America*. New York: Viking, 2007.

Chappell, Sally K. *Cahokia, Mirror of the Cosmos*. Chicago: University of Chicago Press, 2002.

DeNeal, Gary. *Butterfly, Flutter By*. Philadelphia: Dorrance and Company, 1963.

Edmunds, R. David. *Tecumseh and the Quest for Indian Leadership*. New York: Little, Brown and Co., 1984.

Fadler, T. P. *Memoirs of a French Village: A Chronicle of Old Prairie du Rocher, 1772–1972*. Publisher unknown, 1972.

Ferguson, Gillum. "Cache River Massacre in Context." *Springhouse* 21, no. 1 (2004).

Hall, James. *Letters from the West, 1828*. London: Henry Colburn, 1828.

Hall, Ruby Franklin. *Stories of the Lamb Communities*. Hardin County, IL, n.d.

Hardin County Illinois. Elizabethtown, IL: Hardin County Historical and Genealogical Society, 1987.

Hart, L. K. "Against Hauntology and Historicide." http://julieshiels.com.au/street/Hauntology-and-Historicide.pdf.

Havighurst, Walter. *Upper Mississippi*. New York: Farrar and Rinehart, 1937.

Hill, Jonathan, ed. *History, Power and Identity*. Iowa City: University of Iowa Press, 1996.

History of Gallatin, Saline, Hamilton, Franklin and William Counties, Illinois. Chicago: Good Speed Publishing Co., 1887.

LaDuke, Winona. *All Our Relations.* Boston: South End Press, 1999.

Lewis, Meredith. *The Journals of Captain Merideth Lewis and Sergeant John Ordway.* Madison: Wisconsin Historical Society, 1916.

Mann, Charles. *1491.* New York: Knopf, 2006.

Mayor, Adrienne. *Fossil Legends of the First Americans.* Princeton: Princeton University Press, 2005.

McDermott, J. F. "Conference on the French in the Mississippi River Valley." Collection of papers presented at Southern Illinois University, Edwardsville, 1967, Am-Ill Z285851.

———. "The French in the Mississippi Valley." Papers presented at the 1964 St. Louis conference, Am-Ill Z285824.

Metzger, John. "The Gallatin County Saline and Slavery in Illinois." Master's thesis, Southern Illinois University, 1971.

Miller, Otis. "Indian-White Relations in the Illinois Country, 1789–1818." PhD diss., St. Louis University, 1972.

Morgan, Robert. *Boone: A Biography.* Chapel Hill: Algonquin Press, 2007.

Moyers, William Nelson. "A Story of Southern Illinois." *Journal of the Illinois Historical Society,* 1931.

Musgrave, Jon. *Slaves. Salt, Sex and Mr. Crenshaw.* Marion: Illinois History, 2004.

Owen, David. "Report of the President and Directors to the Stock Holders of the Saline Coal and Manufacturing Company, with a Geological Report." Wrightson and Co. Printers, 1855.

Owens, Robert. *Mr. Jefferson's Hammer.* Norman: University of Oklahoma Press, 2007.

Ragsdale, Fred. *The Contract Tree.* Chicago: Adams Press, 1993.

Reynalds, Gerald. *Woodpecker War.* Florida: Beck Printing, 1972.

"River to River Trail Guide." River to River Trail Society, Harrisburg, IL, 1995.

Robertson, Lindsay G. *Conquest by Law.* Oxford: Oxford University Press, 2005.

Russell, Herb. "Indian Hater." *Springhouse* 21, no. 1 (2004).

Searles, William. "Crossing Southern Illinois in 1821" *Springhouse* 21, no. 1 (2004).

Sellers, George E. "Aboriginal Pottery of the Salt Springs." *Popular Science Monthly* 11, 1877.

Smith, George. *History of Illinois and Her People.* Chicago: American History Society, 1927.

Sugden, John. *Tecumseh.* New York: Henry Holt, 1997.

Swann, Brian, ed. *I Tell You Now*. Lincoln: University of Nebraska Press, 1989.

Wainwright, Nicholas. *George Croghan Wilderness Diplomat*. Chapel Hill: University of North Carolina Press, 1959.

Warren, Stephen. *The Shawnees and Their Neighbors*. Urbana: University of Illinois Press, 2005.

Chapter Three

Adams, Sean. *Old Dominion, Industrial Commonwealth*. Baltimore: John Hopkins University Press, 2004.

Ashe, Thomas. *Travels in America*. London: Richard Phillips, 1808.

Birkbeck, Morris. "An Appeal to the People of Illinois on the Question of a Convention." *Magazine of History* 131, vol. 33 (1927).

Blackmore, J. "African Americans and Race Relations in Gallatin County, Illinois from the 18th Century to 1870." PhD diss., Northern Illinois University, 1996.

Bonnell, Clarence, ed. *Saline County: A Century of History, 1847–1947*. Harrisburg, IL: Saline County Historical Society, 1947.

Brown, William H. *An Historical Sketch of the Early Movement in Illinois for the Legalization of Slavery*. Chicago: Fergus Print, 1876.

Carter, Clarence. *The Territorial Papers of the United States, Volume 17*. National Archives and Records Services, 1950.

Coleman, McAlister. *Men and Coal*. New York: Arno/New York Times, 1969.

Cornelius, James. *John Hart Crenshaw and Hickory Hill: Final Report for the Historic Sites Division, Illinois Historic Preservation Agency*. Springfield: Illinois Historic Preservation Agency, 2002.

Database of Servitude and Emancipation Records (1722–1863). Illinois State Archives, http://www.sos.state.il.us/departments/archives/servant.html.

Dillon, Merton L. "Sources of Early Antislavery Thought in Illinois." *Illinois State Historical Society Journal* 50, 1957.

———. "John Mason Peck: A Study of Historical Rationalization." *Illinois State Historical Society Journal* 50 (1957).

Edstrom, James. "A Mighty Contest: The Jefferson-Lemen Compact Reevaluated." *Journal of the Illinois State Historical Society* 97 (Autumn 2004).

Edwards, Ninian, and William Wirt. *History of Illinois, from 1778 to 1833; and Life and Times of Ninian Edwards*. Springfield: Illinois State Journal Co., 1870.

Ferguson, Gillum. "Harrisburg's Founding Fathers." *Springhouse* 25, no. 1 (2008).

Ford, Thomas. *A History of Illinois From Its Commencement as a State in 1818 to 1847*. Urbana: University of Illinois Press, 1995.

"Gallatin Salines." correspondence, 1818–1828. Illinois State Archives, Springfield, IL.

Harrelson, Ralph. "Emancipation Baptist Churches West of the Third Principal Meridian in the Saline Association." *Springhouse*, 1987.

Harris, Dwight. *History of Negro Servitude in Illinois*. Chicago: McClurg and Co., 1904.

History of Gallatin, Saline, Hamilton, Franklin and William Counties, Illinois. Chicago: Good Speed Publishing Co., 1887.

Lemen, Joseph B. "The Jefferson-Lemen Anti-Slavery Pact." Transactions of the Illinois State Historical Society, Springfield, IL, 1908.

Levin, Pat U. "Kinships, Communities, and Conflicts: Bethel Creek Primitive Baptist Church." PhD diss., University of Pennsylvania, 1995.

Lewis, Ronald L. *Coal, Iron and Slaves*. Westport: Greenwood Press, 1979.

Martin, Terrance, and Mary McCorvie. "Archaeological Investigations at the Fair View Farm Site: A Historic Farmstead in the Shawnee Hills of Southern Illinois." Cultural Resources Management Report No. 135, American Resources Group, Carbondale, IL, 1989.

McRoberts, Flynn. "Owner Leases Property with a Warning; Slave Secrets Buried in Historical Cemetery." *Chicago Tribune*, January 13, 2003.

Metzger, John. "The Gallatin County Saline and Slavery in Illinois." Master's thesis, Southern Illinois University, 1971.

Micheaux, Oscar. *The Homesteader*. Sioux City: Western Book Supply Publishers, 1917.

Morgan, Lynda. *Emancipation in Virginia's Tobacco Belt*. Athens: University of Georgia Press, 1992.

Musgrave, Jon. *Egyptian Tales of Southern Illinois, Vol. 2*. Marion: IllinoisHistory.com, 2002.

———. *Handbook of Old Gallatin County and Southeastern Illinois*. Marion: Illinoishistory.com, 2002.

———. *Slaves, Salt, Sex and Mr. Crenshaw*. Marion: Illinois History, 2004.

Nelson, Ronald. "Elder Stephen Stilley Dedication." Unpublished manuscript, Ron Nelson personal papers.

———, ed. *History of the Regular Baptists of Southern Illinois 1877*. Elizabethtown, IL: Nelson Pub., 1984.

———. "History of The Saline District Friends to Humanity Association of Emancipation Baptist Churches Principally of Southeastern Illinois." *Springhouse* 12, no. 2 (1995).

———. *The Life and Works of William Rondeau: "The Old Backwoods Preacher."* Hartford, KY: McDowell Publications, 1979.

————, ed. *The Roar of God's Thunder: An Autobiography, John Blanchard.* Elizabethtown, IL, 1978.

————. "Stilleys of Eagle Mountain." Unpublished manuscript, 1983.

Nelson, Ronald, and Doris Nelson. *History of Liberty Baptist Church, Saline County, IL, 1832–1996.* Utica, KY: McDowell Publications, 1996.

Quaffed, Milo. *Pictures of Illinois One Hundred Years Ago.* Chicago: R. R. Donnelley and Sons, 1918.

Peck, John M. *Memoir of John M. Peck.* Carbondale: Southern Illinois University Press, 1965.

Reynolds, Roy. *Illinois Baptist,* July 28, 1976.

Ricke, Dennis. "Illinois Blacks Through the Civil War, A Struggle for Equality." Masters thesis, Southern Illinois University, 1970.

Schmook, Rebecca. *Gallatin County, IL Slave Register 1815–1839.* Harrisburg, IL: Saline County Genealogical Society, 1994.

Smith, George. *History of Illinois and Her People.* Chicago: American History Society, 1927.

————. *A History of Southern Illinois.* Chicago: Lewis Publishing, 1912.

————. "Salines of Southern Illinois." Transactions of the Illinois State Historical Society, Springfield, IL, 1904.

Trotter, Joe Jr. *Coal, Class and Color.* Urbana: University of Illinois, 1999.

Trouillot, Michel-Rolph. *Silencing the Past.* Boston: Beacon Press, 1995.

Van Broekhoven, D. "Illinois Baptists and the Agitation Over Slavery." *American Baptist Quarterly* 22, 2003.

Chapter Four

Alinsky, Saul. *John L. Lewis.* New York: Putnam Sons, 1949.

Angle, Paul. *Bloody Williamson: A Chapter in American Lawlessness.* New York: Knopf, 1952.

Arrillaga, Pauline. "Utah Mine Owner Candid, Combative." *Seattle Times,* August 9, 2007.

Ballowe, James. "The Work of Our Fathers." *Chicago Reader,* June 30, 1995.

Biggers, Jeff. "In Coal Blood." Salon.com, August 2007.

Bonnell, Clarence, ed. *Saline County: A Century of History, 1847–1947.* Harrisburg, IL: Saline County Historical Society, 1947.

Cartlidge, Oscar. *Fifty Years of Coal Mining.* Charleston, WV: Rose City Press, 1936.

Changnon, Stanley. *Coal and Railroads in Illinois.* Mahomet, IL: Changnon Rails, 2000.

Chaplin, Ronald. "Spatial Changes in Coal Employment Within Southern Illinois 1900–1960." Masters thesis, Southern Illinois University, 1961.

Coal in Illinois. 1907 Annual Report, Illinois Department of Commerce.

"Coal Field Hell-Raiser." *No Backward Step: The Struggle for Democracy in the Illinois Coal Fields*. March 9, 2008, www.minewar.blogspot.com/2008/03/coal-field-hell-raiser.htlm.

Davidson, Lee. "How Much Is a Miner's Life Worth?" *Deseret News*, November 4, 2007.

Derickson, Alan. *Black Lung*. Ithaca: Cornell University Press, 1998.

Directory of Coal Mines. Gallatin County, Saline County, 2008.

Eavenson, Howard. *The First Century and a Quarter of American Coal Industry*. Pittsburgh: Koppers Building, 1942.

"Feds Blame Mine Operator for Fatal Collapse." CNN, July 24, 2008. http://www.cnn.com/2008/US/07/24/mine.collapse/index.html.

Fenoli, John Robert. *Era of Conflict in Southern Illinois Coalfields Since 1890*. Carbondale: Southern Illinois University Press, 1962.

Fetherling, Dale. *Mother Jones: The Miner's Angel*. Carbondale: Southern Illinois University Press, 1974.

Feurer, Rosemary, ed. *Remember Virden 1898*. Chicago: Illinois Humanities Council, 1998.

Forrestal Frank. "Coal Boss Murray Attacks UMWA Miners." *Militant*, May 6, 20, 2002.

———. "Mine Boss Murray Has Long Antiworker Record." *Militant*, September 3, 2007.

Goodell, Jeff. *Big Coal: The Dirty Secret Behind America's Energy Future*. Boston: Houghton Mifflin, 2006.

Griswold, John. *A Democracy of Ghosts*. LaGrande, OR: Wordcraft, 2009.

Hartley, Robert, and David Kenny. *Death Underground: The Centralia and West Frankfort Mine Disasters*. Carbondale: Southern Illinois University Press, 2006.

Hawse, Mara Lou, and Dianne Throgmorton, eds. *Tell Me a Story: Memories of Early Life Around the Coalfields of Illinois*. Carbondale: Southern Illinois University Coal Research Center, 1992.

Hudson, Harriet D. "The Progressive Mine Workers of America: A Study in Rival Unionism." Urbana, IL: University of Illinois, Bureau of Economic and Business Research, BEBR bulletin no. 73, 1952.

Illinois Coal Fact Sheet. Illinois Department of Commerce and Economic Opportunity—Coal, http://www.commerce.state.il.us/NR/rdonlyres/ED8AD879–93FE-47E4–8EE9-E30069A721FA/0/Illinoiscoalfacts Dec2006.pdf.

Illinois Coal Industry, Report of the Office of Coal Development, June 2006, http://www.commerce.state.il.us/NR/rdonlyres/1C724CC6-E056 –41A4–836C-1CC8A74BF710/0/TheIllinoisCoalIndustryJune2006.pdf.

Industrial Relations Hearings. U.S. Commission on Industrial Relations, 1912.

Kalisch, Philip. "Death Down Below: Coal Mine Disasters in Three Illinois Counties, 1904–1962." *Journal of the Illinois State Historical Society* 65, no. 1 (Spring 1972).

Keiser, John. "The Union Miners Cemetery at Mt. Olive, Illinois: A Spirit-Thread of Labor History." *Journal of the Illinois State Historical Society* 62, no. 3 (Autumn 1969).

Lantz, Herman R., and J. S. McCrary. *People of Coal Town*. New York: Columbia University Press, 1958.

Leavitt, Noah. "One Nation Underground." Slate.com, February 8, 2006.

Oblinger, Carl D. "Divided Kingdom: Work, Community, and the Mining Wars in the Central Illinois Coal Fields During the Great Depression." Springfield: Illinois State Historical Society, 1991.

O'Hara, Mary. "Let It Fly: The Legacy of Helen Bass Williams." PhD diss., Southern Illinois University, 2004.

Militia, Joe. "Mine Owner's Companies Fined Millions." *Forbes*, August 9, 2007.

"Murray's Illinois Mine Has 2,787 Violations Since 2005." *Salt Lake Tribune*, August 9, *2007.*

Orear, Leslie. "Mother Jones and the Union Miners Cemetery, Mount Olive, Illinois." Chicago: Illinois Labor History Society, 2003.

"Owner of Utah Mine Is a Famously Combative Figure." *Boston Herald*, August 9, 2007.

Prosser, Daniel. "Coal Towns in Egypt: Portrait of an Illinois Mining Region, 1890–1930." PhD diss., Northwestern University, 1973.

Saulny, Susan and Caroyln Marshall. "Mine Owner Has History of Run-Ins on Work Issues." http://www.nytimes.com/2007/08/24/us/24murray .html.

Schull, Ben. "Reports of the Mining Industry of Illinois: The Earliest Records to 1954." Department of Mines and Minerals, Springfield, IL, 1954.

Simon, John Y. "Boom and Bust in Grand Tower." *Springhouse* 20, (2003).

Smith, Barbara Ellen. *Digging Our Own Graves: Coal Miners and the Struggle Over Black Lung Disease*. Philadelphia: Temple University Press, 1987.

Smith, Ellen. "MSHA: High Negligence and Reckless Disregard." *Mine Safety and Health News*, August 10, 2007.

Stout, Steve. "Tragedy in November: The Cherry Mine Disaster." *Journal of the Illinois State Historical Society* 52, no. 1 (February 1979).

Tintori, Karen. *Trapped: The 1909 Cherry Mine Disaster.* New York: Atria Books, 2002.

Webb, Malcolm. *Seven Stranded Coal Towns.* New York: DaCapo Press, 1971.

Wechsler, James. *Labor Baron: Portrait of John L. Lewis.* Westport: Greenwood, 1944.

Wieck, David. *Woman from Spillertown: A Memoir of Agnes Burns Wieck.* Carbondale: Southern Illinois University Press, 1992.

Young, Dallas M. "The Progressive Miners of America: A History of Its Organization." Master's thesis, University of Illinois, 1937.

Chapter Five

"An Intensive Survey of the Eagle Creek Basin." Saline and Gallatin Counties, Illinois 1986–1987. IL EPA, Springfield, IL, March 1988.

"Agricultural Society of the State of Illinois." *Illinois Gazette*, November 20, 1819.

———. May 5, 1821.

Archaeological Survey Short Report, 5405. Illinois Historic Preservation Agency, Springfield, Illinois, 1994.

Ashby, W. "Sustainable Strip-mine Reclamation." *International Journal of Mining, Reclamation and Environment*, 20, June 2006.

Bazzaz, Farhi. "Succession of Abandoned Fields in the Shawnee Hills, Southern Illinois." University of Illinois, 1968.

Beck, Robert. "The Evolution of Illinois's Surface Coal Mine Reclamation Law from Its Beginnings Up to the Take-Over by the Federal Surface Mining Control and Reclamation Act of 1977." *Southern Illinois University Law Journal*, 1981.

Birbeck, Morris, and George Flower. *History of the English Settlement in Edwards County, Illinois, Founded in 1817–1818.* Chicago: Fergus Printing, 1882.

Bonnell, Clarence. Lecture, Illinois Academia of Science, 1916.

———. *Illinois Ozarks.* Harrisburg, IL: Daily Register Printers, 1946.

Boudling, Russell. "Your Rights in the Coalfields." Illinois South Project, Herrin, IL, 1984.

———. "The Lost Harvest: Study of the Surface Mining Act's Failure to Reclaim Prime Farmland in the Midwest." Illinois South Project, Herrin, IL, 1984.

Brown, Willis. *Infidelity to Christianity: Life Sketches of Willis M. Brown*. Moundsville, WV: Gospel Trumpet Company, 1904.

Bryner, Jeanna. "Ancient Rainforest Revealed in Coal Mine." *LiveScience*, April 23, 2007.

"Citizens Guide to Coal Mining and Reclamation in Illinois." Illinois Department of Natural Resources, Mines and Minerals, Springfield, IL, 2007.

Colby, Charles. *Pilot Study of Southern Illinois*. Carbondale: Southern Illinois University Press, 1956.

"Creation of the Shawnee National Forest, 1930–1938." National Forest Service, http://www.fs.fed.us/r9/forests/shawnee/about/history/.

Croxton, W. "Revegetation of Illinois Coal Stripped Land." *Ecology* 9, April 1928.

DeNeal, Gary. "Moonshine Times Gone By." *Springhouse* 26, 2009.

"Eagle Creek Watershed Plan." Saline County Watershed Partnership Planning, 2007.

"Early Days in Saline County." *Saline County Republican*, January 25, 1913.

"Forest Trees of Illinois." Department of Conservation, Springfield, IL, 1949.

Greer, Edna. "Influence of the South on Illinois Prior to 1860." PhD diss., University of Chicago, 1937.

Hall, Elihu. *Anna's War Against River Pirates and Cave Bandits*. Manuscript at Southeastern Illinois College Archives, 1948.

Hall, Ruby Franklin. *Stories of the Lamb Communities*. Hardin County, IL, n.d.

Hendee, Jacob and Courtney Flint. "The Social Context of the Shawnee National Forest in Southern Illinois." Department of Natural Resources and Environmental Sciences, University of Illinois at Urbana-Champaign, http://research.aces.illinois.edu/system/files/SIRAP/final/ShawneeForestSocialContext.pdf.

Holmes, Leslie. "Reclaiming Stripped Lands in Illinois." *Scientific Monthly* 59, 1944.

"Illinois Citizens Guide to Pre-Blasting Surveys." Illinois South, Herrin, IL, 1980.

Miller, Keith. "Building Towns on the Southeastern Illinois Frontier, 1810–1830." PhD diss., Miami University, 1976.

Montrie, Chad. *To Save the Land and People: A History of Opposition to Surface Coal Mining in Appalachia*. Chapel Hill: University of North Carolina Press, 2003.

Myers, Charles. "Amphibians and Reptiles of an Ecologically Disturbed (Strip-mined) Area in Southern Illinois." *American Midland Naturalist,* July 1963.

Neely, Charles. *Tales and Songs of Southern Illinois.* Carbondale: Southern Illinois University Press, 1998.

O'Brien, Darcy. "Death Sends for the Doctor." *Springhouse* 4, no. 1 (1987).

———. *Murder in Little Egypt.* New York: Morrow, 1989.

———. "A Rose in Little Egypt. *Springhouse* 6, 1989.

Orlemann, Eric. *Power Shovels: The World's Mightiest Mining and Construction Escavators.* St. Paul, MN: MBI Publishing, 2003.

"Reforest Illinois." *Chicago Daily Tribune,* May 25, 1930.

Rothert, Otto. *Outlaws of Cave-in-Rock.* Carbondale: Southern Illinois University Press, 1996.

Searles, William. "Memories of a Coal Mining Town, 1928–1942." *Springhouse* 25, 2008.

Smith, George. *A History of Southern Illinois.* Chicago: Lewis Publishing, 1912.

Snively, W. D. *Satan's Ferryman.* New York: Frederick Ungar, 1968.

Soady, Fred. "The Making of the Shawnee." Reprinted from *Forest History,* vol. 9, July, 1963.

"Surface Mining Control and Reclamation Act of 1977: A Thirtieth Anniversary." Oversight Hearing before the Committee on Natural Resources, U.S. House of Representatives, Washington, DC, July 25, 2007.

Toole, Arlie. "Shawnee National Forest." *Egyptian Key,* October 1943.

"Trip to the Mountains." *Saline County Republican,* June 5, 1912.

Wakeley, Ray. "Baseline Presentation and Analysis of Selected Demographic, Social, Economic, and Cultural Characteristics of the People, Delta Mine Expansion Site, Saline County, Illinois, 1975." Report submitted to AMAX Coal Company, Carbondale, IL, October 1975.

Whitecotton, Stephen. "Cultural Resource Survey of Kerr-McGee Mine Lands in Saline County, IL." Center for Archaeological Investigations, Carbondale, IL, 1980.

Worthen, A. *Geological Survey of Illinois.* Boston: Mayer and Co., 1875.

Chapter Six

Ball, Robert. "Wonderful Coal." *Chicago Tribune,* 1892.

Biggers, Jeff. "Blowing Away King Coal." Salon.com, January 29, 2009.

———. "Clean Coal: Don't Try to Shovel That." *Washington Post,* March 2, 2008.

———. "Coal Ash Crisis Management." *Huffington Post,* January 11, 2009.

————. "Coalfield Advocates Respond to Mountaintop Removal Crimes and Misdemeanors." *Huffington Post*, June 11, 2009.

————. "Do Clean Coal Ads Violate FTC-FCC Standards?" *Huffington Post*, February 9, 2009.

————. "Few Honest Words: Obama's First 100 Days of Coal." *Huffington Post*, April 27, 2009.

————. "Jimmy Carter's Next Urgent Mission: Polarized Appalachian Coalfields." *Huffington Post*, July 20, 2009.

Britt, Robert. "New Data Confirms Strong Earthquake Risk to Central US." *LiveScience*, June 22, 2005.

"Coal Victories Across Nation." Sierra Club Beyond Coal Campaign, July 8, 2009, http://www.sierraclub.org/environmentallaw/coal/victories.asp #kill100.

"Disaster in Waiting: Toxic Coal Ash Disposal in Impoundments at Power Plants." Environmental Integrity Project, January 9, 2009.

"DOE Revives FutureGen, Reversing Bush-Era Decision." *New York Times*, June 12, 2009.

"Durbin Meets with FutureGen Alliance to Prepare for Next Congress." Media release, November 20, 2008.

Gee, Quentin, and Nicholas Allen. "US Electricity Policy 2009." University of California, Santa Barbara, 2009.

Gore, Al. "A Generational Challenge to Repower America." July 17, 2008, http://blog.algore.com/2008/07/a_generational_challenge_to_re.html.

Griffith, Katherine. "Egypt's Coal Buck." *Egyptian Key*, 1943.

Hansen, James. "Coal Fired Power Plants Are Death Factories." *UK Guardian*, February 15, 2009.

Illinois Coal Industry, Report of the Office of Coal Development, June 2006, http://www.commerce.state.il.us/NR/rdonlyres/1C724CC6-E056-41A4-836C-1CC8A74BF710/0/TheIllinoisCoalIndustryJune2006.pdf.

"Improving Coal's Image: A National Energy Strategy Imperative." National Coal Council, January 1992, http://www.nationalcoalcouncil.org/Documents/IMPROVING%20COAL%27S%20IMAGE.PDF.

"Latest TVA Ash Spill Site in Alabama Contains Even More Toxic Metals Than Harriman, TN Spill Site From December." Environmental Integrity Project Report, January 2009, http://www.environmental integrity.org/pub590.cfm.

McKibben, Bill. "Earth at 350." *The Nation*, May 12, 2008.

"McKibben and Berry Call for Civil Disobedience at DC Coal Plant, Climate Progress," http://climateprogress.org/2008/12/10/wendell-berry-bill -mckibben-civil-disobedience-washington-dc-coal-plant-march-2/.

"Mortality in Appalachian Coal Mining Regions: The Value of Statistical Life Lost." *Public Health Reports*, July 2009.

"Mountaintop Letdown: President Obama's Decision Will Enrage Environmentalists, but It's the Right One." *Washington Post* ed., June 11, 2009.

Nilles, Bruce. "The Climate Bill Shouldn't Give Coal a Free Pass." *Huffington Post*, July 22, 2009.

Obama, Barack. "Remarks of President Barack Obama—Address to Joint Session of Congress." February 24, 2009, http://www.whitehouse.gov/the_press_office/remarks-of-president-barack-obama-address-to-joint-session-of-congress/.

"Old King Coal Reigns Here." *The Grade Teacher*, March 1950, Bituminous Coal Institute, Washington, DC.

"The Passing of FutureGen: How the World's Premier Clean Coal Technology Project Came to be Abandoned by the Department of Energy." Report by the Majority Staff of the Subcommittee on Investigations and Oversight of the Committee on Science and Technology to Chairman Bart Gordon and Subcommittee Chairman Brad Miller, March 10, 2009.

Rachel Maddow Show. December 10, 2008, http://www.msnbc.msn.com/id/28178085/%20is%20transcript.

Reece, Erik. *Lost Mountain: A Year in the Vanishing Wilderness—Radical Strip Mining and the Devastation of Appalachia*. New York: Riverhead, 2006.

"Research into the Sulfur Problems of Illinois Coal." Coal Research Center, Southern Illinois University, Carbondale, IL, 1987.

Romm, Joseph. "FutureGen Was NeverGen from the Start." *Gristmill*, March 12, 2009.

"Secretary Chu Announces Agreement on FutureGen Project." June 12, 2009, http://www.energy.gov/news2009/7454.htm.

Smith, Rebecca. "US Foresees a Thinner Cushion of Coal." *Wall Street Journal*, June 8, 2009.

"Stalled Clean Coal Plant Moving Ahead in Illinois." Associated Press, June 12, 2009.

Tankersley, Jim. "Under House Energy Bill, Coal Won't Be Going Away." *LA Times*, June 22, 2009.

"To Hawthorn Friend and Family." Hawthorn Group newsletter, December 2008. http://www.hawthorngroup.com/newsletter/index.BAK.html.

Walsh, Bryan. "What the Energy Bill Really Means for CO2 Emissions." *Time*, June 27, 2009.

Ward, Ken, Jr. "Flattened: Most Mountaintop Mines Left as Pasture." *Charleston Gazette*, August 9, 1998.

————. "Mining the Mountains Series." *Charleston Gazette*, www.wvgazette
.com/static/series/mining.

————. "Mountaintop Removal Forests Return Could Take Centuries."
Charleston Gazette, May 2, 2001.

————. "Secret EPA Study: Big Cancer Risks from Coal-Ash Ponds."
Charleston Gazette, http://blogs.wvgazette.com/coaltattoo/?s=
Secret+EPA+Study%3A+Big+Cancer+Risks+from+Coal-Ash+Ponds.

ACKNOWLEDGMENTS

*Sopratutto, grazie Carla, Diego, e Massimo, per la vostra pazienza
e sostegno mi hanno inspurato sul nostro torrente dall'aquila.*

This book would not have been possible without the assistance of numerous people who have dedicated their lives to preserving the land and heritage in southern Illinois.

Special thanks go to my uncle Richard and aunt Jerretta Followell, who spent years in obtaining and preserving the records, photos, and chronicles of the life and times of our family on Eagle Creek, and its demise to the coal companies, with the doggedness of investigative reporters.

Gary DeNeal, publisher of *Springhouse* magazine, generously gave his time and ideas, and access to his private library, and roamed the back hills, forests, and valleys over several years with me. *Springhouse Magazine* remains a singular fountain of stories and wisdom in the Shawnee Hills. Likewise, Ron Nelson and Hovie Stunson, two of the most extraordinary historians in southern Illinois, spent innumerable hours guiding me through the complexities of the region's past and present-day coalfield realities. Any errors and misinterpretations, of course, are my own and do not reflect the insight of these native sons. I am also indebted to Barney Bush, Barry Vinyard, and Sandy Frohock for their genealogical endeavors and contributions.

Special thanks go to the entire staff at the Harrisburg Public Library, who treated my requests with remarkable patience, and to the librarians at Western Illinois University, who tolerated my racks of interlibrary loans. Thanks, as well, to the librarians at Southern Illinois University, Southeastern Illinois College, the Shawneetown, Herrin, Marion, Carbondale, and Eldorado Public Libraries, the Abraham Lincoln Presidential Library in Springfield, the Illinois State Archives, and the Library of Congress.

My work on the coalfields in southern Illinois also emerged from my longtime writing and activism in the Appalachian coalfields, where mountaintop removal continues to be one of the most egregious human rights and environmental violations in our time. I have been fortunate to be surrounded by a community of coalfield residents and activists who have inspired me with their resilience, courage, and relentless efforts to save the land and people. Thank you so much for your life's work and dedication: Judy Bonds, Larry Gibson, Bo Webb, Vernon Haltom, Ed Wiley, Maria Gunnoe, Lorelei Scarbro, Teri Blanton, Rick Moore, Bob Kincaid, Vivian Stockman and OVEC, Ken Hechler, Jack Spadaro, Elisa Young, Chuck Nelson, Kathy Selvage, *Charleston Gazette* reporter Ken Ward, Chad Montrie, Silas House, Jason Howard, Kate Larkin, and many, many other courageous American citizens. For more information on how we can end this nightmare in Appalachia, visit www.ilovemountains.org; or see the various citizens' organizations at work with the Alliance for Appalachia; or check out the work of the Sierra Club's Beyond Coal Campaign and the Rainforest Action Network.

Thanks to my mountain posse and editors, Brian Lee Knopp, John Morton, J. W. Randolph, Rory McImoil, Cassie Robinson, and the Appalachian Voices staff.

Special thanks to my theater production partner Stephanie Pistello, who has been critical in taking my work and writing to a new stage, and to musician Ben Sollee for his amazing pipes and inspiration.

Thanks, also, to the editors at the *Nation* magazine, *Washington Post*, *Salon.com*, *Huffington Post*, *Grist*, *AlterNet*, *Common Dreams*, *New America Media*, the *Heartland Café Journal*, and National Public Radio and Public Radio International, for publishing my writing on coal, mountaintop removal, and the Appalachian and southern Illinois coalfields, where various excerpts first appeared in different forms.

I would like to express my deep gratitude to my editor, Ruth Baldwin, and Nation Books editorial director Carl Bromley for their fine work and support, and for giving me a chance to explore a dark legacy that has been buried for too long. Special thanks to copy editor Gray Cutler and project editor Laura Esterman for putting the book into shape.

Finally, this book would not have been possible without the support of my family, who made the difficult and painful journey back to Eagle Creek with me over these years. My folks, as always, have been indefatigable supporters of my errant ways.

Onward, shipmates.

INDEX